Equity and Efficiency?

for Anna

Equity and Efficiency?
School Management in an
International Context

Lynn Davies

 The Falmer Press

(A member of the Taylor & Francis Group)
London • New York • Philadelphia

UK	The Falmer Press, Falmer House, Barcombe, Lewes, East Sussex, BN8 5DL
USA	The Falmer Press, Taylor & Francis Inc., 1900 Frost Road, Suite 101, Bristol, PA 19007

British Library Cataloguing in Publication Data
Davies, Lynn *1944–*
  Equity and efficiency?: school management in an
  international context
  1. Schools. Management
  I. Title
  371.21

  ISBN 1–85000–658–X
  ISBN 1–85000–659–8 pbk

Library of Congress Cataloging-in-Publication Data
Davies, Lynn.
    Equity and efficiency?: school management in an international
  context/Lynn Davies
      p.   cm.
    Includes bibliographical references.
    ISBN 1–85000–658–X—
    ISBN 1–85000–659–8 (pbk)
    1. Educational equalization. 2. School management and
  organization. 3. Education—Aims and objectives. I. Title.
  LC212.D38   1989
  371.2—dc20

Jacket design by Caroline Archer

Typeset in 11/13 Bembo by
Chapterhouse, The Cloisters, Formby L37 3PX

Printed and bound in Great Britain by Taylor & Francis (Printers) Ltd.
Basingstoke on paper which has a specified pH value on final paper
manufacture of not less than 7.5 and is therefore 'acid-free'.

Contents

Acknowledgments

My appreciation should be expressed to the International Management Course members 1988 and 1989 at the University of Birmingham, for working through early drafts and chapters. I am grateful for their helpful suggestions and insights, and for their essential requests for clarification.

Charles Aliu	Christine Asiimwe
Abdallah Ahmed Buwayhid	Angus Cheung Yiu Sing
Carol Emery	Joannes Gaduon
Abdullatif Garaybeh	John Hobbs
Christopher Karombano	Angela Kan Wai-Yan
John Kwok-Wai Lau	Kamlesh Manghra
Emma May Kwan Ling	Sibusiso Mazibuko
Catherine Mugerwa	David Osborne
Rose Richardson	Sally Robertson
John Stokes	

My grateful thanks also to colleagues who have read and commented on various chapters of this book: Clive Harber, Roland Meighan, Rex Oram and Roger Robinson. The final responsibility, as they say, is entirely mine.

Acknowledgments are also due to the following authors and publishers for permission to reproduce material in this book: Berita Publishing Sdn Bhd, Malaysia, for the *Lots of Lat* cartoons; the Commonwealth Secretariat, for extracts from *The Commonwealth Casebook for School Administrators*; the Development Education Centre for cartoons from *Thin Black Lines: Political Cartoons and Development Education*; the journal of *Educational Management and Administration* and B. Tipton, for article extracts; the *Independent* newspaper; *Management in Education* and Naylor for cartoons; NFER-Nelson for extracts from *Education For Capability*; Pergamon Press for extracts from the *International Journal of Educational Development*; Times Newspapers and G. Haigh for the article, "Nipscratting? No Thanks", *Times Educational Supplement*; The Women's Press and Dale Spender for the poem, "Gender and Marketable Skills: Who underachieves at maths and science?" reproduced from *Learning to Lose*.

Glossary

AMMA	Assistant Masters and Mistresses Association. One of the four UK Teachers' Unions, with mainly secondary membership.
Assisted Places Scheme	Provision of the UK 1980 Education Act for pupils to attend Independent schools without being charged tuition or examination fees, which will be met by the Government.
Bureaucracy	Originally a description of a large scale organisation characterized by formal rules, impersonal procedures, a centralization of authority and the specialization of tasks and abilities. Now has derogatory overtones of red tape, delay, and mystifying procedures.
CTC	City Technology College.
Criterion-referenced	Performance which is measured against a set standard or criterion, as opposed to 'norm-referenced' or 'norm-related' assessment which measures performance against the average for a group.
CRE	Commission for Racial Equality, UK.
Cultural Capital	The 'banking' in the home of values, styles and work orientations of the dominant educational culture; this capital is a particularly useful investment when cultural values are expected at school but not directly taught.
Deviance	Literally, behaviour which deviates from the expected; in education, refers to behaviour seen as troublesome, disruptive, difficult, or problematic in some way.
EEC	European Economic Community.
Efficiency	A variety of definitions surrounding the notion of getting things done. Sometimes a distinction is made between *effectiveness* as the extent to which goals are achieved and *efficiency* as the extent to which goals are achieved with the minimum expenditure of scarce resources.

EO	Equal Opportunities. Can refer to desires to provide equal access to valued goods such as education, or to equal treatment or even to equal outcomes.
ESL	English as a Second Language. Refers to the teaching of English to those in an English-speaking country who have previously learned another language. Contrasts with EFL (English as a Foreign Language) which refers to the teaching or English to students in a country where the mother-tongue is not English.
ESR	Education for Self-Reliance.
EWP	Education with Production.
Ethnic	'concerning nations or races . . . pertaining to the customs, dress, food etc. of a particular group or cult; belonging or pertaining to a particular racial group' (Chambers Dictionary 1988). 'Ethnicity' is used therefore to signify both culture and race.
Ethnographic	Research which seeks to understand the culture of a small social setting through participant observation, interview, dialogue etc; originally the anthropological research technique.
GCSE	General Certificate of Secondary Education, UK. Has replaced GCE.
Harambee	Literally means 'let's pull together'. Schools in Kenya organised on a self-help basis by communities which consider government provision inadequate.
Harassment	(sexual) The formal definition is: unwanted, unreciprocated and continued sexual advances, propositions or physical contacts, which are injurious to work performance or career. May include frequent use of sexist jokes and putdowns. (racial) Includes verbal or written racist comments; derogatory name-calling and racist insults; frequent use of racist jokes and putdowns.
Hegemony	Leadership; dominance; preponderant influence.
HOD	Head of Department.
Human capital	The idea that investment in people's education, health or welfare by a nation can produce a return on that investment, as with financial investments.
ILEA	Inner London Education Authority. Now disbanded.
IT	Information Technology. The convergence of electronics, computing and communication. Generally includes the use of

computers, microcomputers, information networks, data banks etc.

LEA | Local Education Authority, UK. There are 103 LEAs with permanent local government staff. Each LEA has an Education Committee consisting in the main of elected Councillors but also with coopted members.

LFM | Local Financial Mangement. The devolution of budgets to schools.

Localization | The move by developing or colonized societies to replace expatriate or 'foreign' staff by local staff.

MSC | Manpower Services Commission, UK. Established by the Employment and Training Act 1973 to provide public training and employment services and make provisions for unemployed young people and longer-term unemployed. Officially separate from Government, but accountable to the Secretary of State and with personnel policies controlled by the Civil Service Department.

Meritocracy | A term coined to contrast with 'aristocracy', and meaning a social system whereby the élite would be composed only of people with merit or talent, rather than people there on the basis of birth or wealth.

Meritocratic | Refers to selection procedures which are based purely on 'objective' definitions of merit, and make no allowances for 'ascriptive' characteristics such as family, gender, race or age.

Multicultural | 'a society made up of many distinct cultural groups' (Chambers Dictionary 1988). In education, 'multicultura- lism' is generally used to signify a positive acknowledgement of this diversity, and an attempt to encourage tolerance and cultural awareness.

NUT | National Union of Teachers, UK.

Patriarchal | Literally, governing a family by paternal right. A patriarchal society is usually defined as one where power and decision- making is concentrated in the hands of men, and where decisions are made primarily in the interests of the male.

Plural | 'a society in which different ethnic (etc.) groups preserve their own customs or hold equal power' (Chambers Dictionary 1988). Can also refer to political pluralism, that is power being held by different goups in different arenas (business, government administration, political parties, labour organizations etc.)

Racism   'The belief that race is the primary determinant of human traits and capacities or that racial differences produce an inherent superiority of a particular race (Longmans Dictionary). See also harassment.

Relativism   To maintain that there are no universal standards of good or bad, right or wrong; that there is no such thing as objective knowledge of reality independent of the knower.

SSCEP   Secondary Schools Community Extension Project, Papua New Guinea.

Sexism   'discrimination against, stereotyping of, patronizing or otherwise offensive behaviour towards (originally women, now women and men) on the grounds of sex' (Chambers Dictionary). See also harassment.
Racism, sexism or classism can be defined as the individual, collective or institutional treatment of, or attitudes towards people based on shared stereotypes which are oppressive or limiting.

SHA   Secondary Heads Association.

TGAT   Task Group on Assessment and Testing. Set up to develop the assessment requirements of the Education Reform Act, 1988, and the National Curriculum.

Tripartite   The education system of UK before 'comprehensivisation', which comprised three levels: academic, technical and vocational.

TVEI   Technical and Vocational Education Initiative. A national pilot scheme in UK to stimulate provision of technical and vocational education of 14–18 year-olds, administered by the MSC.

Ujaama   Literally, 'familyhood'. The Tanzanian model of African socialism.

Voucher system   System experimented with in US whereby parents are given vouchers by the local body responsible for education, and can then 'spend' them on behalf of children at institutions of their choice. Institutions then cash them in with the issuing body. Supposedly a way of ensuring parental choice, among private or State schools, and channelling extra resources to popular schools.

WASC   West African School Certificate.

YTS   Youth Training Scheme.

Chapter 1

Dilemmas in the Management of Equality and Efficiency

The purpose and objectives of special education should be: a) to give concrete meaning to the idea of equalising educational opportunities for all children, their physical, mental, emotional disabilities notwithstanding; . . . c) to provide opportunities for exceptionally gifted children to develop at their own pace in the interest of the nation's economic and technicological development. (Nigeria, National Policy on Education, 1981)

The result [of the National Curriculum] will be higher expectations and more effective progression and continuity throughout the years of full-time education . . . The National Curriculum Council . . . is expected to take account of cultural diversity and the need for the school curriculum to promote equality of opportunity for all pupils regardless of ethnic origin and gender, and to cater for those with special educational needs. (UK, National Curriculum Council, 1989)

Inherent in the educational policies of most countries are concerns to make education both more efficient and more equitable. Schools and colleges are asked to be efficient, both 'externally' in terms of serving the country's economy, and 'internally' in terms of providing full value for the money expended on them. Education is desired at the same time to be equitable, either in providing 'equal' chances to the current school-aged population, or in redressing previous imbalances in the distribution of a country's resources. In theory, these two pursuits of efficiency* and equity are not incompatible: a shift in expenditure towards technical/vocational education, for example, could both serve a country's need for skilled labour *and* narrow the gap between academically trained élites and less 'productive' personnel.

In practice, the harmonization of equity and efficiency is much less feasible. From Foster's (1965) research onwards, we have examples of the subversion of well-intentioned vocational education programmes in many parts of the world, as individuals view opportunities in narrower personal mobility terms rather than the larger scale manpower considerations. Similarly, the notion of an 'equal right' for every individual to ten or twelve years compulsory schooling is demonstrated to have a counterproductive effect on overall life chances (unless there is an available and absorptive labour market), in that it increases qualification inflation and creates a pool of 'overqualified' labour (Dore, 1976). Finally, the 'rationalization' of education because of economic recession leads to cutbacks which disproportionately take their toll on already disadvantaged groups (Hunt, 1987). In times of scarce resources, efficiency becomes defined as that which appears to provide the best investment: in the interests of conservation, countries cut back the percentage of entrants to secondary levels of education (as in Tanzania, or the Gambia); delay programmes of special education (as in Zambia, or, until recently, Pakistan); concentrate funds on the 'able' or the 'gifted' (as in the UK Assisted Places scheme). It would seem that egalitarianism, however defined, is a luxury to be afforded in an already booming economy, or with an already buoyant labour market. With the new disjunctures between educational qualifications and employment rewards in many parts of the world (Lauglo and Lillis, 1988), there is little evidence that increasing educational provision after primary level will actually create many jobs or minimise gross social disparities.

This apparently pessimistic scenario is now well-trodden and continues to engage economists and social scientists in individual countries as well as in the large aid agencies. Less well explored internationally is the effect of such planning dilemmas at the level of everyday school processes, that is, for those involved in the management of teaching and learning. Management is often portrayed in textbooks as a series of technical activities which promote 'the goals of the school', or 'educational objectives', as if these were sets of complementary, internally consistent values agreed by all significant parties. If the potentiality for discord is recognized by such texts, it tends to be relegated to a section on 'conflict resolution': again, contestation is seen as a soluble phenomenon, to be tackled by managerial skill or expertise, rather than as a fundamental underscoring of educational enterprises because of intrinsic contradictions within most capitalist democracies.

I will argue, therefore, that many of the problems of school management are not reducible to individual tensions or sub-cultural value clashes within the institution: they relate instead to wider dilemmas within the political formation, which are reproduced in terms of incompatible ideologies at the school level. Schools must balance the selection and ranking function of education with the legitimating norms of socialization into a common culture, of non-discrimination and of equal rights. Put more simply, they have to make students more the same while at the same time making them more different. The final examination system of most countries is, unlike driving tests, designed to 'fail' whatever percentage is currently appropriate. There would be little point in school-leaving examinations if everyone passed them equally well; individuals want to succeed, but do not want everyone else to succeed, as this

> There was embarrassed amusement
> among American educators last year,
> when a West Virginia watchdog group
> revealed that all primary schoolchil-
> dren in the United States were above
> average in their standardized test re-
> sults.
> *Times Educational Supplement*,
> 8 April 1988.

would devalue the currency. Individually rational behaviour such as ambition does not necessarily translate into mass rational outcomes. Any examiners' meeting where anxieties are expressed if there are 'too many' first class degrees will demonstrate the shallowness of any expressed national concern to raise overall standards of perfor-mance. There are in most countries vested interests in artificially depressing the numbers achieving 'excellence'.

Just as every national system has its own mechanisms and timings for 'warming up' sufficient students to create a motivated pool for selection and for 'cooling out' those who will in the end not be chosen (Hopper, 1971), each school too must balance and mananage the warming up and cooling out of groups of students, given that success (in terms of entry to the élite) is a rationed commodity. This dilemma is traditionally resolved by some notion of 'equal opportunity': that schools will provide the *access* to knowlege and skills, but the ultimate take-up of this provision will rest with individuals and their abilities or motivation. Teachers will operate quite happily on the twin premises of impartiality in their treatment and 'healthy' competition for the students. This works relatively unproblematically as long as three conditions hold:

1. that school qualifications have a strong 'fit' with work opportunities;
2. that success and failure appear to be randomly distributed among different populations, with particular categories such as lower social class, female or ethnic minority students not over-represented in certain positions in school or in work;
3. that students want to enter the race, they accept it as fair, and will individually internalize and appropriate any failure as their own respons-ibility.

These conditions are clearly linked, and I will argue that there is a contemporary breakdown of each of them which is leading to tensions, if not crises, in the operations of educational establishments. (One might here want to make a distinction between primary and secondary schooling, but for the moment I will not differentiate, given that 'primary' in many parts of the world includes students up to the ages of 14 or 15, who will be going directly into the labour market or unemployment).

Taking employment first, there is now an increasing disjuncture between school accreditation and the possibility of paid work. Large unemployment levels are not historically uncommon in many parts of the world, but universal education is a relatively recent phenomenon: the promise of social mobility through education was fulfillable as long as few went to school, or as long as some sort of job was available for everyone which was linked to qualifications — or lack of them. Now, neither of those situations necessarily hold, and the combination of mass schooling and a shrinking labour market means that formal education can no longer guarantee employment. The ability to move into remunerative work hinges on other factors than paper qualifications, and thus the second condition breaks down. The notion of a 'pure meritocracy'* (where careers are solely dependent on merit or talent rather than background) is exposed as mythical, and background attributes such as race, tribe, family connections or gender come increasingly to determine allocation to social positions once more. In the old sociological jargon, positions become 'ascribed' rather than 'achieved', and there is increasing recognition by students and teachers of the structured inequality of many societies which makes the dice loaded against certain groups.

> Our schools are, in a sense, factories, in which the raw products (children) are to be shaped and fashioned into products to meet the various demands of life. The specifications for manufacturing come from the demands of twentieth-century civilisation and it is the business of the school to build its pupils according to the specifications laid down. This demands good tools, specialised machinery, continuous measurement of production to see if it is according to specifications, the elimination of waste in manufacture and a large variety in the output.
> (Cubberley, 1916)

Thus the third condition, of acceptance of meritocracy and methods of competition as fair, is also breaking down. There is a crisis of legitimation within the assessment of students, which is leading to reevaluation of the means of appraisal of student performance in many nations. This is interestingly taking different shapes in different countries: UK is experiencing the resurgence of the testing movement, with the emphasis on benchmark tests at age 7, 11 and 14, in order to centralize and standardize, to make schools accountable, and supposedly to raise basic standards. In France, the reverse process is happening, with moves to decentralize the system, and to shift to criterion-referenced* pupil profiles rather than norm-related tests as evidence of school achievement. Yet either move could be interpreted as a response to the problem of legitimizing the school selection function and to the crises in student motivation. Any focus on the testing and appraisal mechanisms within schooling can act to draw attention away from the ultimate relationship schools have to an inequitable or stratified society.

Similar 'masking' operations have been exposed with regard to current management ideologies. A new 'critical theory' of educational management is emerging which traces the transfer of 'scientific management' from industrial corporations to school organization, and argues that such processes act as a technology for control of workers (Bates, 1983). The language of rationality, efficiency and cost-effectiveness disguises the increased colonization of workers by subordinating their human needs to a higher 'objective' truth about economic needs. By presenting 'management' as an expert process, relying on scientific skills and discrete processes, work tasks become fragmented and the decision-making capacity of the teacher is reduced. As Bowles and Gintis argued for the US over a decade ago:

> The concentration of decision making power in the hands of administrators and the quest for economic rationalization had the same disastrous consequences for teachers that bureaucracy and rationalization of production had on most other workers. In the interests of scientific management, control of curriculum, evaluation, counselling, selection of texts, and methods of teaching were placed in the hands of experts. A host of specialists arose to deal with minute fragments of the teaching job. The tasks of thinking, making decisions and understanding the goals of education were placed in the hands of high level administrators. Ostensibly to facilitate administrative efficiency, schools became large and more impersonal. The possibility of intimate or complicated classroom relationships gave way to the social relations of the production line. (Bowles and Gintis, 1976, pp. 204–5)

'Scientific' management may not have spread to all parts of the Third World, but the warnings are there about its effect on the classroom teacher. School organizational problems are presented as *technical* problems, which ignore the power relationships and the structured inequalities around which schools are organized. The use of 'line management', or complex hierarchies of senior management teams, corresponds to the industrial sector's division of labour and clear distinctions between management and workers. The uncritical acceptance of industrial or bureaucratic metaphors within educational institutions means a tying of these institutions to the corporate sector, and provides the means for similar sorts of control mechanisms both of the schools and within the schools. Providing management training only for Heads and senior staff cements a divide between the work of teaching and the work of organizing teaching, in a way that in fact has not traditionally been associated with the enterprise of education in many parts of the world.

> Executives sometimes mention "Our people are our greatest asset". What a stupid remark. People are not an Asset. I believe people *are* the company and that people, not things, will be the focus of business in the future.
> (Anita Roddick, Director, The Body Shop)

Teachers, professionalism and management

Thus questions of teachers' professionalism, and the relationship between teachers and the state, hinge around economic issues and the need to exert control over the teaching force. As Ozga argues in *Schoolwork: Approaches to the Labour Process of Teaching* (1988):

> In times of economic crisis, foreign competition and political dissensus, the central state tends towards strong, directive management which imposes controls on teacher recruitment, training, salaries and status, and curriculum and examination content. In relatively relaxed periods, when resources available for education are sufficient to permit a broad interpretation of priorities, and there is at least the appearance of consensus, management is less crisis-led, appears more relaxed, is more strategic in nature and consequently relies heavily on the promotion of teacher professionalism as a form of control. (Introduction, p.x)

The ideology of professionalism fosters 'worker compliance' and cooption, and has been used historically as an antidote to unionism. The 'professional' teacher is relied on to do unspecified amounts of work without counting hours or insisting on a tight fit between production and reward. Coopting teachers into the policy-making process at national and local levels avoids hostility and organized resistance. Yet the image of professionalism of course implies teachers valuing individual and school autonomy and seeing decisions on curriculum content as their domain. It can invoke resistance to what is seen as state interference in 'expert' educational matters. What becomes instructive therefore is to see how each country manages these dilemmas surrounding the control of the teaching workforce, and to examine the relationship between conceptions of the work of teaching and degrees or types of centralization in education. The intricate debates as to whether teaching is a profession or a semi-profession cannot be seen outside the economic and political context which defines and conditions teachers' actions at any one period or place. New stresses on accountability, and/or financial autonomy, the challenge to 'command' models of school organization, will bring to the fore the political relationship of teachers to the community and to the State. Yet as Polan in a recent book *The Democratic School* argues:

> ...the main obstacle to such developments are teachers themselves, or rather teachers' dismaying level of political ignorance. I do not mean ignorance about the PSBR, the poll tax, SDI, the history of marxism, the activities of the NUT, or any such 'political' issues. I mean their ignorance of their own capacities as political actors. I mean their capacity, through communication — argument, debate, initiative, conflict, action — to change the environment they inhabit — including its most fundamental practices. (Polan, 1989, p. 36)

Teachers' apparent neglect of their political power must be explained and explored. The premises on which this book rests are therefore that

1. Management in schools should be seen against the background of the uneasy tensions in the needs of the state between 'warming up' and 'cooling out' different numbers of students, that is in regulating ambition;
2. Those managerial ideologies and training which rest on top-down, technicist 'skills' approaches are not designed to highlight structured inequalities reflected in the school such as social class, race or gender;
3. Changes in the assessment and appraisal of both teachers and students are integrally linked to national economic considerations and concerns for State control and State legitimacy;
4. Schools are political arenas which can utilize the communication of tension so as to generate radical structural change within their organization, if not outside it.

The aim is therefore to use considerations of divisions such as gender and race to force a reexamination of conceptions of school management and the important issues surrounding it. The book will take a 'teachers' work' approach, which looks at questions of the control of work and the labour process; at social relations within teaching; at the notion of 'career'; at the 'teacher as manager'; and at notions of productivity in education.

It is important to tackle first the basic question of who makes decisions in education. Clearly the management structure of a school, and its ethos and range of objectives will link strongly with the amount of power and decision-making accorded to it, or wrested from its ultimate 'owners'. The next chapter therefore looks at the meanings attached to 'centralization' or 'decentalization' in order to establish whether similar distinctions can be applied to the internal management of the school, and what the linkages between external and internal control are. Chapter 3 then moves on to consider the impact of a different form of 'external influence', that of the structuring of the wider society. It examines the relationship of socio-economic divisions, or social class, to educational outcomes, and details the various management policies implied in attempts to counteract the influence of 'the home'. The fourth chapter focuses more specifically on the question of women in educational administration, as this raises issues not just of female representation at senior levels, but of the challenge to our taken-for-granted, but possibly masculinist and authoritarian notions of 'efficient' management. Race, ethnicity and language are tackled in Chapter 5, as this is a particularly controversial area both in terms of basic definitions of 'race', 'minority', 'racism' and 'multiculturalism', and in terms of the variety of policy approaches internationally. Tied up with inequities in social class, gender and race is the global problem of the divide between mental and manual work, and the classification of students (and their teachers) into different categories of workers. Attempts to mediate this divide are therefore explored in Chapter 6.

The discussion then begins to add the further dimension of the needs of teachers as individuals and as professional workers. Structured inequalities and hierarchies of knowledge will affect them as much as the students, and Chapter 7 explores management strategies which appraise and build on staff needs rather than relegating teachers to the status of simple 'resources' or 'variables' in students' achievement. Neither teachers nor students should be seen, however, as mere victims of the system, and Chapter 8 acknowledges the variability of people's response to their educational environment by examining deviance, subversion, humour and corruption, and exploring their management implications. The penultimate chapter focuses directly on specific policy initiatives for what has been termed 'equal opportunities', while arguing for a replacement of this term and its implicit ideologies by the notion of 'equal rights' policies. It also highlights the contestation and dilemmas around the implementation of school initiatives which seek to challenge both discrimination and concepts of a 'natural' meritocracy. Finally a demand is made for different conceptions of school management based on family images. The argument is for approaches which are equitable, flexible, user-friendly, gender-inclusive but inevitably more politicized than the older 'skills-based' models.

> The aim of education is to induce the largest amount of neurosis that the individual can bear without cracking up.
> (W. H. Auden)

Throughout the book, an attempt is made to present the issues as 'international' and to give examples from a range of countries. The main focus is however on UK and certain Third World areas, for reasons pertaining to the past and current experience of the writer, but also to perceptions of 'gaps' in existing literature. Equity issues in education are comparatively well-explored in the United States, Australasia and in many countries of Europe; they are less apparent, particularly at the level of everyday school management, in countries of Africa and South East Asia. Yet it is the contention of this book that such structural divisions affect the lives of teachers and students in ways that demand urgent reconceptualization of school management, and should entail a reluctance to accept uncritically 'western' models of effective school organization. The exercises and case-studies that follow each chapter are thus intended to enable readers to apply concepts and ideas to their own situations; they have been 'road-tested' on our international students at the School of Education, University of Birmingham, whose contribution should be clearly acknowledged.

There are finally numerous problems of trying to address an international audience, not least the vocabulary and abbreviations used. A glossary of terms is thus provided at the front, and words or phrases to be found in this glossary are indicated on first major use by an asterisk. In the main the now international convention has been adopted of using the word 'student' to apply to any learner of any age, although 'pupils' and 'children' will also figure at times. 'Teacher' is still fortunately a word with worldwide understanding and use, although it may not be long before scientific management deems that we should be termed 'Level Two Curriculum Transmitter' or 'Module Coordinator Number 37'. Let us unite as teachers while we can.

EXERCISE 1: DISCRIMINATION

Clearly as teachers and managers we must all discriminate in our treatment of students and staff, according to our perception of their 'needs'. The question to decide is whether discrimination is 'positive' (in the interests of an individual or group who would otherwise be disadvantaged) or 'negative' (giving an individual or group less favourable treatment on the basis of an irrelevant attribute such as skin colour). Negative discrimination can be direct or indirect: typical definitions would be:

> '*Direct discrimination* consists of treating a person, on racial grounds, less favourably than others are or would be treated in the same or similar circumstances. Segregating a person from others on racial grounds constitutes less favourable treatment.'
>
> '*Indirect discrimination* consists of applying . . . a requirement or condition which, although applied equally to persons of all racial groups, is such that a considerably smaller proportion of a particular racial group can comply with it and it cannot be shown to be justifiable on other than racial grounds. Possible examples are:
> — a rule about clothing or uniforms which disproportionately disadvantages a racial group and cannot be justified;
> — an employer who requires higher language standards than are needed for safe and effective performance of the job.' (UK Code of Practice based on Race Relations Act 1976)

By replacing the word 'racial' with other relevent categories of discrimination, such as 'sex' or 'background', assess whether the following treatments constitute either: no discrimination; positive discrimination; negative direct discrimination; or negative indirect discrimination.

	No Discrim.	Positive Discrim.	Negative Direct	Discrim. Indirect
1. School uniform				
2. Giving more help to a 'slow' reader				
3. A professional job description that stipulates 'under 35'				
4. Ethnic quota system for school entry to rectify previous imbalance				
5. Additional help for 'gifted' children				
6. A union meeting that starts at 5 p.m. (i.e. after work)				
7. A 'blacks-only' management course				
8. Computer club for boys only				
9. Computer club for girls only				
10. Language requirement for entry to higher education				

Chapter 2

Centralization, Decentralization and Control

The aim of this discussion is to relate overall patterns of national control of education to the activity of management in schools. It should be noted that I do not refer to the 'task' of management, as this itself stems from a technicist view of management as an achievable entity like a pile of ironing, with clear boundaries and recognizable goals. Instead, I see school management as a social activity engaged in by people with varying degrees of power and with differing, shifting or unarticulated objectives. While some changes in the national administration of education (such as centralizing curriculum) will have obvious consequences for the work and goals of teachers, the implications for the management *structures* of individual schools are perhaps less immediately clear, and need exploring. Similarly, while the effects on social equality of different patterns of educational control have sometimes been identified at the system level, we need also to examine them at the school level, to establish whether there are connections between the distribution of power and the educational outcomes for students.

First we should briefly clarify the various definitions and conceptions of 'centralization' and 'decentralization', at the national level.

Centralization refers to shifts towards greater government control, or church control or supranational control. (The term 'state' control can often be used for government control, although this may be confusing for countries which distinguish federal from individual state government, as in Nigeria.) In this discussion therefore, 'government' is used to refer to the central power of elected representatives plus the permanent machinery of administration. Education systems can secondly be church centralized, if for example the Roman Catholic church controls the operation of its schools throughout a country. Thirdly, supranational control refers to the administration of schools by an agency outside the country, as in mission schools.

Decentralization is generally conceived as a willingness to broaden or change the distribution of educational power, or conveys the meaning of a transfer of decision-making from the nation state to some socially organic local community. However, there are traditionally three sorts of distinctions made regarding decentralization processes:

(a) *deconcentration*: the creation of regional or field offices, with staff representing the central authority and facilitating the implementation of central directives. This may give *greater* control by the centre over peripheral parts. Many African governments first centralized their administration shortly after Independence by curtailing local government powers, and then deconcentrated authority again, to strengthen the influence of the ruling party at local level (Bray, 1985).

(b) *delegation*: the transferring of more degrees of decision-making to local levels, or to other bodies or training agencies, while maintaining authority in central government. A central authority can however withdraw powers delegated without new legislation.

(c) *devolution*: the creation of local bodies with legal status and/or locally elected officers. These can raise tax revenues and spend them.

I would add a fourth 'definition', that of:

(d) *privatization*: the allowing of 'market forces' to determine the operation of educational institutions.

Internationally, there have been shifts in all directions, with some systems centralizing, some decentralizing, some doing both and some doing neither. The fashion appeared to be more towards decentralization, but there have been swings back to re-centralization in some countries. Distinctions must also be made between the effects of 'top-down' decentralization innovated by the central authority, and 'bottom-up' decentralization demanded by local interest, as Stromquist (1986) found in Peru. Effects will also clearly depend on the cultural history of a country, and the degree of acceptance of hierarchical authority and accepted deference patterns.

The reasons or purposes for a move in either direction are also complex, and it becomes difficult to distinguish the administrative, economic and the political imperatives. Any distinction between reasons and purposes also becomes blurred. For the present, simple lists will do.

Decentralization is attempted for some combination of the following:

(a) to allow a more 'efficient' use of educational and community resources
(b) to promote community participation as an individually fulfilling activity and human right
(c) to reduce hostility to national governments and their policies
(d) to concede to demands for local control
(e) to avoid the negative impact of industrialization and urbanization and bring life back to rural or inner-city communities
(f) to undermine the power of one group by promoting another (e.g. the promotion of parent power is analyzed as a means to undermine the professional power of teachers)

(g) because of a loss of faith in national education
(h) to promote the ideology of free-enterprise economics or consumer choice
(i) to break up large power bases by making smaller ones
(j) to reduce the financial burden on central government.

Centralization or recentralization is preferred for some or all of the following:

(a) fear of loss of control, or threat by radicalized groups or unions
(b) to implement coherent or equitable policies
(c) to effect standardization in output, enabling employment mobility
(d) to avoid multiplication of tiers or duplication of effort
(e) to lower costs and speed up activity
(f) to avoid or monitor corruption
(g) a perception of lack of experienced managers and decision-takers at local levels
(g) difficulty in drawing boundaries or locating communities
(i) a perception of people being unused to involvement, and needing training (e.g. parents)
(j) difficulty in defining 'community representatives', for example whether peasant associations or local officials, and deciding which combination of disparate groups best represents community interests
(k) lack of appeal of decentralization to *any* participants — bureaucrats, teachers, or parents.

The key questions therefore in terms of the effects on equity emerge as: firstly, the purpose for concentrating or diffusing power; secondly the area or issue within education which is centralized or decentralized; and thirdly the unit for local control. While there is a traditional, almost romanticized association between decentralization and democracy, the evidence for this is by no means clear:

> Wide representation can occur within centralised systems. Teacher unions operate at national level within most countries . . . . The equation of centralisation with autocratic policy-making and of decentralization with participation does not survive closer examination. (Lauglo & Mclean, 1985, p. 5)

It is clearly impossible to talk in a vacuum about control until we know what is being decided: whether finance, buildings, curriculum, assessment, teacher recruitment, training and salaries, or the dates of half-term holidays. Similar obvious difficulties emerge in defining 'local' or 'the community'. These can be symbolic or geographic realities, and we cannot compare a recognizable 'village' in a Third World country with a local authority in UK (which may range from 100,000 to $3\frac{1}{2}$ million people) and analyse them equivalently as 'communities'.

Decentralization may also set up intermediate authorities — regional or zonal areas. It may become confusing even to try to distinguish 'centralized' from 'localized': Bray sums up the ambiguities in interpretation well:

> Ambiguity also arises within the government framework. For example higher education can be decentralised in the sense that it is independent of the Ministry of Education or even the government, yet also highly centralized if there is only one university and all major decisions are taken by the Vice-Chancellor and Council. Again, technical education is often decentralized in the sense that it is controlled by several bodies outside the Ministry of Education, yet it can still be very centralized in so far as powers are concentrated in the headquarters of these establishments.
>
> Similarly, even within a Ministry of Education structures may be simultaneously described as centralized and decentralized. For example separate directorates for primary and secondary education may be decentralized if they are autonomous to a very high degree but may be centralized if all major decisions are taken at the top. Alternatively, India's education system gives considerable autonomy to the state governments and in that sense is decentralized; however within the states, some of which are very large, there is considerable centralization . . . . Again, elsewhere many decisions may be taken in regional headquarters rather than in the capital city, but it is usual to find significant centralist strings, especially in relation to the budget. Further, although creations of provincial governments may seem to be a decentralizing move when viewed from the national headquarters or from the provinces themselves, such moves may be accompanied by a reduction in the powers of local governments and of school head-teachers. The interpretation of a move thus depends on the viewpoint of the observer. It cannot be assumed that administrative changes are decentralist merely because their architects describe them that way. (Bray, 1985, p. 185)

We should also draw the distinction between the strength of educational control and its location. In comparing France and England, Broadfoot comments:

> The tendency to equate strong control with a high degree of centralization is misleading for it fails to take into account less obvious and generally much more powerful sources of control and constraint . . . this tendency has led to an over-preoccupation with administrative variables in the study of differences between educational systems and a consequent disregard for how that control is actually mediated and ultimately experienced by teachers in the schools. (Broadfoot, 1985, p. 105)

It is to these school experiences and interpretations that we should now turn.

Implications for school management of shifts in control

Four tendencies will be examined here in terms of their effects on school management and ultimately on equity: two are 'centralizing' ones: technical-rational management and national curricula; and two appear as 'decentralizing' ones: financial devolution and consumer choice.

1. Technical-rational management

The economic recession which has struck many countries has often led to a reemphasis of the vocational and investment function of education in terms of providing a skilled and controllable labour force for international competitiveness. The tightening bond between education and business all over the world has been well demonstrated by Hunt (1987) in *The Incorporation of Education*. Through case studies of USA, UK, Australia, Europe, Malaysia and Singapore, Hunt shows how educational institutions are being 'incorporated' into productive systems of activity, how powerful business interests are able to control ideologies of schooling and 'relevance'. Even at the higher education level, the central concern becomes the profitability from the application of knowledge, with notions of service to the public through dissemination of knowledge replaced by exclusive rights to access by funding groups. The result of such an economic, profit-based rhetoric has been to make education increasingly divisive, with people employing strategies 'that favoured one's self or group and directed the burden of more difficult circumstances elsewhere, but ultimately onto poorer, less powerful or effective people' (Hunt, 1987, p. 127).

The impact of the 'new rationality' in educational thinking is very clear in the transfer of industrial management models to schools and colleges. Bates (1984) contrasts 'educational evaluation' with 'managerial evaluation', with the latter having little to do with the processes by which individuals learn, and everything to do with sorting, classification, allocation and control. Ironically, the previous 'efficiency' of education in producing larger numbers of qualified people for fewer opportunities has led to the escalation of admission requirements to jobs and higher education, and the need by governments to dampen demand and foster the belief that standards are falling rather than rising. Hence the 'return to basics' ideology that currently characterizes many countries and the resurgence of the 'testing movement' to provide accountability and ensure consistent standards. This movement was well written up in Broadfoot's (1984) collection *Selection, Certification and Control*; UK is now experiencing extensions of that accountability ethic in terms of demands for standardized performance criteria for schools, systematic appraisal of teachers and comparative league tables of pupil achievement.

Increased official testing and measurement does not in itself of course lead to higher standards. Teachers have always used tests, either for diagnostic or control purposes, and the imposition of national tests has more to do with standardization and the deskilling of teachers than with increasing the extent of individually diagnostic and remedial screening for pupils. The obvious effect on schools is that teachers begin to teach to the tests, and the tests determine the curriculum rather than merely being a summative evaluation of preceding practices. Such phenomena have been well demonstrated internationally by books such as Dore's *The Diploma Disease* (1976) and Oxenham's *Education versus Qualifications?* (1984).

Linked to the accountability ethic is the spread of various forms of 'corporate management' or 'rational management'. Corporate management and planning originated in American business in the 1950s, and were introduced into British public sector management during the 1960s in order to counter what was seen as excessive departmentalism in local authorities (Bains, 1972). The emphasis is on a unified set of objectives and processes, with specialized structures devised that are 'appropriate' to these processes, such as a corporate planning unit or policy analysis group. In a school, the notion of a headteacher as the 'chief executive' who steers the 'senior management team' is a direct translation of this approach, which attempts to forge an interdisciplinary and total plan for the school rather than subject departments individually competing or negotiating for their share of resources. The aim is consensus over long-term action programmes, with the key management tasks being to establish priorities and measure achievement in relation to the stated objectives.

While such an approach does indeed sound incontrovertible, the consequences of its introduction have led to severe criticism, at least at the local government level. Grey (1982) summarises the main drawbacks as firstly 'an almost complete exclusion of members from policy-making', and secondly a centralization of power within the organization. The tendency appears to be to emphasise the role of officers over members, and a 'depoliticization' of decision-making through the belief that what makes a structure 'appropriate' depends on environmental conditions and not human choice (Greenwood, Hinings and Ranson, 1975). It would seem that the definition of what is 'rational' is unlikely to be devolved to junior members of the organization, often because of fear of loss of control. Stewart observed of local authorities that 'Some management teams have become afraid to expose conflict, lest they seem to deny some strange theory that corporate management means consensus must be achieved at all cost'. He continues 'consensus is just one enemy; but perhaps the biggest enemy is boredom. Some management teams meet too often and consider too many items. Chief officers sit patiently through items that should never be before them, contributing little more than a yawn or an irrelevant comment' (Stewart, 1976). While there are fewer such empirical studies of schools to demonstrate the workings of corporate management in practice, Stewart's description may find some resonances among those involved in interdepartmental committees within the education sector. Given the intrinsically contradictory nature of education functions as outlined in

Chapter 1, it would be even more difficult to achieve agreement over priorities than it would with regard to, say, health, or transport; but of course that is the very appeal of the 'corporate plan' to those who seek to control education. It implies the existence of universal rationality and joint objectives in a system which contains neither.

Thus the sociological critiques of newer management styles in education stem from concerns over the attempted identification of both a singularity of purpose and an equally standardized way of assessing its achievement, with little acknowledgment of the essentially political nature of such definitions. Corporate management techniques, and tighter central control through assessment, appraisal and accountability inevitably lead to norm-related ideals of 'good practice', and the highlighting of 'performance criteria' by which individuals and schools are to be compared and judged. This has clear effects on pupil differentiation and on teacher differentiation and reward, with the older notions of diversity or that 'everyone is good at something' giving way to recipe checklists both for management practice and for participants' activities. A review of Davidson's *Essential Management Checklists* in the journal *Management in Education* (1987) extols its virtues thus: 'Providing managers with a complete checklist system to manage the many situations which may arise during the business day, this book replaces long passages of management theory with easy to digest information that can be applied immediately'. Am I (a) alone, (b) paranoid or (c) forward-looking in finding the idea of management-by-ticklist a sinister and dehumanizing development?

> The current popularity of management courses for aspirant teachers is yet one more illustration of the demise of the traditionally anarchic English education system which was nevertheless tightly internally controlled by ideological networks of moral and professional accountability to clients and colleagues respectively .... In its place is an increasingly centralized bureaucratic structure in which formal, contractual accountability reinforces a managerial and hierarchical ethos oriented to technically defined goals and in which the individual is increasingly powerless to exercise personal choice or judgement.
> (Broadfoot 1985)

Centralized standard testing of cohorts of children, like IQ tests, reveals their ability to do the tests, and little else about their overall ambience as a learner in their school. Similarly, any teacher appraisal which is centrally inspired will be contextual, that is, it cannot assess the way teachers will actually respond in the circumstances or context in which they work. Hartley and Broadfoot (1988, p. 49) conclude:

> Arbitrarily-defined performance criteria are extremely unlikely to do more than provide evidence for the excision of the very weakest teachers. Rather than improving the performance of the majority, they are more likely to lower teachers' professional commitment as they lower their morale. The effect of such bureaucratic appraisal is thus likely to be the opposite of that intended.

And just as no IQ test can be value free, doubts have been cast, too, on the possible gender bias of bureaucratized teacher appraisal: such criteria are likely to be drawn up by men, with typical male career and school involvement patterns in mind (Evetts, 1988). The assumption behind standardized rational accountability is that it is possible to be objective about behaviour; and that true objectivity exists outside of any value system. However, as feminists may like to point out, objectivity is just another name for male subjectivity. Centralized accountability and managerially-inspired norms are ways to deny the professional expertise of teachers to evaluate both their students and themselves; they become an incremental way of deskilling teachers.

> Such comparative data [from USA] suggest that the most likely outcome of this kind of policy initiative is demoralization, insecurity and divisiveness. But, whilst the Government [in UK] persists in ignoring the evidence that bureaucratically-inspired testing does not improve standards but rather tends to lower them because it erodes the goodwill which lies at the heart of successful teaching, we are likely to witness an ever more extreme series of centrally-inspired measures, each one designed to make up for the failure of the equally misconceived initiative that preceded it. The basic lessons management theory suggest are that goodwill and democratic participation are a much surer basis for attempts to raise standards than fear and coercion. (Hartley and Broadfoot, 1988, p. 49)

The link between managerial control and assessment can also be demonstrated by the Chinese experience. With the 'diploma disease' now strongly influencing educational development, the former 'people-managed' schools are more subject to central control, urban bias and conflict over educational goals (Robinson, 1988). A broad type of decentralization has shifted to a very narrow one, involving only token participation in low level policies such as construction of school buildings. 'This suggests that the gap between educational experts and masses has widened, and that the Chinese leadership has lost confidence in the capabilities of peasants and local officials to manage

local schools . . . the equation of decentralization with mass control but low quality became an institutionalized fixture of the educational expert mentality.' (Robinson, 1988, p. 182).

The 'expert mentality' is thus one of the most disturbing byproducts of centralization of control. Whether it is expertise in management or in evaluation, the effect is the same: an increasing spiral of lack of confidence in members of an organization to make their own judgements, and a gradual build-up of mystical technical-expert knowledge confined to those with executive powers — whether at school or national level. The result is an intolerance of diversity, yet paradoxically a growth in divisiveness: barriers increase between the managed and the managers, the appraised and the appraisers and between the failures and the successes according to narrowly defined norms of performance for schools, teachers and students.

2. Curriculum

The 'new rationality' is also having its effects on curriculum policy. The issue is not merely the centralization of the curriculum in order to ensure consistency in terms of school experience, but the criteria by which currently 'worthwhile' knowledge is defined, by whom and for whom. This is an age-old question for philosophers of education, but the new trends in many parts of the world merit a renewed political analysis. Various strands will affect the internal management of schools; the 'back to basics' drive reflecting concern over levels of literacy and numeracy; the resurgence of vocationalism to match projected manpower needs; 'technoromanticism' displayed as an uncritical acceptance of the spread of information technology; and the intrusion of the corporate business ethic into curriculum transmission and materials.

All these trends represent a response to a perceived mismatch between the imperatives of the workplace and the products of schools. Regardless of rising levels of literacy and qualifications all over the world, it is convenient to attribute low economic performance to lack of skills in the incoming workforce. The reaction against the so-called progressivism, radicalism and self-reliance of the 1960s and 1970s has been the renewed emphasis on the 3Rs, often through increased output of materials by government curriculum development centres (see for example Malaysia, 1982). The rapid expansion of schooling in Third World countries brought on by attempts at Universal Primary Education and the resultant knock-on effect of expansion of the secondary sector has, ironically, not necessarily opened up opportunities for teachers to participate in curriculum development and change, rather the reverse. Concern about standards, plus increased competition between schools and between students, tends to lead to uniformity in syllabus across educational institutions, at least in the government sector. In analyzing the progress of the 'youth villages' in the Seychelles (planned to be cooperative, participatory and production-oriented), Haffenden observed:

> ... with the project expanding (to in total 4 villages) the maintenance of resources, continuity and academic standards required new teachers to 'fit in' rather than recreate.... Each village was to have an Educational Convenor, and eventually a full group of Assistance Co-ordinators. In addition, such posts of Head of Programme Development, Pedagogical Development Officers and Pedagogical Development Convenors were created. The effect of this was the further distancing of teachers from participating in the curriculum development and thus establishing greater central control. (Haffenden, 1986)

The effects were a return to the more traditional 'academic' emphasis, so that instead of a radical, production-centred curriculum, the National Youth Service became 'a boarding school with some farming added on'. Similar comments have been made about the Brigades in Botswana (Knox and Castles, 1982).

Selection examinations for entry into the white collar labour market are clearly a great centralizing force, but it is interesting to note the variations between countries in terms of who is to attempt the traditionally academic curriculum and who the vocational one. We need firstly to distinguish between the 'weak' academic and the 'strong' academic versions. It has been pointed out that many of the self-help, community-financed schools in the Third World will in fact be providing a 'weak academic' version of the better funded older established institutions, as this is what

Kenya gives Shakespeare seal of non-colonialist approval

Lindsey Hilsum in Nairobi

To study or not to study Shakespeare, that is the question troubling curriculum writers in Kenya. In 1981, the bard was banished from the O- and A-level syllabus as a move "to get rid of the colonial hang-over in independent Kenya."

But on Sunday, the Kenyan president, Mr Daniel Arap Moi, came to his defence. "The Ministry of Education dropped Shakespeare thinking it is colonial but I do not see why it should not be part of our sylla-bus", he said.

"Shakespeare was a man of international experience and even the British cannot claim a right to his writings as their own culture."

One teacher commented: "Shakespeare was declared dead a decade ago. Now he's being resuscitated — it's a bit like Stalin going in and out of favour in the Soviet history books."

Although Kenyan children have not studied Shakespeare in the original since 1981, they have read Swahili translations by the former Tanzanian presi-dent, Dr Julius Nyerere, in their Swahili literature course.

Ministry of Education offi-cials appear not to have been consulted before President Moi's pronouncements, but have to implement them.

Curriculum developers res-ponsible for the 1981 decision refused to comment, fearing, maybe, that after the President has spoken the rest is silence.

The Guardian 12.7.88

parents want rather than vocational schooling (Bray and Lillis, 1988). In spite of reactions against colonial definitions of academic schooling, and attempts to nation-alize and localize curriculum and syllabus, older versions of the foundations of learning still survive. The classic example is Banda's Kamuzu Academy in Malawi, where every student studies Latin and Greek to O-level. The school is founded on the discipline, learning and syllabus of British public schools, a recreation of Eton for the élite boys and girls of the nation. Classics are of course balanced by modern language and science labs, a carpentry workshop and art, drama and music facilities. The aim is unashamedly to create future leaders of Malawi, a 'home-grown administrative élite' (Allen-Mills, 1987). The school has been in existence only seven years, and it remains to be seen how far this will remain an eccentric and unique experiment for the privileged, and how far it will influence the mass of Malawian education. The prediction for the UK is that academically challenging schools will indeed be increasingly the prerogative of the independent and (by definition in UK) the élite sector:

It can not be entirely fanciful for us to see three curricula emerging from the system. The national standardized curriculum for the mass of the population, in poorly funded schools transmitting powerful messages of limited expectations through their shabby buildings and learning resources;

a technically and vocationally oriented curriculum in the city technology colleges, and in the TVEI-influenced levels of the well supported maintained sector schools; and a free floating academically challenging and often innovative curriculum in the independent and grant maintained schools. These would be apt curricula for a system designed to reproduce the increasingly divided society towards which we seem to be heading. (Campbell *et al.*, 1987, p. 376)

In South Africa, however, the vocational versus academic divide naturally reflects their dual system as opposed to the tripartite one of UK. Muller (1987) shows how the 'manpower shortages' argument was the ostensible reason for increasing emphasis on 'skills' in Black education. Earlier investigations into 'differentiated education' had rejected the idea that the labour order should dictate to secondary education who should be 'trained'; yet the de Lange report (HSRC 1981) used manpower projections to point to the need for technical and vocational manpower for Blacks. Muller casts doubts on the actual size of any 'shortages' and on whether a skill emphasis would actually create a buffer black middle class; instead he points to the social rather than technical dimension of 'skill' used in the reports, and the emphasis on values, discipline and *controllable* skills to create a politically more manageable workforce and a reserve army of workers:

> The argument would run that in the past, black education actually failed in an important sense: it failed to effect the necessary differentiated commodification of black labour through education. Some of the results of this failure were a black community inconveniently united against apartheid; less than optimally productive black labour; and underdeveloped local consumer markets. (Muller, 1987, p. 93)

By commodification, Muller refers to the personalization and privatization of 'skill', and the raising of consumption desires and possibilities 'by translating imperfectly articulated yearnings and emancipatory ideas into assimilable commodities.'

Parallel critiques have been made of the 'values' and 'social skills' components of the TVEI* packages in use in UK schools: how far are they liberating and how far merely a 'domestication' of the workforce into the requirements of a capitalist mode of production? The key question for our concern with management is the freedom of teachers to either design, interpret or transform vocational skills-based curricula. The fear expressed by Apple in USA is that:

> The language of efficiency, production, standards, cost-effectiveness, job skills, work discipline and so on — all defined by powerful groups and always threatening to become the dominant way we think about schooling — has began to push aside concerns for a democratic curriculum, teacher autonomy, and class, gender and race equality. (Apple, 1986, p. 154)

However, we should not see the curriculum simply as an instrument of the capitalist — or socialist — classes.

> Education is at once the result of contradictions and the source of new contradictions. It is an arena of conflict over the production of knowledge, ideology, and employment, a place where social movements try to meet their needs and business attempts to reproduce its hegemony. (Carnoy & Levin, 1985)

Much will depend on the critical capacity of teachers with regard to new incursions into method and material. While as Linn (1985) points out, there were considerable debates around the shift from fountain pens to ballpoint pens, and from slide rules to calculators, no such discussion has taken place about the desirability of micro-computers and their implications for teacher pedagogies. Beveridge refers to this as the 'technoromanticism' of publications on information technology, which ignore the political dimension and possible pitfalls. Thus Beynon and MacKay outline the congruence of IT* with certain dominant discourses.

> In the realm of education, computers provide solutions to those concerned about so-called falling standards; they provide the opportunity to teach high-fliers and slow-learners alike; the rhetoric is of pupil control, at a time of government attack on teachers; they are highly relevant; they are needed by the nation, to enhance productivity and outstrip overseas competitors; they enhance national prestige ... and are congruent with Thatcherist notions of self-help and parental power ... ; they motivate otherwise alienated pupils; and they offer solutions to teacher didacticism or inefficiency. (Beynon and MacKay, 1989)

They also point out how IT in education constitutes a major market, with initiatives to put computers into all schools constituting a hidden subsidy to UK manufacturers, in that technology was 'dumped' in school rather than specifically designed for educational needs.

Computers in schools cannot of course be a major priority for many low-income countries, and this discussion should not be developed here; but given the rapid spread of IT, it is timely to create a critical climate whereby schools and teachers do not reify the computer, elevate the machine over human behaviour, and become unaware of the interest groups and economic rationale behind the technological imperative. New jobs and positions of responsibility in schools are indeed created around technology, but we need far more empirical research into the actual effects on learning processes of students before these new tiers in the management of schools assume a taken-for-granted reality.

All curriculum materials, not just computers, can be 'commercial' in the sense that profits can be made from their production. Centralized curriculum materials, if produced by Government printers, will of course minimize the market base to book production, and in that sense would be less linked to the business ethic. Yet any cuts in expenditure forcing reliance on 'self-help' initiatives may mean the incursion of commercial promotions into the classroom. The International Coffee Organization has instigated a course in nine UK colleges leading to a Certificate in Coffee Studies — with one of the assignments including drinking the coffee. Pring (1987) claims this is but the tip of the iceberg, and quotes the National Consumer Council report *Classroom Commercials* which claims that 'increasingly, children and teachers in the classroom are using leaflets, charts, worksheets and videos which have been produced by commercial and industrial enterprises specifically for school pupils and which are distributed to schools free, or at a heavily subsidized price'. Pring points out how the promotion of a privately produced product may therefore occur, even though it might contradict some of the educational messages taught in school — for example in the field of nutrition. One might want to label this kind of sponsorship a 'recentralization' — but this time into the corporate business world of profitability. The introduction of the national curriculum in UK has made no mention of the control of the surrounding materials; privatization would of course not be incongruent with the entrepreneurial, market-led ideology for education which is simultaneously, and contradictorily, current in UK conservative thinking.

The effects on schools of strengthening central control of curriculum must therefore be examined in terms of: a) who it is intended for (whether for privileged or underprivileged sectors of the educational system); b) the rationale behind its inception ('standards', skills, workforce domestication or national unity); and c) the surrounding curriculum materials and technology, their design and diffusion.

The evidence for national curricula providing national cohesion is not in fact strong; nor is the evidence that it will create a unified, committed and participatory workforce of teachers.

Decentralizing trends

1. Financial devolution

The notion of schools managing or generating their own budgets has appeal to both sides of the political spectrum. The monetarist right would support market-inspired, margin-conscious organizations; the liberal left would claim a blow for democracy and freedom from bureaucratic control. The reality of whose interests are served by financial devolution will depend on a number of crucial, if obvious factors.

The first is the sufficiency of the budget that is provided. There would be a clear contrast between the 'independence' of a school that is expected to raise the major part of its budget from community support (as in 'Harambee'* schools in Kenya) and one that is given the total budget by the government but is free to experiment with radical models, such as the Danish Volkschule. The evidence from the Harambee movement is that the existence of self-help institutions side by side with government institutions can actually *increase* inequality between regions and between communities, as well as between the government and the Harambee schools (Mwiria, 1985; Keller, 1980; Bray and Lillis, 1988). Much will depend on the immediate wealth of the community and the way resources are managed. In Kenya, bursars are provided in government schools, accounts clerks in assisted schools, but in unaided schools, no formal provision is made, and Harambee schools find their own financial personnel. 'Their success in doing so dictates how well accounts are submitted and audited. In many cases, it often becomes the responsibility of the heads. Rarely, though, are they qualified for such tasks, and corruption and embezzlement are frequent.' (Lillis, 1987 p. 111). This question of corruption will be returned to in Chapter 8, and its links with the financing of schools.

The second factor is what aspects of finance are devolved, for example, whether fees, teachers' salaries, or buildings. Where education is not free, there are strong arguments for the devolution of responsibility for fees to the school level, if they are not set so high as to create inequality as mentioned previously. Bray (1988b) mentions: a) flexibility for individual circumstances (communities able to operate scholarship schemes; payments by instalment, or at a season of the year when money is more plentiful); and b) the cost of the collection: at government level this is considerable, in terms of mechanisms to receive the money from heads and check whether every child has been accounted for. When head teachers are required to bring money to a central location, they incur travelling expenses and neglect their teaching. At community level, such machinery and checks do not have to be so elaborate.

Swartland and Taylor similarly comment for Botswana:

> The recent standardization of school fees in all secondary schools, motivated by a desire to avoid inequitable differences between government and community schools, also has the effect of removing the freedom of a Board of Governors to fix its own fees in the light of its own needs. One of the strengths of a system of local control in education is the diversity and flexibility which is possible, and the responsiveness to locally perceived needs. Increasing government support too easily turns into conformity and control. It also heightens expectations of what government can and should do, and reinforces a dependent mentality rather than one of self-reliance. Having got subsidies, teachers and buildings from the government, the schools are now asking for film-projectors, security fences, 'official-free' stamps, school vehicles, and graders to level their sports fields. There is no easy escape from the dilemma that the more the government is able to provide, the more the government is expected to do, and the less the community expects to do for itself. (Swartland and Taylor, 1988, p. 151)

Teacher salaries represent a different question. The evidence here is that a devolution of responsibility to fix teachers' salaries is on the whole divisive, for schools as well as for the teachers. Poor schools are unable to pay high salaries, and will attract only unqualified or refugee teachers from neighbouring countries. Self-help schools may find it difficult to pay teachers any salaries, let alone competitive ones (Lillis, 1988, p. 78) and they are unable to offer pension rights or security of tenure. In some ways, this may provide teaching openings for groups who do not have regular qualifications — perhaps ethnic minority groups or females — but the end result is a confirmation of existing structural inequalities.

> Since the push towards the Four Modernisations barefoot doctors and *minban* teachers have been physically beaten by villagers for failing to produce students who pass the exam for entrance into higher schools . . . . Most widespread, however, is the attitude that if peasants have to pay the salaries of the teachers, the teachers must work. And work means labour in the fields. Brigades and villages have been withholding wages from teachers until they perform assigned field work.
> (Robinson, 1988)

'Freedom' to fix salaries can also mean the freedom to have pay differentials according to subject offered. National schemes to provide extra incentives for teachers in 'shortage' subjects are under consideration in UK, but this is not as yet practised by individual schools, even in the independent sector. Again, the outcome is likely to be divisive, as different groupings within the teaching population are not evenly spread among curriculum subjects, and extra pay for Maths and Science, for example, could exacerbate gender differentials in teaching careers. It denies the right for 'equal pay for work of equal value' as established in the European court of law, and legitimizes a hierarchy of knowledge without acknowledging the political or economic interest involved in definitions of 'shortage' or 'excess'.

At present, most schools in the UK are still however dealing with 'small change'. Even so, there are interesting differences in the way budgets are allocated in the school. Three styles of allocation are distinguished by Simkins (1986): patronage, the 'club' culture, with concentration of power at the centre, depending on personal relationships between the head and key members of staff, and using informal soundings to decide priorities; market styles, using clearly defined roles for middle management, who put in formal bids in competition; and collegial methods, where heads of department participate in deciding allocations through agreement. The last two styles may use a 'formula' system, looking at comparable ratios such as pupil-periods taught, cost of particular subject areas etc. Significantly, Simkins predicts that with increased financial delegation, less participative approaches are unlikely to survive. Formulae may become more popular. Elsewhere he argues that the issue concerns not the principle of choice but the boundaries — what resource choices lie legitimately in the hands of teachers and heads?

> A case can be made that those responsible for managing schools should be concerned with all the major trade-offs that affect the resourcing of the curriculum. Such trade-offs may only effectively operate at the margins of resourcing. But at those margins choices between, for example, further equipment and materials, additional ancillary staff hours, and supplementary full- or part-time teaching staff could have considerable implications for the nature and quality of curriculum provision. Rather different issues arise, however, when we consider areas such as maintenance of buildings or the management of lettings or catering which some schemes seek to delegate. Choices here do not so obviously directly affect classroom provision, except insofar as more efficient operations might generate savings to supplement capitation or other types of curriculum expenditure. Furthermore management of such activities clearly requires knowledge and judgement which is not obviously part of the normal repertoire of the professional educator. Whether it should be part of the normal repertoire of the educational manager is another matter. (Simkins, 1987, p. 16)

There is clearly reluctance in many educational systems to accord financial managerial status to school principals. In his comparative study of Columbia and Venezuela, Hanson gives a graphic account of the lengthy procedures involved in Venezuelan administration, with a school head having to list annually all the special needs of the school anticipated for the coming year, for example, new maps, paint, repairs for a broken fence or new desks. The lists were forwarded up the district, regional and ministerial hierarchy, with the materials arriving eight months later, one year later, or sometimes never. All requests had to go through the chain of command, even though officials had absolutely no power to act upon them. Hanson comments:

> Many of the administrative procedures utilized in Venezuela seemed to be designed for use in ideal conditions, where everything is predictable and controllable. The highly rule-oriented system guides the actors at the lowest level through their prepared steps. Unfortunately, the administrative

system was not equipped to deal rapidly with unanticipated developments — for example, a damaged school roof or a stolen typewriter. In such situations, because district and regional supervisors had no authority, decisions were ultimately made at the top levels of the ministry. But the decision-making time lag adversely affected the teaching learning process and school plant maintenance. However, it would be inaccurate to say that top ministry officials were not aware that materials wear out and buildings frequently need repairs. They could predict such developments on the basis of experience. *But they always responded as though the developments were completely unexpected.* (my italics) (Hanson, 1986, p. 173)

The first annual snowfall in UK has the same effect of surprise on transport systems: it appears difficult for large bureaucracies to cope with unpredictability, even though that unpredictability is itself predictable. While salaries should remain centralized, the arguments for the devolution of as much day-to-day finance as possible to schools would seem clear, both in the interests of forcing more participation by staff, as Simkins claims, and in the interests of circumventing delay in the interests of students.

2. Consumer choice

The ultimate level of devolution is therefore to the 'client' or 'consumer' of education: students and their parents. The relaxation of controls on private education, as in Pakistan (Jimenez and Tan, 1987), and the 'open enrolment' strategy in UK signals a return to free enterprise economics as a guiding educational principle. Freedom to choose an education has always been a possibility for the wealthy in most countries; more recent market-inspired ideologies seek to extend this principle to all parents, in the interests of the public accountability of the schools. While the notion of voucher systems* waxes and wanes, a deregulation of upper admission limits, or of fixed quotas, means 'popular' schools being able to offer more places to students of their choice, and 'unpopular' schools forced to reconsider their policies or close. The rationale is an attack on any 'forced egalitarianism', such as quotas, or attempts at 'a good mix'. The quota system for entry to various levels of education in many countries was an attempt to compensate for regional inequality (as in Nigeria), for ethnic inequality (as in Malaysia) or for gender inequality (as in Zambia) (see Davies, 1986a, for a previous discussion). There is indeed debate as to whether racial quotas in particular merely compound racism; neither the bussing of children to achieve 'balance' nor the restriction of entry of qualified but over-represented ethnic groups are likely to promote racial harmony if maintained for indefinite periods. Thus the argument for deregulation is that making schools sensitive to their locality — whatever its composition — is ultimately likely to improve the quality of education for all children, regardless of social origin.

The validity of this argument can be examined by reference to a recent case in UK: Dewsbury. Kirklees County Council was technically attempting to achieve a numerical balance among its primary schools to cope with falling rolls. Families in an area which had traditionally sent its children to Overthorpe Primary School were refused entry there, and offered places at Headfield, whose pupils were 85 per cent Asian origin. A year long battle ensued, with parents refusing to send their children to Headfield, and instigating a Do-It-Yourself education for twenty-two children in the upper room of the Thornhill Lees Hotel. Central government refused to intervene. The rebel parents denied racism, emphasizing instead that there were empty classrooms at Overthorpe, the traditional feeder school. Kirklees County Council too denied that it was trying to restrict admissions to achieve a racial mix, as this is forbidden in the Race Relations Act. Yet that this was a racialized question is undeniable, with parents privately expressing anxieties about the culture, values and standards of a predominantly, to them, 'alien' school, and claiming it failed to provide a proper act of collective (i.e. Christian) worship. The outcome was a 'victory' for the parents, on a technicality that Kirklees had not followed statutory procedures requiring it to advertize its intended admissions policy in local newspapers. The incident was seen as a test case, and a forerunner of the 'opting out' provisions of the new Education Act whereby schools are able to choose whether to operate independently of local authority control. Press and Trade Union comments thus highlighted the racial implications of 'open' admissions, in words such as 'green light for segregation' (local secretary, National Union of Teachers); 'Dewsbury triumph glosses over bigotry' (*Sunday Times*, 17.7.88). Freedom of choice is seen as likely to ensure freedom by schools and parents to be racist, sexist or even classist in their negotiations as to school admissions.

The overall dilemma is well summarized by Campbell *et al.*, (1987):

The new policies for opting out schools and city technology colleges, and for open enrolment at least offer the opportunity for currently disadvantaged groups, especially in the inner cities, to take somewhat more control over the content and direction of their children's schooling. If the direction is towards more formal teaching methods, and firmer forms of externally imposed discipline; and if the curriculum content becomes pulled back into more recognized forms of subjects, and away from integrated approaches, or more directly vocationally oriented, it may be a matter of regret to curriculum theorists, but that would be a small price to pay for an increased sense among minority group parents that the system had become more openly responsive to their perceived needs and under their control. The most obvious beneficiaries under this scenario would be the groups in the inner cities that feel most strongly that their religious, linguistic, and cultural preferences are badly supported in the maintained sector schools, which have necessarily to be pluralist and secular or to provide, if voluntary (i.e. denominational), a single religious emphasis. A more sinister aspect of this assertion of parental and community choice is that it may come to be exercised on grounds of social and racial prejudice, with parents jumping at the opportunity provided by open enrolment to legitimize the removal of their children from schools with a multi-ethnic intake and multicultural approaches. Ghettoization of schooling would be reinforced, not reduced. (Campbell *et al.*, 1987, p. 374)

If parental 'choice' directly through market principles is a doubtful avenue to equality, would increased rights through the medium of governorship of schools be less divisive? Increasing governors' powers is a trend to be examined closely. Papua New Guinea makes a good case study: Bray (1988a) found that although Boards of Governors were supposed to be 'broadly representative of their communities', there were gender, age, residential and ethnic disparities. There were few female members, reflecting traditional patterns where women are ascribed few decision-making roles. On the other hand, most schools did have a good range of occupations among their Board members, with communities not seeming to consider it necessary for Board members to have attended school themselves, and a large percentage being illiterate. The suggestion that pupils might be represented was not however taken up, again as it would not fit with social patterns which do not give youths decision-making roles of this kind. Geographic representation was carefully organized, although complaints were heard that representatives from distant villages did not attend meetings. Representation from the main ethnic groups was organized less carefully, although there were efforts by some urban schools to do this (Bray, 1988a).

The importance of equity in representation depends of course on the actual powers of any governing body or parents' association. A policeman school governor was recently debarred by the Court of Appeal in UK from serving on an appointments committee, on the grounds that he would have access to confidential and sensitive information about members of the public (*Times Educational Supplement*, 19 August, 1988). In Papua New Guinea, however, Boards of Governors in any case saw construction and maintenance as their principal role: they were reminded of this by the teachers, who were perhaps less enthusiastic about Boards assuming responsibility for pupil enrolment and discipline. At another level still, parents' associations were widely seen as labour forces to be mobilized when it was time to build classrooms, cut the grass or repair toilets (Bray, 1988a).

The relationship between professionals and laity is always going to be a problematic one, for as Pascal (1987) points out in her study of democratized primary school government in Birmingham, 'it is difficult for part-time amateurs to govern full-time professionals in a meaningful way' (p. 198). Nonetheless changing circumstances mean that professionals now have to 'sell' their services to the population and tailor provision to some extent the views of their clients. A dominant interest has to adapt to the pressures of a plurality of legitimate interests and devolve a certain degree of power to them. In Pascal's analysis, however, this explains the current conflict between centralist and devolutionary trends in UK, as:

> a certain degree of devolution is necessary to maintain the control of the dominant interest. The present situation in which governing bodies are apparently being handed more power can therefore be interpreted as a means of diffusing power at a local level. This acts to diminish the chance of any interest challenging the central authority which is at the time increasing its control in key areas of policy and decision-making (Pascal, 1987, p. 200).

Nonetheless, Pascal noted that although there was some conflict between 'professionals' and 'laity' on the governing bodies, 'there were indications that governing bodies which embodied an equitable blend of interests engaged in important, appropriate and meaningful tasks could be a vehicle for the resolution of this.' Conflict was generated where one interest was able to dominate to the exclusion of others, particularly in 'professionally-based' issues such as curriculum development, but there was little evidence of conflict in other areas such as liaison.

The arguments would therefore appear the obvious ones that for governing bodies to be effective in representing a plurality of interests, they must themselves be equitable, and they must have tasks and roles which do not continually permit one area of expertise to dominate. Such tasks must nonetheless have a real significance in the pedagogic and community objectives of the school. But then a tension is to be expected between governors' evaluation/monitoring roles and their expected support roles for the school. If governors are to participate in the call for increased accountability of schools, their internal relationships and the range of relationships with the school will need serious discussion.

With regard to the whole question of devolution to the consumers, 'accountability' is a double-edged sword. If it leads to league table rankings of schools and powerful parents able to exercise class interest or racial prejudice in choosing a school, then this appears to be divisive socially and educationally. If it leads to schools being more attuned to the plurality of needs and desires in their catchment area, then this would seem to be an equalizing effort. The research in Australia by Connell and colleagues revealed differences in the Head's role as between independent schools that must respond to the market and are daily accountable to parents, and 'working class' government schools with a given clientele, where parents have little sense of ownership or participation in school objectives (Connell *et al.*, 1982). If accountability extends the sensitive school/home relationships that characterize ruling class schools to their working class counterparts, then this can only be productive; but this cannot be achieved through individual parents competing unequally with each other for favoured school places. It can be achieved only through the parents of an existing school population entering some democratic process of representation or consultation whereby conflicts of interest can be brought to the surface and honestly, if time-consumingly, disputed.

Conclusion

This discussion of recent aspects of centralist or decentralist moves within educational management has confirmed that neither move is of itself likely to reduce or extend inequality. We saw that certain centralizing initiatives around curriculum and workplace orientations were likely to increase social divisions. We also saw that decentralist tendencies around financial delegation and consumer choice were not without problems in terms of their allowing powerful interests a freer rein. To explain this, we should return to the list of motives for either direction. It would appear that if the impetus for either move is primarily economic, then less powerful groups will suffer disproportionately in terms of either receiving resources or participating in decisions. If on the other hand the aims are creative, specifically egalitarian and well-funded, then they can either permit experimentation and diversity which can favour minority groups, or they can maintain overall policy-oriented principles which proscribe domination of one group by another — or they can do both simultaneously.

While the tendencies under the current world climate are likely to be the economic rather than the expansionary ones, the outlook is not necessarily all bleak for those managing schools. The tricks are the usual transformatory ones of realigning aims: schools in UK for example, will appropriate MSC* funding, supposedly centralizing, to their own ends. Decentralizing moves can be used to galvanize the community, and governors, into making more demands on government and to spread knowledge of political or welfare rights. National curricula, on the other hand, are harder to divert; as with increased emphasis on particular types of religious education, they will begin to influence the type of staff appointed, and the perceived value of 'extra' curricular activities. The climate cannot but put greater demands on schools to achieve cost-cutting and standardization, and the subversive creativity of managers will be at a premium.

EXERCISE 2: THE CONTROL OF SCHOOLS

The following are case-studies or viewpoints on various aspects of the 'control' of schools. The first refers to the move towards local financial management in UK; the second to increased powers of parent governors; the third to problems in Commonwealth countries relating to community and parent involvement in school policy and financing.

Reading and comparing these may enable reflection on the effects on equity of
a) devolving school budgets to Heads and Boards of Governors,
b) devolving parts of school financing to the 'community',
c) devolving power to parents and parent governors,
d) the likely decisions that a Head may make to resolve the tensions described.

Nipscratting? No thanks

Gerald Haigh is a slightly surprising early candidate for local financial management

Volunteering to be one of our education authority's pilot schools for local financial management was bound to cause the odd ripple among my fellow heads. I have never thought of myself, after all, as one of the authority's whiz kids. Why, I still call most of the advisory team Mr or Mrs, and look askance when a colleague catches an adviser by the arm at a meeting and leads him aside saying, "A word in you ear, Spike . . . "

Already through, my mere existence as a volunteer has comforted many. "If Gerald can get through this unscathed then anybody can," one previously sceptical head was heard to declare. In such ways are even the least of us called to serve.

The truth is that I feel very positive about LFM. To enhance the status of individual schools by giving them the freedom to manage their affairs seems to me an inevitable historical development only coincidentally tied up with the policies of the present Government.

Of course, we have some genuine worries. Our school, for example, carries a salary bill inflated by safeguarding. Among those protected is yours truly. Will I, at some stage when all the transitional arrangements run out, have to decide whether to ask the governors to continue to safeguard me at the expense of other sectors of the budget? Well, probably — but sufficient unto the day and difficult examples do not really affect the soundness of the basic principle.

My colleagues on the staff are worried. I know, at the thought that I might disappear from the timetable, from the curriculum and generally from view, while I wrestle with columns of figures. Whatever happens, though I have absolutely no intention of becoming a sort of clerk-bursar to the establishment. Management yes; number-crunching no.

One problem of LFM, mind you, will be not so much the heads who fear it but the heads who take to it like ducks to water. Already the legends grow — of the head who searches tirelessly through the sanitaryware catalogues until he finds a urinal which only flushes when someone breaks a beam. "With what?" we all chorused when we heard the story. "This was not made clear," was the disappointing answer.

And if that is too apocryphal for you, just refer to Richard Jameson, who writes with apparent approval of the Cambridgeshire head who made all his children sit with their coats on so he could afford another teacher (*TES*, July 9). This according to Mr Jameson, "said it all". It sure did. I want to point out that I have no intention of getting into this kind of workhouse economics, best described as what my father would have called "nipscratting".

We can all surely see, though, that there will be heads who will weep for joy at the challenges posed by LFM, which may yet provide for the apotheosis of those colleagues who want to see a full exercise book before issuing a new one. Calculators at the high port they will prowl their schools switching off lights, cutting pencils in half and pondering the cost-effectiveness of — as an ex-colonial head with whom I worked longed to do — deterring vandals by establishing a family of baboons in the school grounds.

Incidentally, we need to be cautious about one thing. Cambridgeshire may have been, up to now, the Mecca for LFM students. We have all gasped at the story of the Cambridgeshire head who gives you a good lunch, tells you about LFM and then hands you a bill. ("That will do nicely.") We need to remind ourselves, though, that no existing LFM scheme comes up to the requirements now set by the Government. A good authority will now get its act together, in the light, not so much an anecdote and the limited experience of other areas, but of its own particular needs. I am not sure I should even visit one of the existing schemes, for events, surely, are fast overtaking them. And in any case I can't afford it.

Gerald Haigh is head of Henry Bellairs Middle School, Bedworth, Warwickshire.

The Progress of a Governors' Meeting

Tunnel vision

A Governors' Meeting is in progress. We are on the item 'The Report of the Headteacher' and a newly appointed Head is discussing staffing. There is a problem about admissions for the coming Autumn term consequent on changes by the Borough to the boundaries of the catchment area and unforeseen promises made by the outgoing Head. Agreement to supply a mobile classroom and additional teachers to cope with the temporary expansion has been secured from the authority. However, all this has necessitated a wholescale re-structuring of staffing arrangements. One result, mentioned in passing, is that the highly respected teacher Y who traditionally takes class X will float during the coming year so that her expertise is generally available to the considerable number of new teachers on the staff. A sound enough plan. Suddenly it enters my mind that next year my child will be in class X. The idea that she would be having teacher Y at that point in her primary school career was something to which we had looked forward. So I sit dwelling upon this news, and coping with a burning desire to ask a myriad of questions about the replacement teacher, before regaining 'consciousness' and returning my attention to the meeting.

Communications

An item is being wound up. The chairperson turns to the parent governors and says: 'Now that is something you could find out for us from the parents whilst standing around in the playground.' My anxiety level rises. My social science training reminds me about stratified random samples and the problem that the views of non-respondents are as important as those of respondents.

The school roll is in the region of 200: allowing for siblings, the parent governors have a constituency of some 320 parents. Although it has a nucleus of parents actively involved in it, and school events are well supported by parents in general, the school has neither a parent nor parent-teacher association. (On each occasion such structures have been suggested they have failed to find favour.) The several attempts on the part of the other parent governor and myself to hold meetings with parents, whether in or out of school-time, and even with the enticement of a speaker, have produced at best a turnout of perhaps 12, and at worst one. We have never had a client for our weekly morning surgeries. And yet the 'playground' (in these days of 'open' schools parents are more likely to wait for their children in the school's precious, small, circulation areas) is just as unlikely to put us in touch with parents in paid employment or those having to deliver various children (theirs and those of others) to various classes or even schools. Employed parents either will not be there or if they are, like those in the second category, will be too harassed to stop to talk. Together these must constitute the majority of the parents. When putting myself forward to be a parent governor. I did not anticipate having to regularly organise market surveys and referenda. My anxiety level rises another degree.

Ideology

A discussion is taking place on the pressure for places in this small school. A local authority representative, and prominent local politician, offers the information that the problem should solve itself if the proposal for a new private preparatory school in the locality goes through. Immediately I want to ask how the governing body of a state school can regard such a socially divisive arrangement as a 'solution'. But how in the theory of parent participation is a parent governor expected to handle issues that take one into the thick of current political agendas? Am I supposed to somehow be apolitical? Yet how can I invoice a view corresponding to that on one side or another of the local or central political agenda and yet appear to be unaligned? And should I try to appear unaligned when I have a political position? Instead would it not be more honest to declare my political interests rather as Members of Parliament are supposed to declare their extra-parliamentary interests? But where and when? As matters stand nothing is asked of a parent governor candidate other than that a short paragraph be submitted with the nomination form outlining his or her case for being elected. One can easily avoid all mention of contentious matters, partly political or otherwise.

Hobby Horses

We have reached 'Any Other Business'. My daughter is keen on school uniform. She wants me to put pressure on the Head to get everyone into it. The issue is not one to which I should have given any thought, left to my own devices. But with my daughter's intervention I have been stimulated into paying it some attention.

I find myself in favour of school uniform. However, I have no idea what other parents think. on the other hand I'm not a delegate. But put against all the other issues that currently beset state schools, core curriculum, testing, financial autonomy, staff shortages in certain areas, and so forth, it seems a trivial matter. Moreover, is a Governors' Meeting the right place to bring it up? And should I do it under 'Any other business'? After all it is hardly an emergency. I hold my tongue. My daughter, on quizzing me, loses some faith in the parent governor idea.

I have not found being a parent governor straight-forward.

Firstly, the parent governor's *qualifications* for the job, having a child at the school, is paradoxically in part a weakness. One must rise above being a parent of a particular child. Ideally one should have as much knowledge as possible of *all* the children on the roll. Thus the parent governor's credentials for the job are weaker in this respect than those of others who will have such broad knowledge, namely the staff. Moreover, they, unlike the parents, will have been *trained* to understand children en masse. What is more, many teachers will also be parents and thus can draw upon their parenting experience when necessary.

Secondly, in principle the parent governor needs to be a 'typical' parent if having parents in the decision-making process is to add a recognisably new dimension to it. If the parent governor is not 'typical' then it is not parents who are represented but various other factors that are characteristic of the particular parent who is elected. From the current example it seems that many parents will never make themselves known to their governors. Thus, short of conducting a house-to-house search, it is difficult for the parent governor to even attempt to represent their wishes. The idea is in any case, inherently over-ambitious. Familiarity with even the circle of parents with whom one daily interacts, is enough to suggest that the social situations and educational ideologies of parents at all but a few seconds in the State sector, will be too diverse to be capable of being distilled into a concept of a 'typical' parent which has any concrete use to it.

If there is no such thing as a collective ideology that can be drawn upon for parent government, how can anyone act as a parent governor other than through his or her existing framework of thought? The more the parent governor attempts to divert him or herself of an existing identity, the less there is to bring to the task of parent government, given there is little to put in its place. Parent governors, therefore, are likely to be indistinguishable from representatives of other interests, be they main-stream political parties, small businesses, the campaign for the abolition of museum charges, school uniform, or whatever. Herein emerges the problem of closet ideologies. The question arises, therefore, of whether we wish school decision-making bodies to be filled with representatives of miscellaneous causes in this unplanned and perhaps covert way.

Indeed, this question merges into an all-round one of the qualifications of parents for educational decision-making. If so much of a parent governor's contribution to the process of school government will have to derive from qualities he or she possesses over and above those to do with being 'a typical parent of a particular child at the school', then the current method of appointing parent governors is a hit or miss affair altogether. It is salutary to consider the stark contrast between what is required of parents and what is required of teachers and educational administrators to establish a right to participate in the educational process. The latter will have proven knowledge of the field of education. They will have been tried and tested through exam-inations and appointment and promotion proce-dures. Those who wish to be parent governors have no such requirements placed upon them. And it is as well to remind ourselves that parent governors too are involved in making decisions for other people's children: their own children are a tiny fraction of the total.

Thus even if parent governors are not in the thrall of what might be regarded as 'inappropriate' ideologists, if unversed in committee procedures and/or educational issues the wisest of them will barely have come to grips with their task before the next election (of governors) occurs or their children have left the school. At worst this suggests that schools will be buffeted around as successive waves of new parent governors take up their position. At best a heavy and continuous burden is placed on teachers and education officers to 'train' them for a job, ironically, they could do themselves. There is certainly a place for parental participation in schooling but the model that is emerging shows a lack of detailed thought on the part of those who have created it.

Extracts from B. Tipton 'Reflections of a Parent Governor', *Educational Management and Administration*, 17 January 1989

3. Case-studies from *The Commonwealth Casebook for School Administrators* Commonwealth Secretariat, 1982

THE NONCONFORMIST

In order to husband the scarce resources for Primary Education in the island republic of San Sebastian it is customary to insist that the parents of each village should build and maintain the school.

Because of the growth in numbers in the north of the island the school at Herato needed two extra classrooms. Led by William, the headteacher, the members of staff took part in the building operation together with all but one of the men of the village.

The exception, Hamoto, believing that the government and not the village people should provide the school rooms declined to help and instead went fishing. This did not prevent him from presenting his second son for enrolment as soon as the new building was ready.

A meeting of the School Committee condemned Hamoto's actions in no uncertain terms. The chairman was deputed to wait on the headteacher and insist that Hamoto's son not be enrolled. He was also instructed to inform the headteacher that, should the boy be enrolled, the other parents would withdraw their support from the school.

William found himself in a dilemma. Ministry regulations obliged him to admit Hamoto's son who had reached the age of 6 years. Ministry regulations also obliged him to take serious note of any decisions of his School Committee. It would reflect badly on his own competence should the parent body carry out its threat.

FUNDS AND DECISIONS

Motatin school has borrowed $100,000 from the bank for a new dormitory block and construction has already started. To repay the loan a fund-raising project has been launched. The target for the first year of the project has been set at $10,000.

Miss White, the principal, delegated responsibility for organising fund-raising through individual classes to the head tutor, Mrs Lau. Mrs Lau left the decision on the means of raising funds to form teachers and classes. Decisions from each class on methods to be used were passed to the head tutor. Mrs Lau was not satisfied with some of the decisions taken and kept those classes back in the assembly hall after morning devotions. She grumbled at everybody and showed her dissatisfaction with the decisions reached. Finally she informed the classes that they had to hold a concert to which all parents should come and donate at least $5.00. The classes thought this was too much. They had decided that each class member would donate $2.00 towards the fund.

Mrs Moa, one of the form teachers, was unhappy with the head tutor's action in forcing the students to hold a concert. She went and talked with the principal. Miss White said that whatever the classes had decided to do should be done. She also said that the head tutor's directive should be ignored.

Unfortunately Mrs Lau was a most influential person and would certainly do what she had decided. Mrs Moa, on the other hand, was determined to do what she and her class had decided.

ESL

It is the policy in a certain island country to teach English as a second language. The authorities have spent a good deal of money in providing resources and in sponsoring in-service courses in the Tate method. While the local language is still used in primary schools it tends to be replaced by English as the language of instruction in the second form of the secondary schools.

Raurenti, the headmaster of a village primary school, fully accepts the policy of his Ministry in relation to the teaching of English but he is encountering a good deal of opposition from the village elders. He is further troubled by the imperfect English used by some of this teachers and the evident boredom of some of the children during English lessons.

At a meeting between the teachers and the parents the matter comes to a head when Sione, an influential elder, is openly critical of the teaching of English to his grandson – ''so encouraging the boy to discard his own language''. The village is divided in its feelings and, as Raurenti hopes to persuade the people to build a new classroom for which he needs their co-operation he feels great concern.

'LAY IS BEAUTIFUL'

The idea that lay people should play an active part in the governance of schools is commonly held in Third World countries. Many examples could be given of the activities of school Boards that have made major contributions to the welfare and direction of their schools. There could be, however, some doubts in relation to the Board of Governors of Ntali Secondary School.

It would be fair to say that, while this Board is well-intentioned it does not share the objectives and ideals of the principal. In particular it believes in economy and staffs the school on the basis of cheap pay. The result is that a conglomeration of doubtfully qualified people staff the school.

As an inevitable result the educational standards of the school are low, examination results are poor and there is a good deal of unrest amongst the parents because of this.

To add to the principal's anxieties the Board has appointed one of its own members to act as Bursar. He had not been slow to exploit the power of his office and indeed is suspected of conspiring with certain members of staff to weaken the principal's position and so improve his own.

Several former principals have solved their problems by moving to another school but Bennett Kay, the present incumbent, is determined not to be defeated.

WHO SHOULD FIX IT?

A District Education Officer was being shown around a primary school by the headteacher. One of the classrooms at the school was badly in need of maintenance and the District Education Officer made a note of this. Two other classrooms in permanent materials were in good order except for ceiling panels which were hanging loose. The District Education Officer asked why these had not been repaired and the headteacher replied that he had reported the matter but no maintenance had been carried out yet. The District Education Officer suggested that perhaps the headteacher or his staff could do such minor repairs but the headteacher replied that the people of the community became cross when the staff maintained the building because they knew if they waited government would eventually pay the men of the village to carry out the repairs.

Chapter 3

Social Divisions: Do Schools Make a Difference?

The previous chapter tried to locate the immediate management goals of a school within the wider context of who controls educational provision, and at what level. The other way to link macro, or broad, issues and micro, or small-scale ones, is to examine and relate outcomes: what is the relationship between patterns of social inequality such as income or power and the processes of schooling? The contemporary debating question is usually phrased as 'Do schools make a difference?' Does it in fact matter whether schools are centralized or decentralized, progressive or traditional, selective or non-selective, for will not the main divisions in society reproduce themselves on the whole? The various positions in this debate should first be traced before focusing on the implications and policy options for the school manager.

This chapter takes socio-economic divisions as its primary focus, but shows parallels and intersections with gender and race where it is appropriate. Across the world there are clearly a number of descriptors of a society's inequalities in wealth, status and power — social class, socio-economic status, income differentials. The following analysis uses the terms interchangeably. While hours of fun can be had distinguishing subjective and objective definitions of 'class', or disputing its relevance as a concept to Third World situations, I have found enough basic consensual understanding among Third World practitioners to enable it to be left as a shorthand term where necessary. Translating 'class' into whatever working terms are used to understand socio-economic divisions in different countries will on the other hand not hurt the arguments in the inevitably summary way they are presented here. Four different interpretations of the relationship between schooling and social position or class need first examining.

(i) Schools as irrelevant or helpless

A persuasive and, for schools, disheartening analysis originates in the USA, where data analysts such as Jencks claim that home variables are more important than school variables in determining levels of academic achievement. 'Qualitative differences between high schools seem to explain about 2 per cent of the variation in students' educational attainment . . . school resources do not appear to influence students' educational attainment at all' (Jencks, *et al.* 1972). In UK, the Department of Education and Science stated in 1983 that as far as public examination results were concerned, as much as three-quarters of the variation between local authorities could be explained by the social composition of the population, and secondary school expenditure added 'a negligible further amount to this proportion' (Little, 1986).

Sociological analyses from virtually every country will produce the not unsurprising finding that children from 'good' homes tend to do better at school than children from 'poor' homes, which has led to an infinite paradise for students busy carving up 'Factors in Educational Achievement'. The emphasis on levels of parental education, facilities in the home, encouragement to study, language, diet, sleep, career orientation, that is on everything in the background from role models to inside lavatories, has meant a focus on the 'deprivation' or conversely 'support' of the home. The result is implicit support for Jencks' assertion that 'the characteristics of a school's output depend largely on a single input, namely, the characteristics of the entering children. Everything else, the school budget, its policies, the characteristics of the teacher — is either secondary or completely irrelevant.' The implication is that it is unrealistic to expect schools to equalize income or power differentials, in the long term; it would be more effective for governments to do this directly, through employment quotas, wage control or welfare benefits. Similar explanations for continuing gender differences in achievement are found in the research on sex role conditioning which portrays the crushing impact of parental and media influences. In computer jargon, the message would be 'garbage in, garbage out': schools are seen as relatively powerless to counteract the strong effects of home socialization and material differentials, and however sophisticated they are as hardware (the machine), are only as good as their software (the discs). Faced with such 'evidence', teachers are relegated to the role of at worst childminders or at best referees in a game with loaded dice.

(ii) School as photocopier or reproducer

A more sinister explanation for continued and patterned inequalities of school outcomes is provided by the 'reproduction' argument usually associated with Marxist analysis. Here schools are not seen as neutral channels through which the sedimentation of society slowly passes, but are conduits which themselves consolidate and solidify the layers. Furthermore, this is not just an unfortunate incapacity to act as mixer, but reflects the assigned function of schooling in a capitalist society actually to maintain a divided workforce. It is essential that the ideologies of the pursuit of profit without the sharing of profit are transmitted and internalized, and the school plays an integral role in confirming identities of 'success' and 'failure', so that the mass of future employed labour does not question its position in the overall labour process. The correspondences between the hierarchies or 'ability' divisions of school and the hierarchies or income/power divisions of the workplace are therefore non-accidental, and act deliberately to prepare students for the authority relationships they are to encounter in industrial or bureaucratic life. Similarly, gender reproduction occurs when girls and boys are prepared differentially in school for paid-work or domestic roles, and absorb ideologies of family roles and domestic consumerism which support the masculinist, capitalist enterprise. Patterns of ethnic inequality are reproduced when 'minority' group children find themselves in lower streams, responding to different teacher expectations and progressing to lower status jobs or training schemes.

Under this analysis, schools are not 'irrelevant' but on the contrary deeply relevant to the continuation of a particular mode of production and/or to a patriarchal* or racist society. The debates within this overall framework centre round the relative importance of the official and the hidden curriculum in the process of reproduction. For European writers such as Bourdieu, strongly aware of the impact of the traditional French curriculum, the official choice of discourse and subjects for study acts to exclude those without the appropriate 'cultural capital'* to master it; for Bowles and Gintis in USA, the hidden curriculum of learned roles and relationships, the organization of the school itself, becomes instead the key focus for analysis. Either way, in the extreme or 'deterministic' versions of reproduction analysis, teachers become mere 'agents' of state, capitalist or masculinist control, who through their classifying and career-channelling functions become unwitting or even witting collaborators in the maintenance of the hegemony* of dominant groups.

(iii) School as producer

An interesting variant of this is the notion that schools not merely reproduce but actively produce a class system. Connell *et al.* in *Making The Difference: Schools, Families and Social Divisions* (1982) tackle the question of differences between private and state schools in the Australian context. They identify crucial mechanisms in the operation of the schools which become significant in class formation. For private schools, independent does not mean isolated, as this extract shows:

> Marnie Paton puts it beautifully, talking about Regatta Day when she and her friends turn out to watch the boys' school battle for rowing honours: 'I think that's the greatest gathering of private schools, because everybody goes there . . . and you just see so many people you know. That's what I mean by 'united' . . . . Most of our parents' friends have children that go to private schools, and so we know lots and lots of people.' All of this seems to obey the rules: drawing lines, knotting networks, defining 'Them' and

'Us'. The ruling class school creates ruling-class solidarity. But it isn't as simple as that. Why, for instance, is there the need for all this network construction and solidarity-formation? And what are we to make of the official self-image of these schools, which typically reject social exclusiveness and stress that they draw families 'from all walks of life'? (p. 151)

The answers to these questions for the authors lie in the diversity and change within ruling class. New groups are recruited or force their way in, as pastoralism declines, manufacturing rises and falls, multinational corporations appear and expand, new professions develop and old ones are transformed. The school's task is to create a unity out of this heterogeneity. 'Internal conflicts of interest, ideology and outlook are a permanent, necessary feature of the ruling class; and overcoming their effects by evolving and imposing a common educational practice is a permanent, necessary task of the ruling-class school'. Hence there is the heavy stress on the school's identity and loyalty to it, and the stress on the social network among ruling class schools.

Fees for schooling are in themselves socially divisive (Bray, 1988b), but social class differences between independent and government schools are less clear in many Third World countries, given that government schools may be more prestigious than private ones, and may also be fee-paying. However, it may be that in selective systems where not all children receive secondary education, the secondary schools themselves act as producers of a new social stratification, especially where their intake is the first generation formally educated. Differences between those receiving 'western' type education and those restricted to vernacular education are usually cited as being particularly divisive, in that networks of common interest and learned values form which are similar to Connell's 'ruling class' networks. Teachers would have vested interests in providing upward social movement for their students, as it reflects on their 'success';

"IT WAS ALL NKRUMAH'S FAULT. IF HE HADN'T SENT SO MANY TO SCHOOL THERE WOULDN'T HAVE BEEN SO MANY USELESS ARGUMENTS TODAY"

one of the problems of the self-reliance initiatives in Tanzania was that teachers found difficulty in diminishing the stress on examinations, seeing the main function of the school as providing upward mobility for 'bright village boys' (Raikes, 1978). In Ghana, Weis (1983) demonstrated that the relationship between the social background of the student and the quality of the school attended became more pronounced as the system expanded, indicating signs of the emergence of a more rigid and closed class structure than had existed previously. Oppong and Abu comment:

> Educated parents have been increasingly aware of this fact and have striven to ensure the entry of their children into élite secondary schools, placing a high value upon academic achievement and entry into the professions, which in the sixties and seventies led to incomes far above those of the labouring poor, though not necessarily higher than those of successful traders and entrepreneurs. (Oppong and Abu 1987, p. 22)

The school's role in the production of a class system is thus not a simple one of linear allocation to an economic position, but means active involvement with a country's status differentials attached to diverse occupations.

The notion of schooling as a producer of social differentials is supported by the research on primary and community education in the Third World. UPE (Universal Primary Education), while seeming fundamentally egalitarian, has been found to create both regional and gender disparities (Watson, 1988). The 'Harambee' schools of Kenya which aimed to expand educational opportunity by capitalizing on community financing and support have been marked by an increasing polarization in outcomes, depending clearly on the ability of the community to pay for and manage their schools (Lillis, 1987, p. 115). An interesting parallel can be drawn with the new City Technology Colleges in UK: the colleges, which were to be centres of excellence financially supported by business and industry, did in fact take £33 million from State funds in 1988, because of reluctance by industry to support the scheme. The disproportionate spending on these few élite schools drains money, students and 'good' teachers from other parts of the State system, and instead of, as claimed, raising standards generally by stimulating competition, will inevitably act to damage schools in the locality. The point about the CTCs is that they do not merely reproduce an existing élite, but with their policy of taking students from across the spectrum of society will act to create a new 'technologically' oriented élite, further differentiated from the mass of secondary school leavers than are even mainstream sixth form leavers.

(iv) Schools as redistributors

In some contrast to the above perspectives is the research tradition which claims a potentially much more autonomous role for each school than as part of a system primarily caught up in the production or reproduction of social divisions. A belief that schools do make a difference to life chances stems from the comparative exploration of outcomes from each institution, balancing student intake against final performance. Research by in the UK by Rutter *et al.* (1979) and Reynolds (1976), and in the USA by Purkey and Smith (1983), demonstrates that schools with remarkably similar intakes of students can achieve measurably dissimilar results, with such differences in final outcomes being attributable to a range of variations in the climate and organizational features of the school. Lists of characteristics of 'effective' schools can thus be produced, such as that by Hopkins (1987), introducing the OECD International School Improvement Project: curriculum-focused school leadership; supportive climate within the school; emphasis on curriculum and teaching; clear goals and high expectations for students; a system for monitoring performance and achievement; ongoing staff development and in-service training; parental involvement and support; local authority support. There is nothing startling about such factors; in some ways they amount to little more than a circular description saying that effective schools have effective organisation. Even the more subtle 'process' factors outlined by Fullan (1985) — for example, a feel for the process of leadership; genuine caring for individuals; intense interaction and communication; collaborative planning — also begin to sound self-evident; the puzzle is why all schools do not or have not adopted such common-sense values.

The answer lies not just with the surface luck factors of having a 'good' head-teacher, with a 'feel' for leadership, but relates much more to the unique contra-dictions within mass schooling referred to earlier. Schools have taken on the twin functions of socialization and selection; we have come to take this so much for granted that its comparative recency in the history of human organization is forgotten. Schools all over the world are remarkably similar in organization and goals: large cohorts of students under one teacher who has a rationed amount of 'gifts'. Two major features thus explain why 'quality' or 'improvement' for all schools is hard or even impossible to attain: these features are differentiation and discipline. In spite of the rhetoric of raising standards across the board, there are vested interests in preserving the notion of 'low ability'. The growing armies of experts on 'special needs' education are a factor in the maintenance of an acceptance of significant divides in the ways children respond to learning, for the experts would not want to do themselves out of a job; but their presence is a symptom, not a cause of the labelling syndrome in education systems. Given the rationed nature of qualifications and élite positions, the system as a whole must fail a certain percentage. If one school has more 'successes', then these must be bought at the expense of more 'failures' by another school. The results of the new GCSE examination in UK have brought many worms out of the woodwork with regard to the 'standardization' of marking: as Kingdon and Stobart (1988) drily put it: 'an unexpectedly high or low proportion [getting a certain grade] will stimulate a reconsideration of that particular grade boundary'. In other words, the examination is still a ranking device aiming to ensure a normal 'spread' of distribution along the pass-fail continuum.

The alternatives in relating this fact to students are either to give them a sound political understanding of structural divisions and the power bases within society; or to convince them that inequalities are the result of a very wide spread in 'ability', 'intelligence', 'capability' or whatever the latest descriptor is. It is unsurprising that the latter alternative comes to be the more popular; political education is a threatening force, both for governments and for classroom teachers. The preference is for a continuation of the con-game: that if you all work hard, you can all succeed. Everyone, students and teachers, know at one level that this is not true; but a suspension of disbelief occurs whereby classroom motivation and order can be achieved by blindly joining in the competition, a game which is simultaneously common and individualistic. Failure to achieve in the long term can then be attributed to lack of ability and/or motivation on the part of the student, not of the teacher or indeed of the system.

This is the uniqueness of classrooms and their ethos. A Health Service can have the genuine aim of full health for all the population; doctors do not have to contend with a surgery full of people who must be simultaneously motivated to compete to get well, knowing that they will be measured against others in the surgery in their ability to do so. Doctors would refuse to work under such conditions. They would see it as inhumane if they were to publicly blame a sick person for not trying to get well, and exhort them to be more like their healthier neighbour. They would see it as unprofessional if in the end they were permitted to see only a certain fixed percentage achieving full health. Yet this is what classrooms have become: a place of daily or even hourly classification and diagnosis made public, and a place where one's achievement of educational health is always going to be relative to the achievement of one's peers, whether in the same class, or in the system as a whole. We would not speak of 'equal opportunities' to be healthy, for in that context we would realize the implications of rationing and competition, and see these as undesirable as ultimate social goals. But 'equal opportunities' has come to be seen as an end goal in education, not even just as a preliminary strategy. As such, it is just as, if not more, divisive than a rigidly selective system, as will be argued later.

In some ways it is astonishing that we should have come to accept such an ethos for what purports to be education, a public and universal good. In other ways, of course, it is understandable, given the importance of the need by power groups — whether of class, or gender, or race — in any society to find a way of maintaining ideologically a gradation of inequalities, and of the need by any complex society to find a cheap way of producing a suitable workforce. The link between 'education' and certification is not easily broken: China attempted to do so by making job entry not conditional on school success; the result was a breakdown of motivation, and a conviction by students that school was a waste of time (Unger, 1984). Schooling appears inexorably bound up with work and occupational rewards, in ways that neither students nor teachers seem to wish to deny.

Returning then to why all schools do not adopt the 'obvious' process factors which appear to lead to student achievement, we realize the burden differentiation and discipline place on schools. It is difficult to be universally 'caring', that is responsible for welfare, if you must attribute student failure to deficits in the students themselves. It is difficult to have high expectations of all students if the determinants of success are narrowly defined and narrowly distributed. It is difficult to have 'intense interaction' with large cohorts of students. It is particularly difficult to have a consensus on goals when the goals are themselves internally contradictory. The uneasy tensions in classrooms because of the con-game mean that some teachers are forced back on an increasing spiral of control: we know from the research that 'effective' schools have fewer rules, less coercion, less physical punishment and more respect for their students (see Reynolds, 1976); but this is difficult for teachers to achieve when their daily function in not to value students equally and yet to have to keep them all responsive. Ironically, the 'effective' schools may be those who gain high individual achievement by deemphasizing individual achievement: they take more responsibility themselves for student outcomes by more lesson preparation, punctual teachers and careful planning, and they attempt to subvert the ranking function of schooling by operating on the assumption of successful outcomes for as many as possible. Although praised by governments, it might be argued that 'effective' schools are in fact having a crack at the system; they are the true subversives. What would happen if all schools did become effective is open to speculation. At the moment effective schools are acceptable because they are involved in the production of the élite; but by definition not all can become members of an élite.

A synthesis?

It is not impossible, therefore, to reconcile all these apparently contradictory positions on whether schools make a difference to social outcomes. Firstly there is the question of the social and educational system from which the data come. When home backgrounds are very dissimilar, but schools are broadly similar in their basic provision, as in the United States, then it is likely that these background factors will take prominence. When, as in some Third World areas, homes may be similar but the schools very differently provided for in terms of materials, teachers or even desks, then it is obvious that between-school differences will be found which appear independent of social intake.

Secondly there is the phenomenon that it is possible to have upward or downward mobility of individuals while the structure of stratification remains the same, that is, there are still the same proportions in the working, middle or ruling classes, but they are occupied by different families in each generation. Therefore one can see a 'good' school providing an avenue for success for an individual or even a group of students, and thus appearing to make a difference; but if the overall number of opportunities for success remain the same, then this success will be bought at the expense of another individual or group's failure, and the social reproduction theorists will claim that schools make little difference to the general pattern of unequal distribution of resources. The differences between schools determine the composition of the hierarchy afresh each year, but do not challenge the existence of the hierarchy itself. In this way schools are not a mirror of society, but a refractor, redistributing life chances rather than reproducing them, but retaining the structural correspondences between school and work.

Thirdly is the complication that the structure of society may be changing in advance of the school's contribution. The middle or skilled class must expand in response to new technology or different modes of production. Hunt, for example, argues that the restructuring of education and work in Malaysia in order to give more opportunities to ethnic Malay groups, is as much a class as a racial question; the major issue is a contest between Malay and Chinese élites in the context of a changing system of production, and with the transformation to capitalism requiring a more substantial middle class. He finds that Malays are now relatively secure as the dominant group, but that in spite of increasing affluence overall there is excessive accumulation of opportunities and benefits by an already advantaged people. 'Any further development in that direction would seem to be towards a more class-divided society, with a closer coalition of élites but possibly with a continuing focus on ethnic consciousness to divide a working class' (Hunt, 1987, p. 108). Thus a school's role in apparently restructuring opportunities must be examined at each layer of a class system, and the particular intersections with race and gender taken into account at each point before claiming a really transformative role for schools.

Fourthly is the clear question of the measures by which schools are compared or deemed 'effective'. Much of the debate centres round the statistical methods and data used in the input/output studies. Controlling for intake is normally done on some combination of socio-economic level and cognitive ability; outcomes are measured on a range of variables such as examination performance, verbal reasoning quotient, school attendance rates, or delinquency figures. These can be taken as a fair proxy measure of potential social class membership, given the link between educational credentials and occupations; yet the 'effective schools' research does not yet use the degree of social class or gender equity *within* the school as an indictor of success. It does not measure social skills, political awareness, responsibility for others, cooperativeness, or peace initiatives; if these are mentioned it is in terms of their efficacy towards other ends, namely individual achievement and group conformity. It is significant, for example, that in the study of Scottish schools by Willms and Cuttance (1985) it was found that few schools were particularly effective for low ability pupils but not high ability pupils,

> A special system of schools, reserved for children whose parents have larger bank accounts than their neighbours, exists in no other country on the same scale as in England. It is at once an educational monstrosity and a grave national misfortune... It is socially disastrous, for it does more than any other single cause, except capitalism itself, to perpetuate the division of the nation into classes of which one is almost unintelligible to the other.
>
> (R. H. Tawney, *Equality*, 1931)

or vice versa: the good news is that schools that are effective for one group are also effective for the other. The bad news is that differentials remain the same, and that 'good' schools are not seen in terms of their desire to minimize 'ability' as a classificatory principle and to diversify 'talent' and its accompanying curricula.

Schools can and do make a difference — but exactly by differentiating, by exacerbating and producing class differences. One of the early critiques of the interventionist projects such as Girls Into Science and Technology (GIST) is that it operated on an uncritical acceptance of masculinist definitions of 'science', and merely changed girls into substitute males rather than asserting female values and activities as equally 'scientific'. Other critiques have centred round the class base to such projects: by aiming at potentially high achieving girls, they act in the end to do little for the mass of females, and divide women on a class base (Kessler *et al.*, 1985). Thus while schools can be internally 'efficient' in terms of raising measurable outcomes for some or even all of their students, the question is whether they are 'efficacious' in terms of realigning society. The human capital theorists would claim that a more skilled workforce and an ambitious élite will expand the economy which will benefit all in the end; there will be a trickle down effect. The evidence for this is, however, slight: links between school achievement and productivity and economic performance are notoriously and increasingly hard to ascertain; there is also no evidence that qualified people brought up in an atmosphere of individualistic competition will suddenly begin using their positions to benefit others. Rather the tendency is for consolidation of position, and a continued use of the school system to bring benefits for the next generation. In a refinement of Connell's Australian research on the differences between independent and government schools, Hatton (1985) traces how certain government primary schools can be 'coopted' by professional parents and transformed into the functional equivalent of prestigious preparatory schools, through intervention about staffing and curriculum. Children of low status parents in other schools suffered adversely as a consequence of the actions of these high status parents, with an over-concentration of inexperienced teachers and more uncertainty about curriculum innovation.

The interim conclusion is then that formal schooling does affect social class positioning — but rarely in terms of moving towards a classless society or minimizing class differentials. How have governments interpreted or tried to challenge these trends?

Policies to challenge social divisions through education

In their education policy documents, many countries have a statement about equality, with aims selecting from current class, race, gender, or regional disparities (Davies, 1986a). We would need to see how or whether this rhetoric is translated into specific policies, either at system or school level. In terms of social class, the system level policies are usually some form of positive attack against poverty: in the UK, the Educational Priority Areas, which were low-income areas in the inner cities, received extra funding and staffing. The American Headstart programme attempted to intervene in the early socialization experience of children from low-income families by providing intensive educational inputs to prepare them for formal schooling. Both programmes were based on a compensatory principle, that good education could balance out the material, attitudinal or linguistic deprivations that characterized poor groups. Such programmes have inevitably come under attack from all sides: there would of course be those who see positive discrimination as fundamentally inegalitarian; but the most telling counterarguments are those which point out the diversionary features of compensatory education. Focusing efforts on the early education experience of poor groups is to draw attention away from the structural features which created their poverty; the implication is that a 'better' education for these groups and individuals can change these circumstances, when it might be argued that the focus should instead be on those who control the distribution of wealth. The end result of interventionist philosophy is to blame the poor for their poverty; and when the programmes failed, as they had to, the attitudinal and motivational characteristics of the poor could simply be targetted as too intractable to change. Being the object of interventionist programmes can mean a no-win situation for low-income groups: if individuals do succeed, then this is confirmation that the poor can be assisted to pull themselves up by their bootstraps; if they fail, they are anyway beyond help. Either way, the responsibility appears finally theirs, to provide the 'right' kind of socialisation experiences which will enable mobility through the system. Nowhere is the admission that structural inequity arises from very different causes than access to pre-school picture books, subordinate clauses and manipulative toys.

The labelling effects which are associated with compensatory programmes are now well documented, with attacks made on attributing 'deficits' and 'deprivations' to cultures which are different rather than substandard. The reaction to such ideology was to focus more on formal school curriculum and teaching methods, the middle-class bias of which acted to 'disadvantage' working-class groups. The question was rephrased into a far more political and historical one: 'not how do working-class kids fail, but how did the education that working-class kids fail at come to be provided?' (Young, 1972). The beginnings were made in some schools on subverting the ascendency of the middle classes on decisions as to what constituted 'school' knowledge, by introducing and accepting elements of working class culture — literature, music, sport, history. Valuing, rather than changing the culture which children bring to school, implies valuing the knowledge and experience they hold, and the logic of this entails a questioning of traditional transmission styles by teachers. Democratic and participatory relationships are more appropriate for cultural respect than ones which support the imposition by the teacher of 'dominant' or 'expert' values and ideas. Hence schools such as Risinghill in UK in the early 1960s were the first in the state system to create a School Council giving students an opportunity to participate in the government of the school. Yet we should not underestimate the resistance by parents and teachers to any undermining of the meritocratic ideology of schooling. Hargreaves (1982) maintains that the continued popularity of academic, competitive curriculum was due to the belief that it opened the door 'to better jobs' — which in one sense is true. We return to the old dilemma that what is a rational belief at the individual level is not rational at the group level: while academic curricula do serve the minority of the working-class people successful within it, they do not foster the interests of the working-class as a whole. The same dilemma is found with regard to rural or 'relevant' education in the Third World. While this may serve well the immediate community, and act to retain people rather than give them urban, white-collar aspirations, it is not always popular with the clients.

> To us, education meant reading books, writing and talking English and doing arithmetic.... At our homes we had done a lot of ploughing, planting, weeding and harvesting.... We knew how to do these things. What we knew was not education, education was what we did not know.
> (Ndabaningi Sithole)

At Risinghill, Berg observed that 'many of the staff furiously resented meeting the children on equal terms' (Berg, 1968, p. 98). The school, which served the predominantly working-class community of Islington was eventually closed by the

Government in June 1965 after considerable controversy which seems to have centred around the equity policies of the Head, Michael Duane. Although the school had an anti-caning policy and did not expect students to wear uniform, much of the controversy within the school appeared to stem from the divisions between teachers as professionals and teachers as persons. Duane was perhaps ahead of his time; certainly some state schools in UK have experimented with democratic organization and equity policies and have survived. However, the attempt by government to impose a national curriculum and to abolish the Inner London Education Authority can be interpreted as a direct reaction to such potentially radical initiatives.([1])

What then is the current situation with regard to attempts at social reconstruction through education? Compared with gender and race issues, class seems to have been put on the back burner. The Inner London Education Authority report *Race, Sex and Class 1. Achievement in Schools* (1983) states in its final conclusion that 'it is difficult to see how a major improvement in the achievement of children from working-class families could be brought about'; the certainty and direction which characterize ILEA's suggestions for gender and race equality are lacking here, and this lack is symbolized in their non-specific suggestion that 'heads and teachers have to do all they can to help individual pupils . . . to perform as well as possible' (ILEA, 1983, p. 10). The Secondary Heads Association, which published a gender document 'Equality in Schools' in 1985, set up an Equal Opportunities Panel to encompass 'gender, race and class . . . to monitor opportunity issues, and to prepare SHA responses to them' (SHA, 1986). The 1986 document *Equal Opportunities* focused specifically on race; neither of the documents addressed the linkages between gender and class or race and class; by February 1988 SHA had still not responded to the question of class, and had no plans to issue a policy statement. While the bracketing of class, gender and race still occurs, and sociological analyses still confirm the intricate intermixing of the three dimensions in determining school outcomes and occupational life chances, the popular initiatives are those which focus specifically on either gender or race as single issues; we need to examine why this is so.

Firstly, there is the obvious point that gender and racial disparities are immediately recognizable in ways that social class is not. While there can be controversy about categories of ethnic affiliation, by and large the research data demonstrating disparities between men and women, black and white, can be physically and visibly confirmed through observational day-to-day experience. Such evidence is less glaring in terms of multi-layered inequities such as income or status; social class is in any case a sociological artefact and perhaps a Western obsession which does not have resonance in many countries where regional, tribal or language distinctions have greater political salience.

([1]) I am grateful to John Stokes, International Course member 1988, for these insights and for his research on social class policy in UK.

Secondly, and linked to this, is the area of legislation: in UK, as in other countries, there are legal prohibitions only against race or sex discrimination; it would be extremely difficult to design an Act which outlawed discrimination on such shifting sands as class membership. While there needs to be a national climate of perceived needs to attain more equitable outcomes in order for legislation to be enacted, the legislation itself acts to concentrate the mind, and force people into considering their policies and behaviour. It is true that laws cannot change attitudes; but they can prevent the manifestations of those attitudes in terms of actual discriminatory behaviour, and can foster a climate where positive initiatives are seen as acceptable. Many so-called equal opportunities policies in institutions were drawn up mainly to avoid being seen to break the race or sex law; but once in existence they can be used by the groups concerned to demand further 'proactive' moves (Williams, Davies and Cocking, 1989). The increasing case law of successful complaints gives encouragement to the gender and race cause; the cause of social class equality has in contrast a very patchy history, with arguably more failures than successes.

Thirdly, we should not ignore vested interests. We can escape our class background, but never our ascribed gender and colour statuses. A woman academic can have more degrees than a thermometer, but can never escape the female identity; indeed discrimination or patronage based on gender becomes more sharply apparent for the 'educated' woman as other areas of inequality recede. Thus female teachers, researchers and administrators, just like black teachers, researchers and administrators, will always have a vested concern in monitoring policy initiatives and in maintaining networks of support. There was to my recollection an attempt once to set up a 'middle class association', but networks of class are not generally labelled as such, and would not be directly involved in policy formation.

Fourthly, there is the political question of how much threat is presented by initiatives to decrease inequality. Gender policies as currently conceived present little threat to established power, whether patriarchal or capitalist. The programmes which try to get more girls into engineering, science and technology do not always question the overall male-oriented definitions of these activities, and indeed by highlighting them as important, merely confirm the view that what men do is central. Conversely, attempts to raise the status of presently conceived 'feminine' activities and areas of knowledge such as domestic science have met with little success. Boys will still not take these subjects unless cooking is relabelled 'catering science' and carries a prestigious and acceptably male tag. And a greater number of boys or men entering female fields may mean simply a take over of top positions, as can happen in nursing or pre-school education. A juggling of who takes which curriculum subjects in school, and to what level, may not in the end make much difference to the way knowledge is used for power. As argued earlier, making some girls more highly qualified in technological fields does not further the cause of the mass of women for whom technology may mean no more than a tedious and unhealthy job staring at a Visual Display Unit.

Tackling female 'underachievement' is to subscribe to the notion that academic achievement is the crucial function of schooling; within-school compensatory programmes for girls, just like for 'poor' kids, do not threaten authoritarian teaching relationships or the meritocratic principle, and may act to confirm girls as 'deficit' and in need of remediation. Quotas for girls entering secondary schools, as happened in Zambia, may also unwittingly act to confirm their image in teachers' eyes as 'less able'; the real threat in this instance, was the challenge to meritocratic ideal, in that the girls were seen to take places which should have 'rightfully' have gone to the boys (Martin, 1983). Significantly, one area which meets with great resistance in the UK is the creation of access courses, or 'women-only' courses, in higher education. The notion that the traditional 'standards' of entry to university can be by-passed is deeply un-acceptable to those who have had to come up the hard way, and are now residents in 'centres of excellence'. Our survey of Equal Opportunities policies in Higher Education (Williams, Davies and Cocking, 1989) found universities generally resistant to positive discrimination, preferring the apparently 'impartial' competition for entry or promotion. The reason why equity policies can be acceptable at one level is that it is then easy to overturn them using another definition of equality if they become too controversial or too favouritist, or in the end, too effective.

Single issue policies are always going to be more popular, more easily accommo-dated and implemented than multi-issue ones. In spite of the compulsory 'commatiz-ation' of areas of inequality (class comma race comma gender) in policy analysis, the reality of implementation has been in the main to tackle one or at most two at any one time. Curriculum materials can be examined simultaneously for gender and race or class bias (Dixon, 1977); but it is difficult to conceive of any organizational feature of schools which would positively act in the interests of all three 'groupings'. The obvious point is that we all have simultaneous membership in class, gender and race categories, and cannot be 'allocated' to a joint position except on a sort of cumulative 'points' basis or on an intricate matrix of interconnections.

Strategies within schools to tackle class (race, gender) disparities

There has therefore been a great deal of analysis in terms of the various intersections of class and gender, and of class and race. Do patriarchy or capitalism 'fundamentally' explain women's contemporary position? Will the overthrow of the extremes of private ownership have to precede the overthrow of apartheid? Should class solidarity be forged before sisterhood or Black power? These debates are too intricate to embark on here, but they may surface in different forms when school policy on inequality is being decided. Priorities may have to be decided on a pragmatic basis. Let us examine some of the options available.

1. *School improvement:* the attempt would be to improve the school's 'performance'

overall, so that both girls and boys, and students from all social classes and ethnic groups achieve more highly compared to other schools, and to the private sector. Different countries and cultures will generate different factors associated with 'effectiveness': in UK, a broad notion of school climate or 'ethos' appears a manipulable and important source of school difference. Rutter *et al.* (1979) found a number of 'process variables' in the school which affected the four outcomes of attendance, pupil behaviour, examination success and delinquency. They noted that the same teacher actions (such as leaving children to get on with their work) sometimes had quite different results in different schools; and therefore that the school had to be examined as a total social organization. Positive styles of group management and discipline, high expectations overall, a consensus and consistency on values, caring models of relationships by teachers, shared activities between staff and pupils, and a high proportion of children with positions of responsibility, were all associated with 'successful' schools; but the researchers noted that with these, and the many other process variables, 'their combined effect was much more powerful than that of any individual factor considered on its own' (p. 182). The heads of the more successful schools took widely different approaches, and no one style was associated with better outcomes; but they managed to achieve an overall philosophy which permeated all teaching/learning relationships and raised standards throughout.

In some Third World countries, where centralized teacher transfer and allocation is common, it is more difficult for a head to maintain the low teacher turnover which is associated with pupil attainment in the UK studies; the presence or absence of physical resources such as textbooks become key indicators (Vulliamy, 1987b), but again this is not always easy for a head to control. A new Head nonetheless *can* bring about significant change. The efficacy of textbook purchase diminishes after the ratio of books per pupil approaches 1:2 (Psacharapoulos and Woodhall, 1985) and similar, controllable factors to those identified in developed countries play their part: good classroom management; time-on-task; homework; and hours of instruction (Heyneman and Loxley, 1983). Management skills which tackle these factors appear important in producing between-school differences, and the dimensions located by Hall, Mackay and Morgan's study *Headteachers at Work* would seem broad enough to merit consideration by a head in any financial or political situation. These relate to the positive and negative criteria for management produced in the DES research on 'good' schools, that is in communication (of specific educational aims to staff, pupils and parents); human management (displaying sympathetic understanding of staff and pupils); personal qualities (good humour, sense of proportion, being available); and devolution of power (being conscious of the corruption of power, and with power-sharing a keynote of the school). Weaknesses would be measured by absence of schemes of work; inappropriate teacher allocation or teaching styles; absence of curriculum review, teacher appraisal, or detailed pupil assessment policies; inadequate attention to multicultural understanding (Hall, Mackay and Morgan, 1986).

Hence the focus could be on creating an overall purposeful institution, with equity perhaps not targetted directly, and measured in relation to other schools rather than internally.

A concern within the organization to minimize the effects of labelling students appears important, with 'effective' schools showing concern for the whole ability range and persevering with unstreaming (Reynolds and Sullivan, 1987). The aim to produce a 'positive' climate is indicated also by the parallel evidence that in 'good' schools rewards have at least an equal emphasis to punishments. A different way to achieve 'effectiveness' may be to attempt to control the social composition of the school: Heath and Clifford's (1981) research in UK found that, having taken into account family background, the 'balance of intake' was the best predictor of school effectiveness, with lower class students doing better in schools where there was a higher proportion of middle class students. The dilemma of acknowledging the effects of class membership while attempting not to label students accordingly would still have to be resolved.

2. Positive action: this involves the drawing up of school policies which bear in mind the fact that different groupings in the school respond differentially to the same policy. Examples of positive action would be anti-racist strategy to outlaw prejudicial behaviour by any individual; or single-sex grouping for certain subjects such as Maths and Science, where girls have been shown to achieve better than in mixed situations where they may take a deferential or back-seat role to the boys, or where boys openly devalue their achievements (Mahony, 1985). Another example would be outreach work with parents, which by fostering more overall parental participation in education, aims to erode the middle classes' ascendancy in the informed encouragement of children, in parent-teachers association membership, or other factors which are associated with higher student involvement and hence achievement in school. A focus on a broadening of careers advice, and positive links with employers, would again particularly help girls or lower class students or ethnic minority students who would not otherwise have access to a range of career possibilities. Attempts to make curriculum materials gender-neutral or free from class or race bias also come under this category. The achievements of particular groupings of students would be monitored to assess the success of such positive action.

3. Positive discrimination: the difference between this policy and positive action is that target groups are overtly identified as requiring disproportionate amounts of resources, time or access. The compensatory principle robs Peter to pay Paul; smaller classes for 'special needs' or second-language learning groups, special girls-into-engineering programmes, higher pay for teachers in rural or deprived areas would all be examples of discriminating between people on the basis of some ascribed characteristic, and allocating more attention or greater privilege to 'disadvantaged' sectors (and by implication less to advantaged ones). Whereas the first general 'school improvement' approach might try to avoid the stigma attached to 'remedial' or 'disadvantaged' labels, a positive discrimination policy works on the principle that 'it is no more just to treat unequals equally than it is to treat equals unequally', and that it is the school's duty to compensate for previous or current social practices which have left certain groups handicapped in the Great Race Of Life. The problem is knowing when the compensation should stop; a quota may achieve numerical balance, but withdrawing that quota after a certain period does not guarantee that the factors that determined an ascendancy by one group will not predominate once more. Making curricula compulsory for all can obviate the tendency for social influences to predominate over 'choices' of suitable options; but difficult questions are raised over when to relax the stringency. An interesting case-study in Australia found that compulsory science for four years of secondary school led to parity in achievements for girls and boys, but that as soon as science had to be blocked against a language, just for one term, girls did not choose it so frequently, even in subsequent terms when it was not blocked against any competing subject (Harding, *et al.*, 1988). Permanent compulsion to behave in what is seen to be in our interests is one answer to the equality gap, but does little for individual liberty.

4. *Redefining 'success'*: whereas the three previous options leave alone the (middle-class, masculinist?) concepts of 'attainment' or 'merit' and simply attempt to alter numbers or balances of those succeeding in those terms, the more radical option is to alter the definitions of 'achievement' so that the skills or orientations of hitherto disadvantaged groups become a valued asset rather than a handicap. Curriculum 'organic' to working-class community (Connell *et al.*, 1982); a focus on critical future life skills such as knowledge of welfare or legal rights, and political or health awareness; introducing a feminist science, or a new mix of physical and social science will value those humanitarian concerns which supposedly characterise a female response to the scientific world. The very bases of our notions of 'class' come under scrutiny anyway here: it has been pointed out that the old measures of class and mobility are in themselves masculine defined, and are not sensitive to the nuances of female employment (Abbott and Sapsford, 1988).

Redefining success *means* redefining class and the bases for our categorizations of people into strata in any society; yet the task is by no means simple. If schools try to value curricula 'organic' to the working class while traditional academic curricula still operate elsewhere, then such attempts are likely to meet the same fate as vocational education. Evidence from Mexico and Tanzania indicates that unemployment is often higher and salary rates lower amongst students from technical/agricultural education than for those from 'general' education (Watson, 1988), even if such education appears more relevant to them and to their employers. Schools can do little about income differentials in employment. Thus the influential Hargreaves Report of 1985 *Improving Secondary Schools* rejected any 'bi-partism' in the promotion of new curricula more suited to those alienated by schooling, and implied practical experience, community service and artistic endeavours for *all* young people (ILEA, 1985). The trend since then has certainly been towards graded tests and more project-based work in the GCSE; yet the doubts being raised about such assessment focus on the ability of the middle class to once again ensure good results for their children. More work done at home, requiring access to libraries, postal services, reference books and so on, ironically may require more 'cultural capital' than the old-style total recall written rituals.

5. *Minimising examinations and competition:* the logic of a redefinition of success means in the long term not simply testing different skills, but minimizing the certification emphases altogether. Adapting the rules of the competitive game may indeed mean a temporary set-back for those with more counters, but the disadvantage is short-lived; making Bahasa Malaysia compulsory for entry to higher education and jobs proved in itself not a long-term handicap for Chinese aspirations. If success in school was changed tomorrow to be measured by an examination in knowledge of the tabloid newspapers, growing vegetables, reggae music, hairstyling, the history of women's organizations and minority religions, all to be written only in a choice of lower class speech forms or minority languages, I would give it eighteen months before dominant groups once more gained ascendancy in results. Hargreaves suggests abandoning the 16 + examination altogether in UK, similar perhaps to China's attempt to break down the link between school certification and jobs. A more modest proposal is that: 'it will be necessary to limit and fence-off the central, competitive, examination-centred process that currently afflicts education' (Lacey, 1988). Lacey suggests limiting the number of 16+ exams it is legally possible to take and limiting the time it is legally possible for any school to spend on them within the curriculum. He recognises that any reform of this kind would have immediate repercussions on higher education and job recruitment, and therefore that a socialist education policy would need to be co-ordinated with a series of reforms not just of the examination system but of new kinds of work, for example in cooperatives and in social and community work.

Another solution is to replace examinations by profiles and criterion-referenced records of achievement; doubts are inevitably cast however on whether this merely places an even greater instrument of power in teacher's hands (Barnes, 1985), and gives greater rein for preconceptions about 'aptitude' which may not in fact be class, gender or race-neutral.

Dale Spender

Gender and Marketable Skills:
Who underachieves at maths and science?

History tells me
That is is not so long since *languages*
Were considered very important.
Anyone who wanted to get on in the world
Needed languages as an entry qualification
For this was how you sorted those who were capable
From those who were not.

Girls, it seems,
Were not.
They were 'naturally'
Not very good at languages
When languages were required
For leaders.

Today
It is maths and the sciences
Which are considered very important
For those who want to get on in a technological world.
Maths and sciences are the entry qualifications
Which sort those who are capable
From those who are not.

Girls, it seems
Are not.
They are 'naturally'
Not very good at maths and science
While these are required
Of leaders.

Of course,
I could resign myself to accept
That girls are inferior
If it were not for one inconsistency.
Today when languages are not needed,
When they are not used to sort those who are capable
From those who are not,
Girls have come to be 'naturally' good at languages.

Have they progressed so far
In such a short time,
I ask myself?
Are they but one century
Behind?
In the twenty-first century,
Will they become
Very good at maths and sciences?

Possibly.
As long as maths and sciences
Are not required
As entry qualifications!

It is not that girls have changed so much
In the last 100 years,
It is that the entry qualifications
Have changed.

Tomorrow,
If weaving and cake making
Are considered very important
And those who want to get on in the world
Need them as an entry qualification
Because they sort those who are capable
From those who are not.
Girls, it seems
Will not.
They will be 'naturally'
Not very good at weaving and cake making
When they are required
For leaders.

It's a very convenient arrangement.
It's very clever of those who control the entry qualification:
To be able to control nature as well.

For we can chase our own tails
And spend years
Testing girls for their inadequacies
We will not find them,
For we are looking in the wrong place.
The underachievement lies not in the girls,
But in those who do not wish to accept them,
As equals.

Resistance to policy options

These options are not mutually exclusive, and schools have tried various combinations of efforts; but because they are based on different philosophical positions, they are likely to threaten different interests and meet different sorts of resistances. Much depends on whether social class, gender or race are seen as absolute or relational categories. Biological or crude cultural explanations for disparities in achievement between different social levels or between males and females, blacks and whites, will attribute that performance to innate or learned capabilities within individuals. The emphasis is on group difference rather than structural inequality. A relational stance, on the other hand, recognizes that it is impossible to conceptualize lower class except in terms of its relationship to middle or ruling class; similarly, to alter what it means to be a girl must mean to alter our conceptions of what constitutes a boy. I argued in Ball's (1984) book on comprehensive schooling, that gender analysis had been clouded by misleading images, particularly of 'girls' and 'boys' as discrete categories: they were seen as somewhat like gerbils and hamsters, with a 'gap' between them, or occupying different levels in The Great Cage of Life. However, the sexes are in fact locked in a mutually interdependent set of definitions. To be a boy, it is necessary not to be a girl; if we alter expectations of what it is to be a girl, we are also shifting the notions of what it is to be a non-girl, i.e. a boy. Similarly, analyses which stress the differences between lower and middle class orientations draw attention away from the parasitical interlocking in any society whereby a 'middle' class can exist only if there is a 'lower' class to sustain it and give it definition.

It could be predicted then that approaches which are based on the apparent desire to alter the position of one disadvantaged group without touching the chances or lifestyles of the potentially privileged will meet with less resistance than those overtly acknowledging the relational nature of all our social divisions, and their delicate balances. If it can be demonstrated that ethnic minority students can receive more resources without affecting 'majority' students' chances; if girls' achievement begins to equal or surpass boys' without affecting boys' entry into the job market; if we could all become 'middle class', and all, in Harold Wilson's contradictory dream, receive a grammar school education, then 'school improvement' strategies will meet with less resistance from power groups. But when an anti-racist strategy effectively challenges the concepts of 'minority' and 'majority', of 'us' and 'them', and shows how for example 'we' in the UK are a now a multiracial and multishaded society which nonetheless uses racial discrimination to sustain its economy, then attempts to use schooling for more equitable power-sharing between black and white will be seen as highly subversive. When female economic independence is acknowledged as requiring an increase in male domestic and caring roles, this is seen as threatening our fundamental conceptions of masculinity, and spectres of homosexuality are called up if boys must do cooking or parenting courses as well as girls doing metalwork and physics. When the logic of a revaluation of 'lower' class culture leads to a parallel revaluation or devaluation of the automatic superiority of 'middle' class culture, then the whole edifice of 'upward' and 'downward' social definition and mobility is called into question.

We should therefore consider in the following chapters in more detail firstly the likely or actual success or failure of particular aspects of equity strategy in different parts of the world, and secondly what the pragmatic politics are in choosing between socially acceptable but inherently conservative equity policies and potentially unpopular but radically transformative ones.

EXERCISE 3: POLICIES ON STUDENT ACHIEVEMENT

Imagine a situation where it has been found that students from lower socio-economic groups were 'underachieving' in English compared to students from higher income homes. Assuming that a school wishes to adopt a strategy to change this pattern, expand on the policies that they might try if taking up each of the five positions identified in this chapter. I have given some possible examples in each section. Then imagine the possible outcomes or problems that would emerge from the adoption of the various policies.

Overall Strategy	Examples of Policies	Possible Outcomes or Problems
1. School Improvement	– an emphasis on language across the curriculum – additional training or appraisal for teachers of English – –	
2. Positive Action	– encouragement of lower-income groups to use the library – ensuring homework done through provision of a room in school – –	
3. Positive Discrimination	– special English classes for low achievers – larger groups for high achievers and smaller ones for low achievers – –	
4. Redefining Success	– Different definitions of achievement in language; emphasis on oral work, dialect, mother-tongue etc. – –	
5. Minimising Competition and Student 'Difference'	– Peer tutoring, with 'more able' helping 'less able' – language used for community work and political literacy, not for testing and assessment – –	

Chapter 4

Gender and Educational Management

'Women are brighter than men. That's true. But it should be kept very quiet or it ruins the whole racket.' (Anita Loos)

Concerns about gender disparities within education have in fact been longstanding in many parts of the world. In the main, however, they have focused around student performance, particularly in terms of the 'underachievement' of girls. As we have seen, the data on differences in access to various levels of schooling, in dropout rates, in examination results, and in subjects taken have evoked a range of explanations and policies around gender gaps in educational outcomes. The question of gender disparities in the management structures of schools and colleges has received less attention, except to indicate the importance of having qualified women teachers to act as role models for girls. Yet it is the contention of this chapter that the gender balance of the teaching force is an equally important issue in its own right, and not one necessarily to be subsumed under the 'pupil achievement' byline. Female underrepresentation in positions of decision-making and power within education is of crucial concern at four levels: (a) for both boys and girls to be able to see women in decision-making capacities; (b) as a question of equal career rights for teachers; (c) to query masculinist definitions of appropriate management; and (d) to challenge male domination of the selection of school knowledge and curricula.[1]

The point that will be stressed is that it is not just in the interests of girls for women to hold educational power; it is in the interests of the progress of democratic and radical education as a whole, for both sexes.

Evidence

We should look first at the picture of where women and men are to be found within educational systems. Compared to gender differences in student access to schooling or

[1] This chapter includes adaptations of parts of articles on the Third World situation already published elsewhere (Davies 1986b; 1987; 1989), which have been combined with the UK and European material.

in student achievement, gender inequality within teaching itself is an under-researched issue. Statistics can be found which use sex breakdowns for pupils in most countries (Silver, 1985); they can sometimes be found for the teaching force as a whole (Seager and Olson, 1986); but they are not so frequently found in terms of the positions that those teachers hold. The data that are available, however, seem to demonstrate a consistent decline in the proportion of women post-holders as seniority increases. For Third World countries, in Fiji, for example, females are 51 per cent of the teaching profession, yet hold only 28 per cent of posts of responsibility (Siwitibau *et al.*, 1985); in Brunei, 60 per cent of teachers are women but only 2 per cent of Principals (Brunei Department of Education, 1983). In the Phillipines the 77 per cent of female Primary teachers declines to 22 per cent at Principal level, and the 57 per cent of female secondary teachers becomes 17 per cent of female Principals (Derreck, 1979). In Zimbabwe, teaching itself is a male-dominated profession, with the 10 per cent women secondary heads drawn from only 32 per cent women secondary teachers, yet the figures at primary level are even more disproportionate, with a 40 per cent female teaching force declining to a mere 1 per cent of headships (Zimbabwe Government, 1984).

Whether or not therefore the profession is female dominated numerically, formal decision-making is in the hands of men. Where women do hold headships, it is often in the single-sex girls' schools or women's colleges. Educational administration is still seen as a masculine occupation in many countries: some returns to an information request to Zambia which showed 15 per cent of headships being female, listed all the names under the heading 'Headmasters' (Zambia Ministry of Education, 1986). One is reminded of the boys' public schools where the matron was always called 'Sir'. A writer on Malaysian educational management reveals that change was 'much to the credit of the early educational administrators, *men of vision* with practical knowledge and wisdom . . . ' (Chew Tow Yew, 1986, italics added). However, it must be stressed that such apparent male 'supremacy' is not confined to the 'developing' world: in UK a secondary teaching force which is roughly half women now produces only 16 per cent of headteachers (a decrease from the 1973 figure of 20 per cent). It appears to be an international and increasing problem.

Proportions of women also seem to decline as the age or status of the student increases, whatever the 'baseline' figures are. We should first dispel the myth that teaching is a 'feminine' profession all over the world. While this may be true for USA and UK, we can see from Table 1 that teaching is a masculine profession in many countries, 'even' at primary level.

This was a table I drew up from patchy statistics for a previous article (Davies, 1986b), and shows some interesting trends. The proportions at primary level range from 9 per cent in Mauritania to 82 per cent in the Seychelles, but the bulk of countries have fewer than 50 per cent female primary teachers. At secondary level, the figures decline even further, and if the countries shown at third level are typical, then the

Table 1 Distribution of Third World countries by ratio of female teaching staff

Percentage	First level	Second level	Third level
Under 10	Mauritania Nepal	Mauritania Nepal	Malawi Mauritius Sudan
11–20	Afghanistan Congo	Congo Korea Sudan	Cameroon Congo India Iran Korea Sierra Leone
21–30	Cameroon Congo Gabon India Mozambique Papua New Guinea Sierra Leone Uganda Korea	Afghanistan Cameroon China Gabon Gambia Ghana India Mozambique Rwanda Tanzania Tunisia Uganda	Iraq
31–40	China Gambia Chana Malawi Rwanda Sudan Tanzania Tunisia	Botswana Iran Mauritius Papua New Guinea Seychelles Sierra Leone	
41–50	Burundi Iraq Mauritius	Fiji Honduras Iraq Lesotho Swaziland Tonga	
51–60	Fiji Iran Tonga	Costa Rica Panama	
61–70	Botswana		
71–80	Costa Rica Honduras Lesotho Swaziland		
Over 80	Seychelles		

figure of 20 per cent women teachers in further or higher education is unlikely to be exceeded. If we find few female principals or heads, then it could be argued that they start from a much smaller base; teaching in the Third World may be seen as a masculine arena, and women suffer the same entry and discrimination problems as they do when trying to compete in any male field. Yet in many parts of the world, teaching is still seen as one of the few accepted occupations for women, presumably because of its traditional association with the female roles of socialization and caring (and/or because it fits in with their own children's hours and holidays). Because of the monastic nature of girls' secondary boarding schools, it has often been the only place for a woman to pursue a career in countries where purdah is the norm. It may be surprising that the under-representation of women in educational work starts further back than in some western countries; nonetheless, the subsequent decline in the proportions of women as the job status and pay increase shows a parallel curve to that holding in the West. In Britain, women constitute 78 per cent of primary school teachers and 12 per cent of university lecturers; in Iran the figures are 57 per cent and 3.25 per cent respectively; in Cameroon 28 per cent and 2 per cent. Presumably, the younger the student, the more its nurture is associated with the 'natural' female role; and possibly the fewer academic qualifications its progress is deemed to warrant.

> **The NNEB training course . . . is very popular with girls who want to be nannies for a few years but hope to be teachers or Marks and Spencer trainees in the end.**
> From *Harpers and Queen, September, 1988.*

Yet while teaching, like nursing or catering, is seen as 'suitable' for women, there is, as Dove (1986) points out, no statistical evidence that the teaching profession is becoming 'feminized'. Over the period 1970–1982, there has been only a three percentage points rise, from 45–48 per cent, in the proportion of female teachers at first level in all developing countries. Latin America showed a four percentage point decline. The average proportion of secondary teachers rose only one point to 34 per cent. While the recitation of all these statistics may be tedious, I would stress the importance of knowing and publicizing the basic patterns for each country. This is the pool from which future women educational managers are drawn, and there may be a need to establish realistic targets and avoid convictions that equity is just around the corner.

There are of course hiccups in the curves or the ratios, and some interesting differences emerge which point to the intersection of gender with other social divisions. In South Africa, for example, the teaching profession tends to be female dominated numerically, with 66 per cent, 69 per cent and 63 per cent women respectively for Black, White and Coloured sectors. In Indian schools in the same country, the proportion drops to 45 per cent female teachers. Percentages for Principals range from 3.5 per cent female in secondary schools for Indians to 22 per cent female in primary schools for Coloureds, with female heads in White schools occupying an intermediate position (Republic of South Africa, 1984). We clearly have to look at the immediate cultural and political contexts around teaching, as well as attempt to seek out any universal features to do with women's apparent oppression, suppression or even depression.

★ There are currently no female Chief Education Officers in UK.
★ There has never been a woman Vice-Chancellor or Director of a Polytechnic.
★ Only 2% of professors are women, although women hold 15% of posts in Higher Education.
★ The number of women in promoted posts in Further Education has fallen.
★ The average salary for a male teacher is 16% higher than for a female.
★ One third of women teachers are unmarried and only one in three of those who are married has children of school age or below.
★ Attitude surveys done by NUT and ILEA reveal women to be as keen and interested as men in promotion although they do not make as many applications for promotion as men do.
★ Nearly all part-time teaching is done by women; jobsharing schemes should be extended as job-sharing is often at higher salary levels.
★ The present regulations for pensions for women are discriminatory.
★ The Equal Opportunities Commission has recently helped some female employees to win cases concerning equal pay for work of equal value.

Myths and blind alleys

Whenever the above series of apparently gloomy statistics are trotted out, they are immediately countered by the production of Favourite Explanations. Women do not apply for senior positions. Women are socialized into passive and supporting roles. Women lack confidence. It is called the We-would-love-to-have-appointed-a-woman-but-they-didn't-come-forward syndrome. Alternatively, intricate debates ensue as to the relative importance of biology and conditioning. Did she fall or was she pushed? That is to say, is women's relative invisibility in top positions because of hormones, Sindy dolls, OPEC oil prices, underarm odour or the unacceptable face of capitalism? This leads into the bottomless pit of sex differences research. One can relatively easily devise questionnaires to probe teachers' domestic responsibilities, perceptions of career chances, reactions to patriarchy or experiences of sexual harassment. One can equally relatively easily discover statistically significant differences between the sexes on some dimension. Thus some pilot questionnaires of ours for a research project on Women in Educational Administration in the Third World (Davies, 1987a) not surprisingly found women teachers having different ambitions from men, spending more time on domestic tasks, and being more self-critical in their appraisal of their own teaching performance. Given what is already documented about gender-based socialization, this is like doing intricate research to show that taller men wear longer trousers. We already have mountains of research to show that women all over the world display (for whatever reasons) different orientations from men to family, marriage or career. Replicating all this with regard to, say, educational management serves only to confirm a yawning gulf between the sexes which will in the end be used to justify the 'obvious' position of men in power roles. Much of the problem is that such research may not finally be interpreted as 'differences' but as 'deficit'. There is an implicit tendency to present the male-as-norm in management terms, and to see where women differ from this. They are perhaps 'less' ambitious, 'lacking' in confidence, 'over-emotional', 'too' family-centred, or 'underachieving'. The net result is to confirm that ambition, over-confidence, and maximal achievement are universal goods, and that emotions and orientations to family are somehow Barriers and Handicaps.

We get a different picture altogether if we portray a realistic appraisal of one's capabilities as 'normal' and couch male ambition in terms of being 'neurotic about success', or if we say that any displays of love or feeling are beneficial to an organization and that repression of these is bad management practice. Better still, and given the enormous overlap between the sexes in terms of all these traits and experiences, it is perhaps time to play down the 'sex differences' research in favour of a 'commonalities' approach. We need to depict personnel in education as human beings with similar needs and vices, which may be a composite of previously designated 'masculine' and 'feminine' traits. Otherwise we entrench the stereotypes and cause trauma about which sex role norms we are approximating to.

> Headships clearly involve greatly increased responsibility and a change in role. Women's confidence may need to be increased by encouragement and training before sufficient numbers see themselves succeeding in so large a step. In order to become a Head, a women may have to agree with her husband and family to the husband following her career move. However, the group do not consider that these are the most important reasons for women's lack of success. The NUT's recent publication 'Promotion and the Woman Teacher' challenges a number of myths about women's lack of qualifications, lack of ambition, family problems etc. In fact, one third of women teachers are unmarried. It cannot be said that there are not enough exceptional women able to take their fair share of the relatively small number of secondary headships.
> (Women's National Commission, 1983)

Too much attention to internalized 'sex roles' therefore is dangerous for three reasons. Firstly, it draws attention away from the parties currently involved in the reproduction of discrimination, by attributing expected roles to a vague notion of 'the needs of society'. Secondly it blames the woman in particular as not succeeding because of her learned aspirations, conduct patterns or domesticated traits. Thirdly it accentuates the concept of sex difference instead of gender inequality. A critical review of research casts doubt on much of the accepted folk-lore about female lower ambition, or significant differences in aggression (Archer and Lloyd, 1985). Measured differences between the sexes on some socialized trait may be statistically significant, but they are not necessarily educationally significant, and the actually minute differences have little explanatory power for gross inequities in social structures. The fact that the number of women Heads is declining in a country and age where female education and female opportunities have apparently expanded, leads us to investigate more than the previous upbringing of the sexes in order to explain disparities. It is more fruitful to examine the particular and immediate contexts in which exploratory role behaviour is played out, and life chances decided.

Enabling conditions and qualifications

We should look first at the access conditions which determine progress within administrative fields. Differential qualifications may seem important, and can be traced back to segregation at the training level, as in the Middle East, or to alternative 'options' being taken — even without compulsory differentation (Dupont, 1981). Yet even in countries where women are more qualified than men, they still do not exceed men at senior levels (Gambia Ministry, 1982). A recent UNICEF report commented on the paucity of women on its own staff, and noted that 'where educational, experience and language levels among women are higher than men, it hasn't reaped any great gains. Even in UNICEF, the now age-old axiom that women must be better qualified than men for the same job continues to be heard' (UNICEF, 1987). Qualifications are not always a good predictor of long term careers, and may be gained after someone has been selected for leadership. It is more fruitful to focus on specific preparation and sponsorship for management roles. Greenland (1983) noted how in sub-Saharan Africa, women did not participate in leadership training in proportion to their numbers in the primary teaching force. Governments in the first world providing overseas scholarships point to the great range between countries in the proportion of women nominated for such scholarships, and therefore identify discriminatory factors within the sending countries (Commonwealth Secretariat, 1986). Yet immigration rules, entry restrictions to Higher Education and lack of provision for dependents in the receiving countries may also hinder Third World women from taking advanced courses overseas (Goldsmith and Shawcross, 1985). Real and equitable opportunity for job-related administrative training would seem a significant factor, whatever a country's level of development.

The job market

In order to identify the processes through which the selection of potential educational administrators takes place, one should explore the financial and cultural or religious context of teaching. While teachers are professionals with a vocation, they are nonetheless workers in paid employment. Salary scales provide important messages to them and to the public about their perceived worth. In some countries there are still different salary scales for men and women; in South Africa, pay discrimination was removed in 1984, but not for African women teachers. There may be rules about women having to resign from public service on marriage, or being re-employed but at a lower rank. Alternatively, basic salary scales may be the same, but fringe benefits — housing or cost-of-living allowances — may be higher for men than for women. Different salary scales for primary and secondary sectors act as a discriminatory factor if women are concentrated in the younger age range. The School Management and Women Teachers Project in Birmingham found 'a considerable imbalance in the distribution of scale posts between Primary and Secondary schools which could represent a form of indirect discrimination . . . similarly, inconsistencies in gradings of promoted posts where responsibilities are similar could potentially be the basis for complaints under the provisions of the Equal Pay Act' (Al-Khalifa, 1987, p. 2). Given the association in most countries between high pay and high worker value and productivity, any legalized or even illegal disadvantage in remuneration serves to present an image of women as being less suitable for posts involving command over men.

The process is self-reinforcing: low pay (which keeps salary bills down) may be a reason for governments to employ large numbers of women teachers; yet the occupation is then seen to lose status, and it is difficult to fight for higher rewards. The intersection with ethnic background emerges again when we examine for example comparatively recent Namibian policies. A 'special course for women teachers' was to be instituted in Ovamboland, with the admission requirement set at Standard IV. While this may sound like positive discrimination, and what we now see as 'open access' courses, it was yet another means of social control. Women teachers were, as O'Callaghan (1977) pointed out, deliberately being trained for the lower primary classes, 'selected by the educational process for the lowest and worst-paid rungs of the teaching ladder. In addition, the so-called expansion of African education at primary school level was to be accompanied by a lowering of teaching standards.' Women and blacks can be downgraded in one combined move.

Equally important in an understanding of the place of women teachers in a country's political history is the question of religion. The role of Christian missions in perpetuating colonial sex sterotypes regarding suitable curricula for boys and girls can be extended to their possible effects on suitable functions for men and women teachers. Yet the single sex convents were an important arena for women educational administrators, and the increased secularization or the government control of mission schools in many countries may mean a shrinking field for the exercise of female leadership. Segregated education in India similarly gave rise to a large number of women teachers and principals, although Nayar (1986) claims that the segregated inspecting cadres did not in the end help women administrators, as the posts for women were far fewer and led to isolation and stagnation. As elsewhere, India is trying to attract more women into teaching, but this is to aid female enrolment, rather than in the interests of sex equity at the workplace. Finally, in discussing women's position we should not ignore the place of Islam. Muslims differ about whether girls should go to school or be educated at home (Hussain, 1984), and predominantly Muslim countries will also differ in their choice of whether to have single-sex or co-educational schools. However, in Koranic schools everywhere, female teachers are not recruited (Dove, 1986). This could mean that future mothers will prefer to send their children to the State schools or more secular schools that they themselves experienced; but an exclusion of women professionals from a central part of Islamic education does not currently help their careers.

Institutional constraints

Coeducational schools can be a mixed blessing for both students and teachers. The replication of a 'natural' family structure often means the replication of conventional gender divisions. In single sex girls' schools, women teachers will hold administrative and organizational positions, while in boys' schools men will of necessity take pastoral and affective roles. Yet Marland (1982) notes that it is easier for women to get promotion in the three stereotyped fields: 'the young child; "girls"' subjects (even in mixed schools); and pastoral care.' Over ten years ago Byrne castigated the sexual divisions of labour in typical mixed schools:

> Twenty years of staffing has taught me that senior masters, apart from occasionally caning boys, typically deal with school organization, curricular reconstruction, major administration, CSE examinations, and resource allocation, while senior mistresses typically deal with social functions, pregnant schoolgirls, difficult parents, coffee for and entertaining of visitors . . . and school attendance. Equal is not held to mean the same here.' (Byrne, 1978).

My preliminary research in mixed schools in two African countries (Davies, 1987a) demonstrates the same phenomena as in UK: men assume greater responsibility for curriculum, examinations and timetabling, women for counselling, hospitality and support services. Not only is there the same sexual division of labour, but the distribution of the organizational 'spoils' itself may be unbalanced: in Ghana it was found that men teachers were likely to allocate nearly all of a long list of proposed duties to themselves, releasing only 'girls' welfare' and 'hospitality' to the women. Similar sex segregation has been found in Indian schools, symbolized by women being in charge of tea/coffee collections and gift-giving arrangements (Singhal, 1984).

Such allocations lead to a spiral of undervaluation, where women are not given the chance to demonstrate administrative competence, and where men's 'natural' leadership ability is given prominence. In my survey, men were all going to be Director of Education; women were more pragmatic about the possibility of 'reaching the top'. Aspirations are very much rooted in current appraisals of the situation: in UK the reasons often cited for low proportions of senior women is that women do not apply; it is instructive therefore to note that in countries where 'applications' are rare for either sex, and where centralized postings or simply letters informing teachers of their promotions are more the norm, the same gender imbalances still hold. We must look to discriminatory practices at all levels, within the staffroom, by Heads to their subordinates, and by Ministries in their selection procedures. As the Minster of Education for Fiji admitted:

> 'One of the weaknesses in the structure of the headquarters of the Ministry of Education is the absence of women in any decision-making areas. Much as I would like to rectify the situation, sanctified practices instituted by my fellow males for their own perpetuation do not allow me any flexibility' (Siwitibau *et al*, 1985).

It also becomes clear that women must challenge any such abdication of responsibility and locate the real people or practices that may be preventing them achieving — or even visualizing — purposeful career directions.

> The adviser told me I had done well [at interview], but explained to me that next time I should not wear the same round necked blouse I had on with the suit.
> (Woman deputy after headship interview)

The various levels of educational decision-making need to be distinguished when identifying 'blockages' to advancement. Women holding primary headships may be acceptable, but Ghana, for example, is only recently reconsidering its legal directive that all heads of secondary coeducational schools must be men. Similarly in the United States it has been found that affirmative action has enabled female access into the lower administrative levels, but that women are still passed over for promotion to the upper ranks. The networks and allegiances among existing decision-makers at each level must be unmasked and tackled if women are to carve out positions and change the administrative climate.

A significant and symbolic part of institutional ethos may be sexual harassment. The School Management Development and Women Teachers' Project in Birmingham found evidence of frequent incidents of harassment, some so serious they could lead to criminal proceedings.

Women teachers appear to be intimidated from making complaints, especially where the general ethos of the school conveys a negative view of women. When complaints are made, they seem frequently to be trivialised or male managers fail to take action. This problem is compounded by the fact that male teachers responsible for acts of harassment are often of higher status than the women victim:

'I do not think that senior management are interested, they do not see it as very important; they think you are being a bit over-sensitive "wrong time of the month" all that business and you know you should be grateful anyway really' (Secondary teacher) (Al Khalifa 1987, p. 6).

> As I was putting books into the cupboard, a male member of staff came up behind me and put his arms around me. That in itself was bad enough but the fact the he tried to feel my breasts obviously made the incident far worse.
> (Secondary teacher)
>
> A colleague told me she was regularly handled in doorways, found boys' underpants in her schoolbag, and generally had to run the gauntlet in corridors, where her progress would be watched by boys murmuring 'bounce... bounce...bounce'.
> (Secondary teacher)
>
> The male head would kiss us at the slightest provocation. He would put his arm around us or touch our breast if he could get hold – you know without it seeming as though he was doing that.
> (Primary teacher).

Mahony (1985) also identified the same double bind: if a woman says nothing, she appears to condone the harassment; if she comments she is over-reacting, and confirms the stereotype of woman as emotional and unable to take a joke. Black women teachers are especially vulnerable. The significant finding from the Birmingham survey was that there was considerable continuity of experience among girl pupils and women teachers, and that the management response was minimal or non-existent.

The bypassing of such issues by management is paralleled and compounded by the bypassing of women for in-service training, based on stereotyped assumptions about teacher development, career norms, motivation and leadership qualities. Al-Khalifa summarises the findings thus:

> Men teachers are more likely to be supported in undertaking in-service training through access to information, positive encouragement and active facilitation, especially in areas linked to promotion opportunities, because of a widespread belief in men teachers' stronger career orientation;
> (b) women teachers are more likely to be prevented from attending in-service training because cover is not available and because the head refuses permission;
> (c) men teachers are more likely to experience formal and informal sponsorship in career and development opportunities at all stages of their careers, especially from male managers;
> (d) women teachers, especially those with children, are more likely to be overlooked when opportunities for development occur and not to be given career advice, especially by male managers. (p. 8)

The old myths about breadwinning men and childbound women are alive and well in 1980s 'developed' Britain, and institutionalized in training practices.

Management and the family

We should then look very carefully at the old concepts of the 'dual role' for women, and how this affects careers. While not denying the tensions and guilts associated with simultaneously managing a home and a paid job, the dual role for women has become a convenient peg on which to hang a range of explanations for 'underachievement', and has become almost as much a form of 'victim analysis' as sex role socialization. It is, because of pay differentials, more likely to be the woman who follows her spouse if a job demands mobility. It may indeed by as difficult for a woman to relinquish power in the home as it is for men to assume responsibility for domestic management. Women all over the world work notoriously long hours at a great range of activities, some even simultaneously. Yet we should not fall into the trap of seeing this as a social handicap only to be resolved by equal parenting, modern technology or the exploitation of other women to act as substitutes on the domestic field of play. There are strong implications and responsibilities for school management itself.

My African survey did confirm women teachers spending more time on domestic tasks than their male counterparts. Yet female headteachers also spent more time on domestic tasks than male heads, almost as much time as classroom teachers: it would seem that the organization of family life does not necessarily act as a 'barrier' to female careers, but presumably merely entails greater skill at time management. Both men and women teachers saw problems integrating home and school lives, and in matching the demands on their time. The implication is that school management styles or structures should acknowledge the varied roles that we all play, instead of clinging to the traditional managerial assumption of a 40-hour plus week with a non-working spouse at home. The solution to family commitments is not to see them as 'interference', but to begin to view them as a positive attribute in terms of learning management skills.

Child-rearing and maternity leave have traditionally been associated with the notion of a career 'break', but there are signs that this can be changed. Women teachers are increasingly taking minimum maternity leave in order not to jeopardize career prospects, rather than taking a number of years 'off' when children are small (Holmes, 1984). Some authorities in countries such as UK and Australia give increments for child-rearing, seeing this as a positive experience which will enhance teaching performance. Yet elsewhere, women teachers can feel victimized for having children, or for causing 'inconvenience' by taking maternity leave. The increasing number of single-parent families (irrespective of the sex of the parent) has not made a great deal of impact on staff management practices in schools, although there is rhetoric about bearing in mind the effects on the children. It may be timely to get away from the 'dual role' thesis confined to women, and talk instead of the multiple roles that we all assume; it is equally timely for management literature to stop pretending that 'organizational goals' can be pursued in a vacuum without acknowledging and building on the family and life concerns of teaching staff.

The language of entryism

At this point we should also paradoxically cast some doubts on any unquestioning drive to get more women 'into' management. There is the danger of presenting 'management' as the Holy Quest, the utmost pinnacle of ambition. Without care, it is easy to accept uncritically the masculine notions of what management entails, and become obsessed with getting more women into it, like an anxious teenager trying to get into adult films, or an ugly sister into the glass slipper held by the Prince. But are the current conceptions of educational management actually what women should want to infiltrate? Do we want women marching round the school in their executive suits clutching time and motion schedules? It may be equally important to use gender analysis to analyze critically the derivations and implications of some of our ideologies about managerial or leadership styles, and to highlight how a feminist view might lead to a somewhat altered view of the practice of administration.

This is not to claim that women make significantly different leaders once they do get to the 'top'. It might be nice to point to radically altered or trail-blazing style, but the research in fact shows few vast sex differences in the currently espoused leadership 'qualities'. Women and men show equal scores on dimensions such as 'initiation' (setting the goals of the school, and efficiency in implementation). Women do score marginally higher on the 'consideration' dimension (caring for the welfare of staff) in both the West and in countries such as Nigeria (Frasher and Frasher, 1979; Ejiogu, 1982), but they appear to have made little impact on the overall hierarchical nature of typical school administration. This reiterates the point made earlier about the 'sex differences' research being something of a red herring. We cannot claim that simply appointing more women Heads will revolutionize the lives of teachers and pupils. Single-sex girls' schools may be just as traditional or internally competitive as the equivalent boys' or mixed school — albeit unlikely to be as violent.

A problem is that in order to become a school or college head or inspector, a woman may have had to follow very similar routes to her male counterpart. She must have pursued (often more) qualifications, have been socialized into the country's administrative culture, demonstrated her incisiveness and determination. She has probably made sacrifices, perhaps delayed or eschewed child-bearing, or organized a support team of carers at home. None of this is conducive to long-term empathy with the harassed, 'under-achieving' classroom teacher (male or female) who in the attempt to survive from day to day merely ends up rushing about like a gerbil in a bucket.

Definitions of management

It is an irony that educational administration, as a practice, is not at all educational. It teaches nothing to those being adminstered, except perhaps the strategies for countering control and the devices for manipulating the managers. Nor does the theoretical 'discipline' of educational administration have much to say about the underrepresentation of certain groups within it — such as women or ethnic minorities. Those interested in equity in leadership will gain little from most management textbooks, whether written for developed or developing countries. Aspiring women administrators may suffer a temporary discouragement as they penetrate a world where the manager is presented as 'he', where the teaching force is relegated to being merely 'human resources' for the accomplishment of educational goals, or where the elements of 'effective leadership' are extracted exclusively from the traits of past or present male leaders. A recent World Yearbook of Education *The*

Management of Schools (Hoyle and McMahon, 1986) does contain a chapter on 'School Administration: an analysis by gender' by Patricia Schmuck; but this relates mostly to the United States, any mention of gender in the chapters on Third World countries is conspicuously absent. A chapter on UK does contain a mention of gender; but it is last on a list of 'background' features: 'Fourth, women are significantly underrepresented in senior positions in all types of school.' (Bolam, 1986, p. 254). Such omissions or tokenism are critical for two reasons: firstly any management theory which does not recognize the differential constraints on the workforce (of which gender is one such structural dimension) is likely to be lacking in effectiveness; secondly a management perspective which does not treat as problematic the masculine and hence partial derivations of its own ideologies and assumptions is unlikely to become 'gender-inclusive' or 'user-friendly'.

> In this volume, for the sake of consistency, the convention has been adopted of designating promoted teaching staff as 'he' and classroom teachers as 'she'. This is not to be taken to imply an endorsement on the part of the author of current sex bias in the distribution of posts in schools.
> (John Wilson,
> *Appraising Teacher Quality*, 1988)

Focusing on gender imbalances should therefore provoke a fundamental critique of the concept and practice of educational administration itself, rather than spotlight the supposed shortcomings of individual women — or men — as they operate within a given system. There is a parallel here with concerns about female underachievement and wastage in school. Programmes to channel more girls into science and technology have revealed the need for a deeper examination of the abstract and dehumanized notion of 'science' as we conceive it in our curricula. If girls do not like science, do we change girls, or do we redefine 'science'? Similarly, if women do not strive for senior positions, do we remould women or do we begin to question the hierarchically ordered and increasingly technicist notions we have of 'educational administration'? Current critical sociological perspectives provide the clue to this reconceptualisation. A conflict framework would seek to trace the different access to resources such as power that particular groups in organizations have, and to identify in whose real interests an organization operates. It would ask what ideological, financial and emotional mechanisms are used in the distribution of scarce resources, and how power inequalities become legitimized — either within a school, or between a school and its

> Assuming that leadership is formed by and has impact on the
> culture in which it exists, it is not surprising that traditional
> leadership theory was proposed for, researched on and normed on
> male leaders in male-oriented institutions . . . Because theories are
> systems for organizing past and future experience, their value is
> two-fold: they provide a way to pattern or understand what
> happened in the past, and they help us predict what will happen in
> the future. We create worlds reifying experience in theories.
> Leadership theory potentially frames the way that money, status
> and power to change are distributed. By definition, leaders have
> their hand on the levers that move the world. Leadership theory
> that assumes a male perspective, or theory in which male values
> are so deeply embedded as to be invisible, ensures that only males,
> or women adopting male views, will be selected as leaders, will
> continue to lead and thereby set courses, define visions and create
> new worlds. The current realities of organizational life make this
> situation untenable. Intriligator, 1983, *Leadership Revisited*

paymasters. We noted in Chapter 2 the rise of 'rational' scientific management, with
the emphasis on efficiency and performance targets. As Watkins comments, by
presenting school organizational problems as technical problems 'it ignores the power
relationships, class structure and legitimating ideologies around which organisations
are structured' (Watkins, 1983).

Clearly, newer phenomenological approaches to management (which expose
tensions and differing definitions of the situation) have gained some ground over the
last decade (Greenfield, 1973, 1978), but Tipton argues that British and American
educational administration still lacks a firm social science foundation. Questions of the
social class, age, gender or ethnic group of the 'members' of school organizations have
rarely been raised in terms of their own staff interactions, rather in terms of the student
and the effectiveness of learning. 'It is almost as if there is an assumption that anything
that is good for the client must be good for the staff' (Tipton, 1985). A UK exception
is Ball's *The Micropolitics of the School*, which interestingly tackles age and gender
together in examining conflict and change in school organization. He talks of the
'sexual and emotional sub-text' of organizational relationships, which is the hidden
dynamic which conditions perceptions and allegiances. Even where women have
established a right to participate in the formal processes of institutional decision-
making in a school, Ball reminds us of how their problems are not ended:

> There are now numerous studies which demonstrate the ways in which in
> discussion and argument men are able to exert control over topics and
> themes and otherwise dominate, in quantitative and qualitative terms,
> public and private talk. Typically, women's talk is supportive and
> facilitatory when interacting with men; control over the topography of
> conversation is thus surrendered to the men . . . men may meanwhile
> actively assert their own conversation 'rights' by finishing women's

sentences, failing to respond to topics and issues raised by women and interrupting without permission . . . . Within these interactional norms, not unusually women are caught in a double bind. If individual women, or groups, do attempt to assert themselves in discussions or meetings, they are liable to find themselves labelled by men and other women as aggressive, loud-mouthed, essentially unfeminine. Such interactional constraints are policed by the moral arbitration of superordinates and co-workers. (Ball, 1987, p. 78)

Ball recognizes that not all women experience discrimination, nor is there necessarily a sense of combined sisterhood among women teachers. Yet he sees women's groups in schools as likely to become an increasingly potent source of agitation for change in the organizational arena of school micro-politics as the claims of women receive greater publicity and external legitimation.

A gender analysis within educational management theory or practice is not therefore about identifying fundamental sex differences in teachers or administrators. It is not about providing female access to a male-dominated or male-defined occupational hierarchy. Instead it is about locating what women and men teachers bring to education and what they want from the school or organization as a workplace. It is about returning to a sociology of work, and arguing for a management ethos which takes account of the 'total' individual — warts, aspirations, mortgage, 2.4 children and all. Such concerns would examine within each institution the rewards and penalties supplied by each job and by the personnel surrounding it. Any 'gender disparities' investigation arises in identifying whether men and women differ in the amount of recognition and needs fulfilment they get from the organization. This is not a 'blame the victim' analysis which equates female underrepresentation with ingrained female 'tendencies', but a searching appraisal of institutional and managerial practices and how they affect different groupings of workers — female and male, black and white, old and young, unmarried and married. The aim is to phase out separated 'gender' research; we must discover afresh for each institution where gender becomes an issue and where it is less decisive than, say, ethnicity.

The areas for management concern are therefore the vertical division of labour (who occupies which rank); the horizontal division of labour (the academic/pastoral split, the science/arts divide); the allocation of mentoring and encouragement and in-service training; the provision of flexibility so that family concerns do not induce guilt or cover-ups; the dynamics of meetings and discussion which decide informal power processes. Instead of regarding the stereotypical male as the 'normal' worker in education (highly aspiring, sole breadwinner, spouse to care for children), it is instructive to begin from the female-as-norm in conceptualizing the teaching profession. What are her multiple roles? What does she want from work? What does she contribute to educational and national development? What needs does teaching or administration fulfil for her? Could the management and opportunity structure of the school realize these needs and contributions in a better way?

Another instructive rephrasing of questions is to ask not 'why don't women enter management', but 'how did the management that women don't participate in come to be conceived?' If the management structure of a school or college acts to exclude women from formal or informal decision-making, then we should explore that structure and not attempt to change women into surrogate men. In terms of vertical divisions, the new emphasis on 'management training' means, paradoxically, a greater divide between the expert, trained educational leader and the uninitiated classroom teacher. Senior staff are taken out of the classroom, even out of the staffroom, and then have to go on courses to (re)learn 'communication skills'. If we identify the needs of ordinary teachers, however, we may find them also concerned with communication, but not necessarily as defined by a top-down management 'technique'. It is a truism to reiterate that all teachers need managerial skills, for all are concerned with supervising people — albeit of different age groups; and all are concerned with managing time — personally and professionally. Yet confining the expert mystique to the 'senior management team', and denying the bulk of staff real access to decision-making or feelings of control over events, may further entrench existing power and gender divisions.

Horizontally, we may need an administrative structure which allows flexibility and experimentation in the performance of various roles. Factories have long since discovered the benefits of allowing workers to rotate their tasks to alleviate monotony and gain a fuller understanding of, and a stake in, the total production process. Teaching is admittedly more varied in essence than the assembly line, but it can become routinized, especially if personnel become typecast into specialized roles, or at the other end of the scale merely aim at daily survival in coping with the demands of school and home. To permit the cooperative learning of management skills, to enable the maximization of our use of time, to increase women's stake in the organization, and to celebrate rather than denigrate multiple roles, we will probably need a far more flexible, rotational, non-pyramidal style of school administration than is normally the case. Such structures should not of course be decided by men in the interests of women; they must be generated by the thoughts and decisions of women themselves. We shall return to the question of teachers' needs and how they can be identified and acted upon in Chapter 7. We should finally examine some of the initiatives around women and management in the light of the above discussions.

Strategies for change

Strategies for the inclusion of females in decision-making about education have, as we shall see for racial balance, ranged from the coercive to the persuasive. They appear to fall into three main categories: positive discrimination or forceful legislation; training; and institutional development. In the first category an example comes from Holland. The city council of Amsterdam decided that with 70 per cent of women primary teachers leading to only 36 per cent primary heads, and 47 per cent of female secondary teachers providing only 4 per cent secondary heads, new heads should be chosen from women applicants who met the job requirements. The parent-teacher association of the most prestigious school appealed to the Minster of Internal Affairs to overturn the policy (in the interests of 'quality') when their headship became vacant, but the minister declined to intervene (*Times Educational Supplement*, 2 September, 1988). Positive discrimination will always be challenged by those fearing a lowering of standards, even if formal job requirements are still met. It is difficult to convince consumers about femaleness actually being a good qualification for a job in its own right, although the Women's National Commission in UK state the case quite forcefully:

> The Group consider that it would be a grave tragedy for our society if there
> ceased to be a significant number of women heads of schools. Where there is
> a woman head of a mixed school this offers the opportunity for boys and
> girls at a formative stage to have close contact with a woman in a leadership
> role. Women teachers are frequently relegated at best to the second-in-
> command role in schools. The responsibilities of this post are also often
> restricted ('high grade girls' lavatory attendant' as one member of the
> Group expressed it). If unchecked, this will strongly reinforce many girls'
> traditional assumption that management and leadership roles are not for
> them. (Women's National Commission, 1983)

An alternative to positive discrimination or quotas is the use of a Sex Discrimination Act or other forms of legislation whereby behaviour likely to impede women's progress can be sanctioned. Teachers claiming that discriminatory questions were asked at interview can appeal to the law in UK, with complaints made about questions to do with child care, likelihood of maternity and so on. Not only can individual cases be given redress, but the publicity demonstrates that a society is serious about equal rights. A nice example of 'good publicity' legislation comes from Nigeria, where the courts fined a man for impregnating a Form Three student and ordered him to bear the financial responsibility of raising the child as well as the cost of the mother's comple-tion of secondary education after delivery. 'The judge directed the administrators of the school to continue her education notwithstanding her pregnancy. According to Nigerian sources, such cases have not been prosecuted until quite recently — a step forward for Nigerian women' (*The Women's Watch* 1,3, Fall 1987). While the case may not seem immediately relevant to the question of women in management, it is significant that the administration of the school came under the directive, with the implication that there would otherwise be resistance to the mix of motherhood and schooling. The acknowledgment of male responsibility for children, of maternity not being a communicable disease, and of the importance of female education can only be in the interests of women teachers.

The second area to tackle is that of training. This can be both for the women themselves and for selection boards. The Women's National Commission (1983) found discrepancies between local authorities, with some not committed at all to professional development courses, whether for men or women, and others recognizing that special encouragement has to be given to women to train for posts of high responsibility, and attempting to equalize 'or nearly equalize' the numbers of men and women on courses. Some local authorities run professional development courses for women only; others were against positive action. The Commission did not support quota systems, but recommended that LEAs should ensure that:

> — in service training is, as far possible, compatible with family commitments and that teachers (especially women, who have the greatest problem) are consulted to achieve the best compromise.
> — at the stage of 'sifting' applications able women are not excluded simply through lack of an appropriate career profile (e.g. because they have not been deputy heads).
> — training/advice is given the potential members of Selection Committees who should be vigorously reminded that questions raised to women's marital and domestic circumstances are 'out of order'. On the positive side they should also be reminded that women have become successful heads of large mixed schools.
> — in particular, the new National Training Centres for school heads and others should consider how they can meet women's needs in all respects including course arrangements. (p. 9)

A recent document from Strathclyde Department of Education in Scotland, *Sex Equality in the Education Service*, contains similar recommendations, and also includes the need for written guidelines for interviewers; the composition of interviewing panels to contain both sexes; advice offered to heads and principals on the completion of reports on staff seeking promotion; parental leave available to parents of either sex; supplementary training for parents seeking to reenter the profession after a break; and the maintenance of systematic statistics relating to the recruitment and promotion of

> The odds ratio of a woman being hired when there are no women on a selection committee was found to be 20%; when there was at least one women on a screening committee, the odds rose to 35%.
> (Patricia Schmuck)

women within the teaching profession (Strathclyde Department of Education, 1988). This is a far-reaching set of recommendations, and it will be informative to follow their progress.

The arguments for training do not necessarily contradict my earlier reservations about an uncritical acceptance of the ideology of management courses. The important issue here is less the content of the courses but the fact that women have been selected for them and have returned with an experience or a qualification which is useful currency. The confidence-building aspects, and the self-socialization into feeling powerful, are arguably the most salient features, although the time management and decision-making sections can of course be highly functional. Whether the management of organizations can be taught outside the institution in which it is practised is still debatable.

Thus a third area for strategy around women and power derives from work within the school or college itself. Pupils at an experimental girls' school in Jerusalem are taught to pursue a career and build a family. They are encouraged to opt for science, and the parallel course on family studies includes units on choice of partner, stereotypes of women and birth, and on parenting, as well as nutrition, budget management and the environment. The really significant departure from tradition is however the attempt to turn the school into a model of participatory government. All the teachers, pupils and administrative staff are equal members of a school general assembly; an executive committee of four pupils and four teachers then turns its decisions into realistic possibilities. The principal's right of veto is seldom used. The girls are responsible not only for making rules but also for imposing them. A fairness committee, which is made up of four pupils and two teachers, decides on suitable punishments for erring pupils. The Head, Professor Shalvi, has found that 'people assume an extraordinary degree of responsibility when given the chance and that women, like men, must be given that responsibility.' (*Times Educational Supplement*, 15 July 1988).

Work in girls' schools must of course be paralleled by work in boys' schools, if men are to relinquish dominance or power to the newly confident and assertive women, and take equality at work and home seriously. I am interested in the boys' schools that have pioneered courses on parenting and the father's role ('Fifth-formers study joys of fatherhood', *Times Educational Supplement*, 23 December, 1988), and in the boys' schools that study the effects of masculinity or challenge sexual harassment (Mahony, 1985). It is however in mixed schools where the immediate shifts in gender relations will be played out, and where action by groupings of teachers will become apparent. Ball (1987) traces how women staff may bring politics, including feminist politics, into their stance and work, and force defensive reactions from male staff.

> Sexist treatment in the classroom encourages formation of patterns...which give men more dominance and power than women in the working world. But there is a light at the end of the educational tunnel. Classroom biases are not etched in stone, and training can eliminate these patterns. Sixty teachers in our study received four days of training to establish equity in classroom interactions. These trained teachers succeeded in eliminating classroom bias. Although our training focused on equality, it improved overall teaching effectiveness as well. Classes taught by these trained teachers had a higher level of intellectual discussion and contained more effective and precise teacher responses for all students.
> (Sadker and Sadker)

'The concerns of politically conscious women are on the social agenda even if they are manifest, in part at least, through the taunts and jibes of male colleagues. In the micropolitics of the school, feminism is frequently perceived by men, probably accurately, as a threat to their vested interests. It is a threat to their masculinity, and it does represent a challenge to their control of decision-making and organizational consciousness, it is an attempt to redefine the political ethos of the school.' (p. 76)

Similarly, Connell and colleagues in Australia note that teachers are themselves involved in a changed sexual division of labour; and a significant number of the younger women teachers have been influenced by feminism. 'They, with sympathetic male teachers, support the project of careers for girls, and provide a base for counter-sexist campaigns in schools: in careers advising, in the reading matter supplied to young children, in removing promotional barriers for women in their profession, and in teacher organizations' (Connell *et al*, 1982, p. 176). The difference between Ball's and Connell's case-studies are the type of conflicts or allegiances, and whether these are overtly gender-divided: Connell's implies the cooption of 'sympathetic male teachers' as a feature of support for change. The authors are however doubtful whether co-education has meant any relaxation of sexism, and to indite the conservative, hierarchical organization of secondary schooling, 'the patriarchal structures that constitute power and authority as the major axis of relations among people' (p. 178).

We return to my earlier comment that merely replacing men by women at the top of a hierarchical organization will not necessarily create radical change in gender relations or sexism. The focus on gender in management should act to challenge patricarchal worldviews as they are manifested in educational organizations, in particular those that deny participation and responsibility to the mass of their members — male or female.

EXERCISE 4 : PAIRING

What would a 'gender-inclusive' management structure in a school look like? What would we need to make schools 'user-friendly' and take account of the needs and problems of both women and men staff? Try this pairing exercise. On the left are the possible areas that a teacher has to manage in their school life. On the right are some possible organizational features which could help that teacher manage the areas more effectively. They are not in order: is it possible to draw lines to match the two sides up appropriately? Is there more than one set of connections? What would you discard or add?

If you are managing . . .	Organizational features which could help in particular areas
other people	bursars
conflicting demands of home and school	teacher's aids
time	temporary working parties to solve problems
students in class	peer appraisal
decisions	in-school creche
self-esteem	flexi-time
sexism	rotational chairs, convenors, or heads
money	equal opportunities network or group

Chapter 5

Ethnicity, Pluralism and Anti-Racism

There are three intentions for this chapter: firstly to outline some of the explanations and policies around perceived differences in educational outcomes for different ethnic groups; secondly to explore where 'race' issues are significantly different from other areas of potential inequality, such as gender; and thirdly to pinpoint some of the management concerns for schools which are raised by past or present racial inequality in a country. It is not the intention to examine the manifold definitions and interpretations of multiculturalism* as such, as this is an enormous and well-trodden field, particularly if attempting an international framework. The number of glossary items to be asterisked is an indication of the difficulties of definition of 'the field'. The subtleties and political histories of ethnic, language and religious divisions — and their surrounding policies — vary so greatly between different cultures that an overarching analysis appears impossible. Instead I select a few of what could be common areas of concern for schools in plural* societies, in terms of institutional organization and staff development, and deliberately focus on the more contentious issues of racism and racial inequality.

A plural society, or the presence of a number of ethnic groups in a school, do not in themselves constitute a 'problem'. If they become conceived of as problematic, it generally relates to a search for consensual goals for a school or for the education system, that is, the attempted socialization into a common culture or a common framework of opportunity. Hence ethnicity* becomes a 'problem' firstly when there emerge different achievement levels as between ethnic groups; secondly when choices have to be made about language, curriculum and religion in education; thirdly when there is the presence of individual or institutional racism; and fourthly when goals of national unity are not being realized. These four areas are clearly interlinked, if not inseparable; but the focus on one of them as a starting point may evince different explanations and policy measures both within and between countries. Separate schools for children from different ethnic groups, for example, may be seen as a problem or a solution, depending on one's cultural aims. Similarly, a school without much ethnic diversity in a country which is multiracial may be viewed as fortunate or unfortunate, depending on whether the focus is on achievement or on citizenship.

A situation of disparity and division as between ethnic groupings in a school system has therefore been explained by a variety of theories:

(a) cultural deficit (that certain ethnic groups 'lack' the orientations and experiences conducive to educational attainment);

(b) language problems (that certain groups 'suffer' from second language learning or bilingualism);

(c) regional disadvantage (that certain ethnic groups are geographically located in areas which are poorer both in environmental or educational provision);

(d) cultural difference (that different ethnic groups have equally rich and valid cultures, but the school focuses only on a 'mainstream' or single culture);

(e) institutional or societal racism (that the school actively perpetuates negative values attached to membership of certain groups and reproduces the power imbalances of society).

These theories are not mutually exclusive, and policies will be based on various combinations of them. However, we can initially separate different policy ideologies attached to the five positions, which, in some countries, also represent chronological shifts in thinking regarding 'solutions' to pluralism.

(a) A *cultural deficit* position will, as with gender and class, lead to compensatory policies designed to integrate 'underachieving' ethnic groups into dominant educational and cultural values: home-school links, pre-school intervention and parental education are examples. Cultural injections are often linked to the next policy, that is

(b) *linguistic deficit* measures, whereby additional help in mainstream language is provided for immigrant children (as in UK in the 1960s) or for children for whom the language of instruction is not their mother tongue (as in linguistically plural societies).

(c) *regional disadvantage* explanations may lead to quota systems whereby disadvantaged areas are allocated certain percentages of numbers entering different levels of the education system (if this is selective); or they may be linked to the 'bussing' of children to schools away from their locality in order to avoid 'ghetto' schools.

(d) *cultural* (or linguistic) *difference* theories will invoke a pluralistic or bicultural stance, emphasizing the need to give equal value and respect to different cultures, languages, religions and histories and promoting multicultural curricula, multi-faith teaching and mother-tongue learning in school. The focus is on the self-esteem of minority groups as well as the implicit prejudice of dominant groups.

(e) an *institutional racism* interpretation may, on the other hand, claim that many multicultural policies are in themselves racist, in that they tend to portray minority cultures and languages as exotic and marginal; an anti-racist stance aims to tackle the discriminatory features of school organization and of relationships between staff and students as well as any curricular distortions. It is argued that merely exhorting tolerance for 'other people' only underscores the 'otherness' of minority groups, and does little to challenge the racially based economic and political power imbalances which are reflected in the education system.

Schools:	We're all equal here.
Black students:	We *KNOW* we are second-class citizens, in housing, employment and education.
Schools:	Oh, dear. Negative self-image. We must order books with Blacks in them.
Black students:	Can't we talk about the Immigration Laws or the National Front?
Schools:	No that's politics. We'll arrange some Asian and West Indian Cultural Evenings.

(Cole 1986)

A nation may also attempt different combinations of these at different times: UK has moved from the integrationist or assimilationist position of the 1960s (whereby immigrant children were to be made more like white children) through the multiculturalist, pluralist position of the 1970s (aiming at respect and tolerance for a range of cultures) to the anti-racist ideologies of the 1980s which seek to challenge the structural and institutional racism characterizing the UK economy. Even within a broad anti-racist position, there are clearly different strategies: the racism awareness courses for local authority employees (including teachers) have in some authorities given way to more forceful ways to change behaviour, such as contract compliance (whereby firms are not given contracts by the local authorities unless they operate an equal opportunities policy or have targets for adequate representation of ethnic minority workers).

Examples of a different selection of policies would be found in Malaysia and in Israel. Malaysia has used a combination of cultural difference and regional disadvantage positions to arrive at a national unity model which overtly favours the previously underachieving but numerically dominant group: the Malays. Quota systems in favour of rural 'bumiputera' (literally sons of the soil) Malays, Malay as the major language of instruction and business, Islam as the preferred religion, and the promotion of Malay culture and institutional values are all designed by Malays to redress previous Chinese dominance in achievement and power. While other countries have been moving towards multiculturalism and linguistic diversity, Malaysia has been promoting monoculturalism and linguistic homogeneity. The temporarily racist appearance of such policies are justified in the interests of long-term national harmony and integration, and of the achievement of a Malay identity regardless of original ethnic membership. The parallel is to what Banks and Lynch (1986) refer to as 'assimilation', or the idea of the freeing of youths from their

> ethnic identifications and commitments so that they can become full participants in the national culture. When schools foster ethnic commitment and identifications, this retards the academic growth of ethnic youths and contributes to the development of ethnic tensions (p. 13).

While such an approach seems incompatible with a celebration of cultural variety, Horowitz (1988) claims that Israel has at times in its educational history attempted to adopt a mix of approaches simultaneously — with resultant fundamental ambiguities in policy. The education system of Israel never aimed at cultural pluralism, yet it could not ignore ethnic differences in achievement. 'The problem has thus been one of legitimizing the plurality of cultural inputs without legitimizing pluralism as an output' (p. 7).

The two major distinctions in policy seem to be between homogeneity and diversity on the one hand and between persuasion and coercion on the other. Homogeneity would imply a choice of one recognizable cultural identity which would be preferable to other choices (e.g. local rather than colonial, or indigenous rather than immigrant or foreign); diversity would imply a cultural relativism which denies any inbuilt superiority of one religion or life-style or set of values. These tendencies represent of course degrees of difference along two continua rather than absolute positions. An interesting exercise is to attempt to locate countries on a matrix representing the two dimensions: (see Figure 5.1)

Educational and social policies can be devised which acknowledge and celebrate the presence of different ethnic groups and languages, but hope that education in tolerance, cultural awareness and mutual respect will forge a plural society, with different communities existing side by side in a mutual symbiosis and harmony. This would be country (A). Eradicating individual prejudice is seen as the key to progress. This has parallels with what Kirp (1979) calls 'racially inexplicit' policies, which use categories such as 'language provision' or 'cultural adjustment' to tackle problems associated with black students, in a way which avoids a white backlash.

Figure 5.1

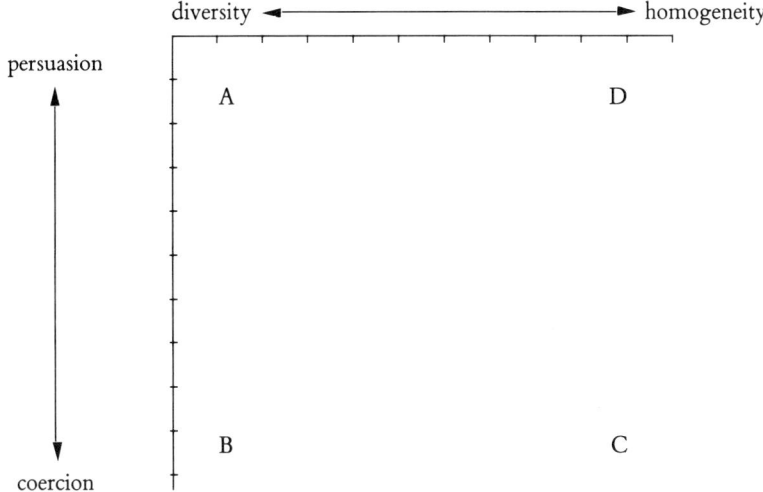

Alternatively, as in country (B), equitable pluralism can be aimed for, but it is acknowledged that this will require a legislative and institutional framework to outlaw discriminatory structures and actively to promote the position of potentially disadvantaged groups. People are seen as naturally self-seeking, and while one cannot change attitudes through legislation, one can prohibit certain behaviours so that racism is signalled and victims are protected. In the context of UK, this has been termed the explicit 'racialisation' of discourse about educational inequality (Troyna and Williams 1986).

That same need for control is reflected in country (C), whereby a legal framework is enacted in order to create in this instance a homogeneity out of a previously inegalitarian diversity. Temporary unevenly distributed resources in favour of subordinate groups, and/or the suppression of certain cultural expressions or languages may feature here.

Unity is also attempted in country (D), but through educational policies such as citizenship, political mobilization, and the stress on a common cultural history, common future priorities and even common enemies. Tribal or colonial affiliations must be subordinated to the new national identity.

Clearly, the options available to a school in contemplating its pupil and staff body, and its responsibilities to the community, will be contingent upon that national framework for action. If there is a Race Relations Act or similar legislative machinery to define and proscribe racism or negative discrimination, then this might act as a backcloth to decisions about staff appointments, treatment of students and provision of curriculum, even if educational choices are not actually specified by law. If there is a national policy which lays down the medium or media of instruction and the way religion is taught, then the school can have little official room for manoeuvre. A policy of permitted diversity, or the absence of a national policy, will enable schools to interpret their role within a multiracial community, and lead to diversity between schools as well as within them. Watson (1985) makes a useful distinction between those interpretations of 'cultural pluralism' which imply separate but equal development for all groups, and those which imply bi- or multiculturalism, whereby each group is expected to learn the language and culture of one or more other group within society. He contrasts the (then) '*laissez-faire*' policies of UK with Australia, Canada and Sweden, who 'have legislated for biculturalism and bilingualism as the true measure of cultural pluralism' (p. 76). School staffs and managers will vary therefore in the degree to which they have experienced in their training any courses in second language teaching, in cultural or racism awareness or in curriculum reform for a plural society.

Countries, and even teacher training institutions, will vary also in whether race issues are seen in the context of equal opportunity as a whole, or whether they are tackled separately. Before looking specifically as certain management issues, it is important to explore with regard to education, how 'race' can be distinguished from other areas of inequality such as gender.

Is race a 'parallel' issue?

First is the question of cultural identity. Even if girls are disadvantaged in certain areas of the curriculum, they are not generally seen as outside the mainstream (even if some girls-into-Maths/Science/Technology strategies are avowedly integrationist). For ethnic minority groups, in spite of a rhetoric about, for example, being part of a multiracial Britain, there may emerge the 'myth of belonging'. This myth, that West Indians were seen as truly British, was highlighted in quotations in the Swann Report:

> Many of us came here with a myth in our minds, the myth of belonging. We have also raised our children to believe that they belong in these societies and cultures (simply because they were born here) only to find that as they grew older, they were seen in the eyes of the host community as a new nation of intruders. Our children are then faced with great traumatic and psychological problems, since they are made to feel that they do not belong here, also they feel that because they were not born in the West Indies they do not belong there either (HMSO, 1985, p. 21).

Linked to this is secondly the question of timespan. We have always had two sexes, but not all countries have always felt they have enjoyed a multiplicity of cultures. Apart from minor skirmishes around whether Eve was created from Adam's rib or vice versa, or whether all mankind is derived from a sole African woman, both sexes have been around a roughly equal amount of time. Yet population balances change rapidly, and migration and immigration patterns lead to marked designations of people as 'indigenous', 'newly arrived', 'second generation national' etc. The 'myth of return', also identified in the Swann Report, additionally acts to colour people's views about rights to citizenship and 'natural' origins. Time scales will determine who constitutes an immigrant worker or child, and influence the perceived necessary length of quota systems or integration policies.

Third is the issue of community membership. An ethnic minority child is a member, normally, of a whole ethnic minority family, which in turn may be subject to discrimination and prejudice. In a predominantly ethnic minority area, minority consciousness may be additionally heightened. The experience of sexism, on the other hand, is not felt as part of a total family or community 'oppression', but as a more individualized and possibly less overt message. Girls are not perceived to have 'language problems' — quite the reverse. Disruptive units in UK may have disproportionate numbers of ethnic minority children, but not disproportionate numbers of girls. Both racial inequality and ethnic minority individuals can be seen as more threatening and problematic than sexual inequality and girls.

Then there are the effects of colonialism in many parts of the world, which are different for race and gender. While it may be argued that Western definitions of 'breadwinner' and 'head of household' have adversely affected the post-colonial status and power of women, independence from colonial rule was primarily a national and racial issue, with any gender liberation seen as a spin-off. The ending of segregated schools for black and white, as in Zimbabwe, or the abolition of colonially-inspired separated racial schools, as in Malaysia, was one first educational task. Because of material, ideological and curricular differences as between segregated school systems, the integration of previously racially divided educational sectors presents far more apparent tensions than ending sex segregation, particularly when one sector has suffered long-term educational disadvantage.

Finally is the basic area of communication and intergroup knowledge. While girls and boys may be seen to inhabit distinct role cultures, they speak the same language, and unless brought up in complete seclusion, will be aware of how it is to be a member of the 'opposite' sex. This may not be true in the case of ethnic groupings, and has led to the sometimes dubious school policies around 'awareness', such as visits to mosques, learning about festivals and attempting international cooking. The danger of patronage in the respect for 'other' cultures is not implicit in gender policy. The 'ethnic additive' approach to multicultural curriculum (Banks and Lynch 1986), whereby bits of 'other' cultures are tacked onto the dominant knowledge base, has not permeated attempts at non-sexist curricula.

The contemporary attention paid to race issues can thus be double-edged. On the one hand, it is clearly beneficial. Gender distinctions are deeper seated and hence more acceptable: teachers can say 'Good morning boys and girls' in a way they cannot say

'Good morning blacks and whites'. They can have boys' names on the register first, followed by girls' names, or make the sexes compete against each other in a way they would not dream of or dare differentiate racially. Sexist language is more permeating of everyday English because of grammatical forms than is racist language, and we are still less sensitized to it. The implicit link between racial inequality and the potentiality for political disturbance means that ethnicity is at least on the agenda for action, even if provision is patchy and piecemeal. On the other hand, the sensitivity around ethnicity issues means it may be seen as more threatening and contentious, and research in educational institutions is less easy to arrange. Bland efforts to sanitize curricular materials may be preferred to overt anti-racist strategy in schools and teacher training colleges.

Finally, we return to the whole issue of whether race issues can be seen in any way as 'parallel' across nations. It may well appear that the juxtaposition of different countries in the attempt at an international perspective is an uneasy and artificial one. Yet it is perhaps just by such an uncomfortable juxtaposition that we realize the different historical bases to our notions of 'discrimination' or 'prejudice'. The parallels are not because of some fundamental 'baseline' to race issues (unless one takes colossal dimensions such as 'power'); but in terms of the similar recognition of the need to understand and engage in the struggle for equal rights — in whatever context. As always, the major reason for studying 'other' problems is better to comprehend 'one's own'.

School management issues

In this search for parallels and for understanding, let us turn to some school management concerns which have been identified as pertaining to issues of race, pluralism and integration. I want to focus attention on the linked areas of headteachers' management experiences; staff management and development; and student management. I do not intend to dwell on curriculum management for two reasons. Firstly, whole libraries have been written about multicultural curricula. Secondly, I would concur with the distinction usually made between multicultural education and anti-racist education (see, for example, Carrington and Short, 1987), and prefer to highlight concerns around the latter. Much multicultural education, as Troyna argues at least for UK, continues 'to draw its inspiration and rationale from white, middle-class professional understandings of how the education system might best respond to the perceived "needs" and "interests" of black students and their parents'. The power relationship between black and white remains unchallenged. Multicultural reforms introduced in the 1970s 'were geared towards a representation of their (presumed) life styles in curriculum designs and teaching aids. What they ignored were the formal and informal racist processes which constrained the educational opportunities available to these students. This, we concluded, was discrimination by proxy. (Troyna, 1987, pp. 308–309). Young's appraisal of Inner London's anti-racist policy notes:

> It (racism) is seen as a fault in the social system by which one is informed as a member of society. Its origins are located in the economic and political dominance of white people over black people in Britain's colonial past. This acknowledgement that power relations must be taken into account for any real understanding of racism to be achieved is a welcome step in the right direction. The more commonly shared understanding of racism, however, continues to limit to the realm of prejudice, where it is associated with intolerance and irrationality. (Young, 1985, p. 31 quoted in Carrington and Short, 1987).

There must be essentially a politicizing of analyses around race and education, in any country. This includes the examination of the structural bases to racism in the school, and the micro-politics of the school itself. The hidden curriculum of staffing, assessment and pupil organization as they interact with ethnicity have received too little attention compared with the effects of formal curriculum. My concern is how past and present ethnic inequalities and racism affect school management. I do not want to mask this by diversions into 'culture'.

Heads' management experience

Racial inequalities can first of all affect the basic style and management history of heads themselves. In Zimbabwe, Maravanyika (1986) draws our attention to the very different management experience black and white heads had under British colonial rule. White education was designed to provide skilled manpower requirements in government, commerce and industry, while black education was intended to provide unskilled and semi-skilled labourers. There were fears that black education, if not controlled, could encourage African nationalism and provoke civil unrest. A European child received thirteen times more *per capita* grant than an African child, and more likelihood of qualified teachers. Significantly for our management concerns, white school heads had far more autonomy than their black counterparts. They could decide curriculum issues and which examination boards to use. The school was seen as part of the local community, with the local Parent-Teacher Association involved in day-to-day activities. (There are parallels with Connell's 'ruling class' schools in Australia today, as mentioned in Chapter 3). African schools on the other hand were managed according to specific instructions given to heads by missionary superintendents and occasionally by government inspectors; schools were deliberately divorced from the life and culture of local African people. Maravanyika summarizes the problems of heads in black areas trying to implement the new socialist transformation after independence in 1980:

> In the black areas, the headmasters who had to manage the change process had no experience in taking independent decisions or in being innovative. They had been schooled in taking specific instructions from school superintendents and carrying them out. Whereas in the past instructions and directives came in the form of circulars, the expected reforms were generally announced at political rallies by politicians and reached some of the teachers through radio, television or the press. The newly appointed black educational administrators, recruited from the rank and file of teachers and college lecturers, were inexperienced in translating policy for purposes of implementation in schools. Moreover, the policy of Africanization of the civil service and other sectors of the economy through a presidential directive resulted in the movement of experienced secondary school teachers from the schools into these other sectors. At the same time, there was a massive expansion of education, but because of this movement of teachers out of the system there were not enough managers left to manage the change process. Primary school teachers and untrained teachers were recruited into the new secondary schools while primary schools recruited largely from the pool of unemployed school leavers. They had enough problems in trying to settle down into their new jobs, let alone in managing change as envisaged by the politicians. (p. 207)

A legacy of racially discriminatory practices with regard to colonialism or apartheid may therefore lead to differences in approaches to school management which act to compound prejudices about 'readiness' for power and responsibility. Personal experience of membership of a particular ethnic group will clearly influence the way a head sees his or her role in future 'integration' and the likelihood of adopting either multicultural or anti-racist approaches. Studies of the attempted implementation of anti-racist measures in the UK have found many of the (predominantly white) heads resistant to such initiatives, preferring assimilationist approaches (Troyna and Ball, 1985). The heads who ignored LEA recommendations for action generally worked in the voluntary sector, or in schools with mainly ethnically homogenous intakes. There has been some modest success with government-funded multicultural projects in the 'white highlands' of UK, but some projects have low status because the staff involved were on low grades (Tomlinson and Coulson, 1988). The problem of convincing heads and teachers that anti-racist education is as important, if not more important, in all-white schools is compounded when the implementers suffer marginal prestige; or when, as Troyna and Williams (1986) point out, initiatives come only from funds such as Section 11 which imply 'special' and hence abnormal status. Heads' and governors' perceptions of the wishes of the community and the resistance level of parents, will play a great part in the interpretation of 'acceptable' policy — particularly, as we saw in Chapter 2, in times of public accountability.

Current or previous segregation of heads, or the underrepresentation of ethnic minority heads in networks or presumably on management training courses, will not advance the cause of pluralism, especially if anti-racism is not tackled routinely within such management courses. As with 'inputs' with regard to gender, there are dangers in itemizing 'multiculturalism' as a single component — assuming it appears at all. In order not to allow heads to dismiss ethnic considerations as 'irrelevant' or 'inappropriate' to their school, race must be tackled as part of a total political analysis of structures of opportunity.

Staff management and development

Whether or not educational institutions have previously been segregated on racial lines, those operating within a multiracial society will face the issue of the ethnic composition and balance of their staff. Just as we saw with regard to gender balance, 'proportional representation' is crucial in terms of promoting equity in career opportunities for teachers and in terms of providing role models for students. Heads may not, however, have much control over appointments of staff; if they do, attempts positively to discriminate in favour of one ethnic group may provoke accusations of bias and racism; and as with all ethnic monitoring, statistics on the ethnic origins of teachers are difficult to obtain and maintain. The problems of ensuring what appears to be an appropriate ethnic balance on a staff should never be underestimated. Nonetheless, it is a concern in many countries, either as a minority representation issue, or as a localization* one. The need to recruit more ethnic minority teachers in UK was clearly set out in the Swann Report (HMSO, 1985), together with the need to collect statistical information on distribution. The Commission for Racial Equality has identified a number of reasons limiting the recruitment of black teachers in UK, which are reported in the Assistant Masters and Mistresses Association Report (AMMA 1987). They quote recruitment methods and procedures – where posts are advertised, the use of word-of-mouth soliciting of applications and the encouragement of applications from within the work force — which while not directly discriminatory, tend to perpetuate existing imbalances. They are cited as an example of 'institutional racism'. 'The experience of black teachers arriving for an interview to find a clear change of apparent attitude when a British-sounding name is seen to go with a black face is commonplace' (AMMA, 1987, p. 95).

The low status of the teaching profession will also act as a disincentive for upwardly aspiring suitably qualified black people. A recent survey in Bradford schools found poor pay, discipline problems, poor promotion opportunities and racism among pupils and staff were discouraging young Asians from teaching (Singh, 1988).

Problems experienced by black teachers, although anecdotal rather than statistical, will act further to deter potential applicants and present management problems for heads. The Swann Report is concerned about the number of black teachers 'stagnating' in the system 'at posts far below their capabilities and experience'. Many are found in ESL* and mother-tongue teaching positions which have a marginal image.

> In extreme cases interviewers have found it difficult to believe that the black candidate is a genuine candidate for the post. That is, of course, not restricted to the teaching profession or to black people. At AMMA's conference 'Positive and negative discrimination in multi-cultural Britain', Jocelyn Barrow, an experienced and respected teacher-trainer and a governor of the BBC, told us how frequently on arriving somewhere for a meeting she is mistaken for the tea-lady.

There is also the question of relationships within the staffroom. AMMA claims that black teachers do not always feel at home in predominantly white staffrooms — either because of real prejudice simply unease at 'difference'. The cultures of the staffroom are compounded where linguistically diverse groups of staff coexist. Observations of staffrooms in Botswana, for example, found at least three languages in operation, with conversations between English-speaking expatriates or between Asian expatriates taking place side by side with the Setswana interchanges between local teachers (Davies, 1988). The point at issue would be the degree to which the informal use of language by teachers acts to include or exclude segments of the staff; a management ethos to induce cohesion and loyalty can be thwarted by mistrust evinced by non-comprehension.

Some language issues thus need addressing at this point. While not wanting to enter the intricate debates around mother-tongue teaching and the pros and cons of bilingualism for students, we could usefully ponder the necessary language proficiencies and responsibilities of teachers. For black teachers in South Africa, the crucial question is seen as proficiency in English, for a number of reasons such as the perception of blacks regarding access to Western European technology and culture, access to the economic and social life of the country, financial implications of producing textbooks in the seven major languages, curricular difficulties in ensuring culturally fair testing materials, semantic and syntactic difficulties in translating learning content into vernacular, and importantly, the political perception of black languages as 'inferior' to an international language. Afrikaans, the other official language, is of course seen as the language of the oppressor (Louw, 1988). In their students' interest, it is therefore recommended for compulsory English to be part of all in-service upgrading programmes for teachers.

In officially integrated systems, on the other hand, where mother-tongue teaching and bilingualism is overtly valued, the issue would be whether teachers should be familiar with the major languages spoken in the school, as well as having some knowledge of techniques of teaching the official language as a second language. Local authorities in UK are changing policies of placing immigrant children in special units, or withdrawing them from conventional lessons for additional English. In the first complaint of its type received by the CRE*, a black teacher in the West Midlands complained that her white pupils were suffering because Asian children were given special treatment, and that Asian parents were opposed to segregated teaching (*Sunday Times*, 20.9.87).

Yet integration on its own does not solve the problem of enabling children to reach the threshold of linguistic competence whereby they can benefit from learning in a second language (Cummins, 1977). A recent study in Hong Kong found the majority of English-medium secondary school students lacked communicative competence and the ability to argue, discuss or explain, compared to Chinese-medium students (Yu and Atkinson, 1988). The argument is that the distinction should be borne in mind between 'balanced' and 'non-balanced' bilingualism (Cummins, 1977), with the latter referring to one very dominant language. Nonetheless, the Hong Kong study did not use dual language instruments for assessing developing-bilingual students; it has been recently demonstrated (Baker, 1988) that intellectual and linguistic achievement can only be validly tested by such means (Baker, 1988). Other benefits from second language study may well have been missed.

It is interesting that Singapore officially endorses an almost segregated pluralism by requiring citizens to 'have' one of four ethnicities shown on their identity card; and it provides education in the four different language systems. Yet unity is fostered by the encouragement of multilingualism, in terms of the languages of Singapore. Foreign language proficiency in UK, on the other hand, looks towards Europe rather than the languages spoken within the country, a bias which is likely to increase with entry to Europe in 1992. The Swedish solution is an official policy of bilingualism and biculturalism: there have been considerable arguments about this, in that many parents and teachers do not want bilingualism *within* school; since 1977 the Swedish government has provided financial assistance for mother tongue or home language teaching and for intensive Swedish classes, and has been willing to provide teachers for both. Special teacher training courses prepare teachers of Swedish as a foreign language. Watson (1985) cites the argument that:

> because of this supportive approach there are very few emotional problems
> related to language difficulties among immigrant groups ... there is
> evidence also that, if parents attempt to become bilingual, this helps their
> children emotionally, socially and academically, whereas if they deny their
> own culture or try to preserve it at the expense of adjusting to life in
> Sweden, there are serious psychological effects on the children. In other
> words adjustments and integration while preserving a bilingual/bicultural
> approach are likely to be the most satisfactory in the long term. (p. 81)

Clearly there will be differences between bilingualism for immigrants adjusting to a
'host' country, and for existing members of a long established multilingual society.
The major point still, however, is not to see bilingualism — of whatever type or
duration — as an automatic 'problem' for the child and the school. Instead its positive
advantages need continuously stressing. The BRITE project (Bilingualism and its
Role In the Teaching of English) at the University of Birmingham has replied strongly
to the English Working Group of TGAT* regarding their paragraph 'Language
Difficulties' which suggests exempting children from tests where the language
problem is 'so severe as to render the assessment unworkable'. BRITE points out a
number of misconceptions: that the continuing identification of pupils whose first
language is not English in terms of 'problem' or 'difficulties' is at best negative and at
worst an expression of a continuing prejudice which devalues the language and culture
of British ethnic minorities; that to consider assessment of these pupils as 'unworkable'
is simply to comment on the current state of testing practice which frequently leads to
division and to the exclusion of linguistically gifted pupils from mainstream
educational practice; to consider low marks in national tests as merely an indication
that special help is needed is out of touch with the political reality of testing, and
assumes a link between bilingualism and Special Educational needs. 'We must stress
that *bilingualism is not a learning difficulty.*' Instead BRITE give illustrations of the
positive aspects: access to other languages spoken in Britain which give possibilities
both for wider understanding and for practical help; the potential for cultural and commercial development by large numbers of young bilinguals; the benefits of greater
intuitive knowledge of language, whereby 'the presence in English lessons of just one
pupil whose mother tongue is not English is an immense resource for a teacher
working on a conscious study of the English language and its usage' (BRITE, 1989,
p. 4).

When considering staff development, the implications of linguistic pluralism
point therefore to the encouragement of teacher proficiency in community languages;
knowledge of the strategies of second-language teaching and learning; 'language
awareness' courses to appraise the benefits of bilingualism; and, returning to the
Bullock Report, awareness both of the linguistic processes by which pupils acquire information and of the reading demands of teachers' own subjects. Again, equitable

pluralism will not be a reality if any language or language speaker is devalued or viewed as a problem to be solved rather than an educational plus.

Student Management

As with the 'problem' of bilingualism, the 'problem' of a multi-ethnic student population is of course a social construction, depending on whose definition of the situation prevails. For schools that have been recently integrated, the problem may be perceived by whites as the influx of black pupils into 'their' schools. A Chief Education Officer in Harare commented in 1981 that the 'pupils who moved into former white schools were fighting a war worse than the liberation war in these schools' (Maravanyike, 1986, p. 206). Similarly, an increased percentage of ethnic minority children in UK schools is perceived by some as 'holding the white children back'. Apparent concerns with progress may mask a very deep racism; a year head was reported as stating 'I find it very difficult to accept the immigrant people and children that I come into contact with. I cannot change my feeling; it is part of my upbringing — I feel that the English culture is being swamped' (Wright, 1985).

The problem is seen to rest with the ethnic minority students themselves, rather than with the structures with have generated disadvantage and prejudice. Even multicultural approaches 'were premised on the assumption that the priority was the management of problems thrown up by the presence of black students rather than the mitigation of problems which they encountered precisely because they were black citizens living in a racist society' (Troyna, 1987, p. 309). While it is indeed important to make the educational experiences of black or minority students more palatable, this should not be seen purely from a control angle; tackling institutional or individual racism is critical not just for a 'harmonious' school, but to provide students with the political insights and strategies necessary to challenge actual or potential racist phenomena outside the school.

Two obvious areas need highlighting, if not floodlighting. The first concerns the organizational and classificatory features of the school, which can compound stereotyping and polarization. We know enough of how teacher expectations are linked to success or failure to be able to understand why certain ethnic groups tend to cluster in particular streams or tracks within an educational system. Avalos (1986) in her vivid ethnography, *Teaching the Children of the Poor*, describes the 'determinist ideologies' at work in Latin America, with teachers fatalistically operating on linguistic pathologies, and assuming non-Spanish children to be almost totally handicapped.

> The racial origin, not just the linguistic background, was also seen as a potential determinant of failure; all sorts of social evils appeared to be associated with being, for example, of Indian descent.

> In the case of Patricia Sanchez...how terrible! They are of Mapuche (Indian) descent; the husband beats his wife in front of the children; they all sleep in the same bed. What a mess! I don't know how they manage! (p. 148)

Avalos describes how the chances of children deemed for such reasons unintelligent were even further lessened by the practice of teachers considering them to have a 'central deficiency', and sending them to diagnostic centres in the hope that they might be recognized as mentally deficient or dyslexic. This thereby excused the teachers from the responsibility of dealing with them.

The following observations have been made in informal conversation by teachers, none of whom could be accused of prejudice or malice.... It has been suggested, for example, that West Indian children are both unusually demanding of teachers' attention and, at the same time, indifferent to the good opinion of their teachers. It has been suggested that they are arrogant and yet have a low opinion of themselves. They have natural 'rhythm' and exceptional physical co-ordination and yet they are clumsy. At school they exhibit a lack of enthusiasm, while managing to be exceptionally exuberent and keen. They are silent, inarticulate and they talk too much. Their parents impose too severe a discipline on them, are over-indulgent and are completely indifferent. It is impossible to get their parents involved in the affairs of the school, yet they interfere too much. A strong, simple Christian faith apparently dominates households where children are never shown any standards.
(Schools Council Working Paper 29).

The over-representation of children of West Indian origin in schools for the educationally subnormal in UK was early recognized (Coard, 1971); and Afro-Caribbean children may now suffer behavioural as well as intellectual fatalism from teachers. Teacher expectations of potential conflict are more rife than with white or other ethnic minority groups (Wright, 1985). The 'myth of a West Indian challenge to authority' identified by Gillborn (1988) meant a parallel conviction by teachers that such pupils could only be underachieving. As one white girl commented with regard to a West Indian boy:

> I mean Paul Dixon . . . I could cause trouble as well as him, if something went wrong while the teacher wasn't there, they'd probably try to blame him, when it could've been *me* . . . Paul and people like that, you know, if they really do settle down to their work then the teacher'll say, "Oh, what's wrong with you, *you're working!*" And taking it out of them *'cause they are working*. And I suppose he thinks "Why bother . . . they're always getting at me". I feel sorry for him in a way. (p. 381)

Some West Indian children in Gillborn's study worked hard to counter the staff tendency to label them in a negative way; others acceded to the labels.

> The scale of the problem facing academically ambitious West Indians was mirrored in their achievements in their final external examinations. Each West Indian in the age grade (both sexes) gained pass grades in either a minimum of five subjects or none at all (a pattern which was unique to West Indian pupils). This tendency to polarise around the extremes of examination achievement reflected the size of the problem facing West Indian pupils in the school: unless they had ability and a suitably low-key response to their situation, they tended to follow a career which . . . led them into further conflicts with staff and ultimately to academic failure. Some West Indian pupils did succeed, but . . . they faced a particularly demanding set of requirements which had little or nothing to do with their academic ability. (p. 383)

The reinforcing nature of such stereotyping and of potential group resistance to negative labels means a vigilant role for management in averting spirals of disaffection. In inner London, a disproportionate number of Afro-Caribbean pupils, both boys and girls, are being suspended from school, according to a report presented to ILEA (*Times Educational Supplement*, 9 September 1988: 'Black pupils most likely to be suspended'). Once the polarization of ethnic groups into streams becomes institutionalized, then the resultant qualification gaps can only reinforce labour market differentials after school, and their contingent racial disadvantage.

A second, but linked issue concerning pupils management is that of racism within the student body. It is worth stressing that this can appear at all levels. There is an apparently widely held but fallacious belief among primary teachers that young children are 'colour blind', and thus incapable of showing racial hostility (Davey, 1983). Even if student racism is acknowledged, the view can still be traced among teachers that racist incidents should be ignored or played down, in order not to 'make things worse' or heighten racial tension. For the victims of racial abuse, such a position is, of course, untenable. When a teacher is in a position of authority, whose assigned function is to determine and promote acceptable behaviours, any conduct which is not overtly sanctioned is implicitly condoned. The message to both perpetrator and victim is that racism is either in order or is insignificant. Neither is likely to deter future offenders. Cohn's (1987) survey of 500 children in London found that the amount and variety of racist abuse increased with age and boys were more regular offenders than girls. Racist names were more common than those referring to sex or physical or mental attributes. The names ranged from the 'creative' to the mundane: "From Spanish omelette to Spear Chucker, from Allah to Zulu. Wooden Spoon and Blue Lagoon, I had to be told, were rhyming slang for 'coon' and four by two meant Jew . . . .One wordless insult is the sound of the whip, heard in corridors and dinner queues, readily recognized as a reference to black slaves, used and perceived as an insult.' The most commonly cited and ranked among the worst were paki, nigger, yid, slag and spastic. Children regarded name calling as an extremely important issue, albeit one they felt powerless to do anything about. There are thus clear implications for management, in terms of providing a well-publicized and agreed system of grievance procedures, automatic sanctions and guidance and support for staff in handling what are very difficult situations. Incidents of physical violence and knifings between pupils, with an overtly racial base, have hit the headlines in UK recently, and they have clearly had a history of verbal ethnic abuse in the school which culminated in physical assault. The presence of anti-racist policies do not in themselves prevent such outbreaks, and it would be naive to assume a cure-all function for the official ethnicity line. As I shall argue later, equity policies must be analyzed and implemented within a total framework of equitable and non-abusive staff-student relationships if they are to have any credibility.

> . . . I attended a middle school where approximately 90% of the pupils were white. The results of this situation were terrifying. The group of black children was bussed to school and then isolated from their neighbourhood. At home they were again isolated from any school contacts. During the four years I spent in that school, not one person attended any after-school activities for fear of walking through the neighbourhood where about 92% of the population were white. It would be literally true to say there was a physical barrier between our homes and our school and the only way in or out was on the coach. At school the situation was the same. The Asians were constantly in fear of being attacked by the several gangs of white boys. As we ran towards the staff room a teacher would come out and disperse the white gang, throw us back into the playground and then walk back as if nothing had happened. The teachers had no idea of what we were experiencing.
>
> Quoted in Swann Report

One cannot of course by coercion alone 'force' students to integrate and respect

> With me like I go into school and I listen to the teacher and I put down just what they want. Christopher Colombus discovered America, I'll put it down, right. Cecil Rhodes, ye know that great imperialist, he was a great man, I'll put it down. We did about the Elizabethans, how great they were. More European stuff; France, equality, liberty and fraternity, we'll put it all down. At that time they had colonies, enslaving people. I'll put down that it was the mark of a new age, the Age of Enlightenment. It wasn't, but I'll put it down for them, so that we can tell them that black people are not stupid. In their terms we can tell them that we can get on. In their terms I come from one of the worst backgrounds but I am just saying to them, I can do it right, and shove your stereotypes up your anus.

(6th form girl, quoted
in: Mac an Ghaill,
*Young Gifted and
Black*, 1988)

*When the missionaries first came
to Africa they had the Bible and
we had the land. They said,
"Let us pray." We closed our eyes.
When we opened them
again we had the Bible and
they had the land.*

ARCHBISHOP DESMOND TUTU
16/12/84

each others' persons and sensitivities. Official quota policies and positive discrimination in favour of some ethnic groups may in fact generate even greater integration problems. A study of secondary school in urban areas of Malaysia came to the conclusion that Chinese pupils in the Chinese schools actually had a greater sense of their national identity as Malaysians and more optimism about their chances of achieving their goals in life than did those in the ethnically mixed secondary schools. Although the latter interacted more with Malays, and thus could be considered more 'integrated', they were also more aware of inter-ethnic competition and tended to view policies in favour of indigenous Malays as having potentially detrimental effects on their future prospects (quoted in Somers Heidhues, 1986). Being confronted with designated 'different' ethnic groups does not automatically break down barriers — any more than it does with gender. In Nigeria, the policy is to establish schools with quotas from different regions, so that students from a variety of ethnic backgrounds are enabled to get to know each other and in theory dispel the ignorance which contributes to prejudice and fear. However, there is evidence that students have tended strongly to socialize with other students from the same ethnic group (Bray and

Cooper, 1979). Bray, Clarke and Stephens comment later 'This need not be seen negatively, for it is natural for students to seek colleagues who share their linguistic and cultural backgrounds' (1986, p. 136); but the authors cite a disturbing study of a Nigerian school which ran into serious administrative problems and in which the students began to organize their own affairs independently of the official hierarchy. They set up their own systems of authority, and each leader had his own group of juniors who washed for him, copied up his notes and received his protection. Such systems were built up within each ethnic group, and 'unhappy were those outside it or those who had none of their own group to protect them'.

A key issue is therefore, in any country, the official protection of the minority, the isolate, as well as monitoring and sanctioning those who create the need for protection. Some schools in UK have introduced a system of logging any incidents with obvious or suspected racial motivation so that senior staff can monitor whether individual pupils feature disproportionately either as perpetrators or victims (AMMA, 1987). For an international conference on 'Equity and Diversity: Challenges for Educational Administrators', Newsam provided an example of one school's 'Unified Policy':

> 1. This school firmly believes that it is vital for all its pupils to develop, as part of their education, a full understanding of the multicultural society in which they live. Part of that understanding will be a demonstrable respect for all people whatever their race or religion. Because a unified consistent approach is essential, the following procedures should be followed in the event of any racist behaviour in the school.
> 2. No incident, however apparently trivial, should be ignored, and every opportunity should be taken to teach positively and against racism.
>
> *Classroom Incidents*
>
> 3. A record of any racist incident, however small, which occurs in the classroom should be given to the Head of House concerned. It should be completed on the Serious Incident Form in the section entitled 'action taken'.
>
> *Corridor Incidents*
> 4. Incidents, including verbal abuse and jostling, should be dealt with by the Heads of House, Deputy Head and Head in that order . . . .
> 5. Graffiti and pamphlets must be dealt with promptly. Stickers, badges and any form of appearance which would offend and cause distress to any ethnic groups, must be brought to the attention of the Head at once.
> 6. If the Heads of House receive several reports of a similar nature for particular pupils, it is their responsibility to initiate the next course of action.

7. Action to be taken could include:
(a) writing to parents
(b) warning of the possibility of suspension; and
(c) in serious situations: suspensions . . . .(Newsam, 1986, p. 23)

Newsam commented that he admired the full statement for the combination of philosophy and detail. I would support it also for its insistence that nothing is ignored, 'however small'. Implicitly condoning nastiness is the best way to ensure its continuation. Policies to interview the offender's parents after any racially motivated incident have the benefit of allowing the school and home to work together for change, (if and this is a big if) they agree the behaviour is unacceptable. Awareness, too, of any racial composition to students' peergroups can help to identify if there is any racial pressure against which they are seeking each other's support.

Conclusion

Yet all the above discussions perhaps only point up the impossibility of providing neat universal policies regarding staff and student relationships in plural communities. When the political backdrop to ethnic diversion is so disparate, how can one compare school management in countries where there is a semi-official policy of discrimination against a minority (the Koreans in Japan, the Chinese in Malaysia), with countries where there is an official policy in favour of a minority (the untouchables in India), and with countries where there is no official policy at all, save a vague commitment to multiculturalism? Rothermund's conclusion is:

> Whenever education is expected to cope with problems which are beyond its reach, such as widespread poverty and extreme social inequality or deeply ingrained ethnic differentiation in terms of region, religion and language, political solutions must be found before educational measures are adopted. Otherwise the educational field just turns into an arena of political conflict and actually accentuates conflict by providing an institutional focus for it rather than contributing to its resolution.' (1986, p. 11)

However, one premise of this book is that schools are sites of political conflict, anyway, and that change occurs when this conflict is recognized and constructively utilized. We cannot indeed force students to 'integrate', but we can examine the hidden curriculum of the school's own messages about power, authority and cultural worth. We can, and must, force the dilemmas out for policy discussion.

If, as we have seen, there is a disparity between heads of different ethnic origins in the amount and type of management experience they have had, then additional training courses seem the answer; yet there is then the danger of creating divisions within ethnic minority professionals, with accusations of a 'sell-out' to the élite

(AMMA, 1987), or, as with gender, blacks acceding to majority or colonial definitions of 'appropriate' leadership experience, training and behaviour. Nonetheless, it would seem imperative that both white and black, majority and minority students see minority communities in positions of authority as teachers, heads and governors. A university course in UK enabling black students with overseas qualifications to gain Qualified Teacher Status was aware of the dangers of the 'black teachers for black kids' approach, and aimed at 'good teachers for all children' (*Times Educational Supplement,* 30.2.88). Black teachers in the White Highlands are, as we saw, equally important if one is to counter the myth that multicultural or antiracist education is relevant only to specifically multiracial schools or 'all-black' schools.

With regard to staff perceptions and treatments of students, a range of strategies have been tried. Racism awareness courses have suffered something of a setback in UK; there is the dilemma of whether we can *force* teachers to go on racism awareness courses or whether that is, as Jeffcoate (1985) argues, an infringement of liberty, of the democratic right to choose. The courses themselves, in their more confrontational form, have been seen to be counterproductive, with teachers feeling harangued and unjustly accused of racist behaviour by outside organizers. More effective may be the discussions and seminars held within the school itself, as part of the self-evaluation process for an institution. Checklists such as those produced by ILEA or AMMA can perhaps evince the right degree of group discomfort without individual hostility and retrenchment, requiring answers such as the following to be answered:

— What ethnic groups are represented in the school or college (including staff?
  How has this pattern changed?
  What responses do these changes call for?
  How do we collect and store this information?
  Who has access to it?
— Do we have a formal statement of policy defining unacceptable racist activities?
  Are there clear procedures for dealing with them?
  Do they work?
— How good are we at knowing about the incidence of racial harassment and tension inside and outside the school?
— Have internal and external examination results been reviewed?
  What is their ethnic pattern?
  Is there any ethnic bunching? What have we done to find out the causes?
  How can we remedy it?
— Which pupils are literate in their mother tongue(s) as well as English?
  Is this bi- or multilingualism given the same esteem as it would be if the other language was French or German?
  Do we have records of pupils' capabilities in different languages?

Do we mention these capabilities in reports and profiles?
What provision is there for pupils to discuss racial and ethnic matters with staff, both formally and informally?
Do the records of employment of our leavers include ethnic details?
What evidence do they give of any racial bias by employers?
What corrective action can we take?
(Taken from ILEA *Education in a multi-ethnic society: an aide-mémoire for the Inspectorate*) (1981)

Doubts were expressed in Chapter 2 about the notion of management-by-ticklist; but the above is not really of the yes/no, have-I-done-this variety. As a set of queries rather than prescriptions, it might be more greatly applicable across a range of countries and national policies. A real difficulty in direct questions such as the above is in fact the political nature of the exploration. First of all, the presence of actual or potential racism in the school must be acknowledged, a stance which will clearly meet resistance. Secondly, attempts publicly to discuss this within the formal timetable, and to provide students with political insights about causation and strategy will be seen as threatening to school and social stability. Carrington and Short (1987) found primary teachers generally apathetic to the teaching of any contentious issue. Yet any pedagogical style which stresses the transmission of knowledge and didacticism, 'where status differences between teachers and pupils are accentuated and where only one viewpoint (i.e. the teacher's) is valid, stands in opposition to democratic and anti-racist principles' (p. 9).

The management implications are immense, in that in tackling the whole of teaching relations, they go far beyond tinkering with the school curriculum and celebrating all the festivals. If political literacy, the exploration of social issues relating to justice and equality, and the challenge to the *status quo* cannot be tackled meaningfully in an authoritarian, teacher-dominated mode, then the whole basis of teacher-student relationships and asymmetries of power need to be examined. I would contend that such macro- and micro-political activity is more important in tackling the structural problems of racial inequality than 'prejudice reduction' through multicultural curricula and multifaith 'tolerance'.

EXERCISE 5: WHAT DO WE KNOW ABOUT ETHNIC PATTERNS?

This 'general knowledge' questionnaire is extracted from one I use on inservice and pre-service courses for teachers, to appraise the extent of our awareness of race dimensions in UK. It generates much discussion about the 'truth' and the implications of various social facts and their distortions, and indicates sometimes a disturbingly low level of concrete knowledge about ethnic minorities in education and society. Ignorance is by no means the only basis for racism, but eradicating ignorance is a good place to start.

You may like to fill in the answers for self-assessment; or if you are not familiar with the UK scene, use this to design a similar one to explore ethnic dimensions in a relevant country. Such questionnaires need continual revision, and may already be dated before completion; but the aim is more to point up areas where we have little idea, or where we are misguided, than to teach absolute statistics.

1. The size of the black* population in Britain is   2.1%
                                             4.5%
(*of 'New Commonwealth' and Pakistani origin) 7.6%
                                           10.1%
2. More white than black people have come to Britain to settle since 1945. True/false
3. Most West Indians came to Britain in 1940–50
                                        1950–60
                                        1960–70
                                        1970–80
4. Most Asians came to Britain in   1940–50
                                        1950–60
                                        1960–70
                                        1970–80
5. West Indians came to get jobs in transport and catering because
    — there was unemployment in the West Indies
    — they heard of opportunities in Britain from friends
    — recruiting offices were opened in Barbados
6. Controls on immigration were first tightened in 1962
                                             1965
                                             1971
                                           1976
7. Britain is still a net importer/exporter of population
8. Britain received 17,000/28,000/39,000/53,000 Ugandan Asians
9. Hong Kong citizens with British passports will automatically be granted right of access to UK up to 1997. True/False
10. In 1981 around 10%/20%/30%/40% of black people here were born in Great Britain
11. The immigrant birth rate is increasing/static/decreasing
12. The proportion of Asians in council housing is smaller/about the same/larger than for the population as a whole.
13. The proportion of West Indians in council housing is smaller/about the same/larger than for the population as a whole.
14. The percentage of school leavers in Birmingham who are black is . . . . %
15. There is evidence that the proportion of black children in a class has a significant influence on the attainment of white pupils. True/false
16. The proportion of West Indian children in schools for children with learning difficulties is half as much/the same/four times as much as for white children
17. More pupils from Caribbean backgrounds are suspended from school than white pupils. True/false
18. The proportion of Asian and white pupils suspended from school is about the same. True/false
19. There is a measurable difference between various 'Asian' groups in terms of examination achievement. True/false

20. Caribbean children, regardless of social class, tend to have lower educational achievements than white children. True/False
21. Local Education Authorities receive grants from central government specifically to meet additional educational needs of minority groups. True/false
22. There is a national policy on multicultural education. True/false
23. Racist abuse increases/decreases with the age of the pupil and is more common from girls/boys
24. The proportion of black teachers in schools is higher/the same/lower than for the population as a whole
25. 57% of white teachers are on the bottom two pay scales. For black teachers the percentage is . . . . . . %

Answers

1. 4.5% (Census figures)
2. True; about 57% white
3. 1950–60
4. 1960–70
5. All three
6. 1962 Commonwealth Immigrants Act
7. Exporter
8. 28,000 in 1973
9. False. Only if a grandparent was born in UK.
10. 40%
11. Decreasing
12. Smaller
13. Smaller
14. 20%
15. False
16. Four times
17. True
18. False: fewer Asians are suspended
19. True
20. False: lower average Caribbean achievement relates to lower average social class
21. False
22. False
23. Increases; boys
24. Lower
25. 78%

Chapter 6

The Mental/Manual Divide

'There is, in Britain, a deeply ingrained belief that practical people must be stupid. It is a belief that will not be changed by the creation of mixed ability classes in comprehensive schools. It is still assumed that the brighter will go on to further study and the dimmer will do practical tasks...we are trapped in a web of conventional ideas about brightness or cleverness.' (Nuttgens, 1986).

This belief is not confined to Britain. Since the advent of formal education, a split has grown up worldwide between academic and practical activities. Not only that, but academic has come to be associated with mental and hence things of the intellect, requiring intelligence, abstract reasoning and brainpower; whilst practical has come to be associated with manual, and capacities of the hand, requiring habituated reflexes, physical agility and brawn. We take this so much for granted that it seems almost tautologous to point out that academic has become mental; yet there is no sacred law that decrees that the academic must equate only with second-hand, desk-bound learning. This chapter looks at the particular problems for schools created by our hardened definitions and distinctions between 'academic', 'intellectual', 'practical' and 'vocational', and examines some of the solutions attempted by various countries to break down the inequalities and inefficiencies caused by dividing children and adults into brain or brawn types. It then continues the pattern of the book of drawing out some management issues, in this case related to the dilemmas and contradictions in current strategies around 'productivity' and 'vocationalism'.

The problems of the dual curriculum have long been recognized, most notably in terms of the divide it creates between an élite oriented to words and a mass of the labour force oriented to 'skills'; of the association of academic with entry to prestigious jobs; of the consequent over-production of academic graduates; of the diploma disease and qualification inflation; of a disdain for manual or agricultural work and workers; of difficulties in 'relevance', and of the lack of creativity and entrepreneurship among the academic products of the education system. These arguments are well rehearsed and researched, and need not be elaborated excessively here. Equally well analyzed are the sometimes vain struggles by various countries over the years to promote the practical or vocational side of schooling in order to address the problems of relevance and economic growth. As long ago as 1965, Foster exposed the 'vocational school fallacy' in educational planning which assumed that individual motivation would equate with national need, and that parents and pupils would happily espouse the education which fed directly into productive work. Instead, as we have seen, consumers have rated work-oriented education as a second-rate alternative to formal academic schooling, and have rightly perceived 'academic' to equal 'vocational', in the sense that it provided access to the sorts of jobs to which they aspired.

In terms of the Third World, Foster has continued to argue that academic rather than community-oriented choice by consumers was a rational one; that problems of school-leaver unemployment, rural-urban drift and students' alienation from village life had their origin in socio-economic factors which curricular changes could do little to alleviate; and that, although formal education played a role in economic development, far too much was being expected of the schools (Vulliamy, 1987a). Foster's views have provoked controversy, with doubts cast on the universal 'instrumentality' of the consumers of education, and on the development and curricular models he suggested. Yet it could equally be argued that insufficient attention has been paid to his warnings, with the result that much well-intentioned community and work-oriented schooling has lost sight of its original ideology and been forced back on a more traditionally academic framework (see Sinclair, M. and Lillis, K., 1980).

We should briefly refresh our memories of some of the more well-known initiatives around what is variously termed 'self-reliance', 'productivity', 'enterprise', or 'technical/vocational initiative'. It is not being suggested that they all mean the same thing, but that they all represent attempts either to promote learning and skills other than academic ones, or to integrate mental and manual into a new vision of schooling.

Education for self-reliance

The main example of education for self-reliance has been Tanzania, based on Nyerere's socialist educational philosophy, ujaama*. Primary and secondary schools were not to be seen simply as academic preparation for further studies, but as an integral part of the community and a preparation for life and service in the village and the rural economy. Students and parents were to be involved in decision-making, and authoritarian teaching methods and control were to give way to democratic community responsibility. With primary schools offering self-contained courses and secondary schools ceasing to be merely a selection process for higher education, students were to be made aware of the obligation to use expensive education to serve the mass of the people. Examinations were to be downgraded in government and public esteem, and combined with teachers' assessments of 'character' and 'willingness to serve' in terms of school and community work. The schools were to teach self-reliance by being self-reliant — growing their own vegetables, maintaining buildings, raising poultry and cattle and participating in self-help projects in the community.

Tanzania's initiatives faltered in some areas because of inadequate preparation of teachers to relinquish an authoritarian role, but also because of the difficulty of educating people to forgo status based on written qualifications. Teachers, as Adams (1981) discovered, were still expected to:

> nurture, examine and select the few for advancement (at the primary and secondary levels) while at the same time to extol the virtues of working and living on the land to the vast majority of their students. The new philosophy appears to have presented an inherently contradictory view of the teacher's role. In addition, like the bureaucrats, their own educational experiences in terms of academic success, selection and promotion leading to secure wage employment would tend inevitably to reinforce the former role and relegate the latter to 'extra-curricular activities'.

Neither would parents necessarily accept the 'complete cycle' approach of primary education, wanting it to lead on to further opportunities, while the vocational implications of self-reliance would appease them only if matched by employment prospects in the rural areas.

Part of the problem was the attempt to implement self-reliance methods across the whole country simultaneously. Other countries have chosen to start with pilot schools, or to use a step-wise approach to educational change. In the Seychelles 'youth village' initiative, mentioned in Chapter 2, volunteer teenagers in three areas were given the task of building a self-reliant village, producing their own food and their own energy, building their own radio station and deriving their own culture. Formal teaching was initially abandoned, and teachers attached instead to working 'blocs' and cooperatives, explaining radio waves to the broadcaster or marine biology to the fishing group. Mental and manual work were to coexist. The aim was to build up areas of socialist relations which would gradually join up and expand. However, as we saw, the original production-centred emphasis became somewhat lost, and the pressure for academic standards and for curricular and timetable control meant a return to more transmission-style teaching methods.

Although the end product of a self-reliant individual would appear to be non-controversial (and indeed fitting well with current ideologies of entrepreneurialism and pulling oneself up by one's bootstraps), the resistances to, and erosion of, the African initiatives show that the philosophy potentially has a revolutionary force. There is a difference between education for self-reliance and education for subsistence. Groups who are self-reliant aim at not continuously needing experts to tell them what to do, or needing certificates telling the world that they can do it. Nor do they want the profits of their labour siphoned off elsewhere. That this could be threatening to established educational and occupational interests is self-evident: the notion of selective self-reliance would be a contradiction in terms, for the educational process aims at the whole community, not just the 'able' or 'bright'. This implies redefining and infinitely expanding our concepts of 'ability'. One cannot have a bottom tier of 'self-reliant' people if others are still taking decisions for them. Moves towards self-reliance have to examine very carefully therefore the question of entrenched interests in the academic qualification spiral.

One attempt to balance the interests of self-reliance and formal assessment is Papua New Guinea's Secondary Schools Community Extension Project (SSCEP). Here the school curriculum has been redesigned to integrate the practical and the intellectual; formal assessment is skill-based, linked to project work in the community. The students spend periods of time at 'outstations' where they, with the teachers, must participate in the solving of community problems. The major thrust of the outstations is educational, not economic: the students are not to become cheap labour, even though the outstations aim at being self-supporting. The interesting feature of SSCEP is the systematic integration of the vocational and the academic. In Tanzania teachers sometimes interpreted self-reliance simply as productive work, which, if anything, impeded the main academic aims of their teaching. The 'character' assessment there tended to become a formality, and academic success was still the accountable and most visible aspect of schools. In the SSCEP project, however, the 'academic' qualification is gained only if the student has demonstrated skill at applying curriculum content to the solution of practical community issues. The SSCEP rationale recognizes the powerful motivating force of selection for further education and salaried employment, but the hope was to turn the extrinsic motivation of exams into longer-term intrinsic motivation, in that the student learns to find the problem-solving application of school curriculum items a rewarding activity in itself. The 'carrot' of exams 'can be used to develop behaviours which will survive the consumption of the carrot' (McNamara, 1982).

It appears to be not a question of trying to make the practical have 'equal status' with the academic (that was shown to fail as long ago as the tripartite system in UK), but of making definitions of academic *derive from* the vocational. If we cannot foresee educational life without exams, then the least we can do is make them criterion-referenced and skill-based, and deny the notion that there can be any useful demonstration of 'pure' theory divorced from the real-life situations that students find themselves in.

Education with production

Initiatives around education for self-reliance are clearly linked to the ideal of service to the community. Another rationale is that all people need intrinsic job satisfaction, yet with automation and high levels of unemployment this becomes increasingly difficult.

Claudius Switzerland

Western countries have thus played with the idea of 'education for leisure', even if Third World countries cannot afford such luxuries, and in general have not been side-tracked down such sterile and potentially socially divisive paths. Instead, there have been initiatives such as the Foundation for Education with Production (FEP), which has more to do with the idea that self-determination comes from the possession of capabilities of social or economic value. The Foundation was set up in 1980 by a group of African educationists, and branches then spread to Europe. The general aim is to equip people to be in charge of their own lives through work which they control: the direction is towards self-employment and cooperatives. The particular school benefits were outlined as follows:

> Giving children employable skills, especially the financial management and business skills now almost completely neglected, which are so vital for self-employment.
> Helping to interest and motivate children by involving them in things which are fun to do and lead to a tangible end product. This would be particularly helpful for those older children in countries like the UK who see little chance of success in gaining certificates.

(especially in developing countries). Contributing towards meeting the costs of the school.

(especially in developing countries). Helping to make learning more meaningful through practical work and experience, as opposed to the all-too-common situation where the teacher stands at the front of the class dictating notes to the pupils. (Knox and Castles, 1982)

With regard to Knox and Castles' second benefit, I have already expressed doubts about any dual system which contrasts practical competence with certificate gaining, but the subsequent points about cost contribution and teacher style have a great deal of salience for our concerns with efficiency and equity.

The historical background to FEP lies with Patrick von Rensburg and the Serowe Brigades in Botswana. In order to meet the problem of the mass of primary-school leavers whose schooling had equipped them for little of practical value, the brigades were established as production units in activities like farming, building, tanning, forestry, sheet metal work, printing, motor maintenance and carpentry. It was hoped to make them provide a focus for rural development, and reduce rural-urban migration through improving living standards and educational opportunities in the countryside. The models provided blueprints for other liberation movements in Zimbabwe, South Africa and Namibia, who all sent cadres to training at Serowe; these in turn helped to develop and sharpen the political ideas of the people in the Brigades. Yet in the 1970s the Serowe models ran into difficulties. The best trainees were being enticed away into the towns; other graduates found it hard to find employment; there were internal conflicts about political aims and management policies; and the use of labour-intensive traditional production methods kept productivity in the self-help groups too low to offer reasonable levels of income to members (Knox and Castles, 1982). The obvious lesson is that educational innovation will fail unless it actively works with the economic and cultural structures surrounding it. At present, there is renewed government interest in the Brigades, and attempts being made through careers work with schools to reverse the decline in the number of girls entering various training areas.

There are continuing examples of education with production in many Third World schools; Jennings (1987), for example, provides a useful analysis of different levels of productive education in the West Indian context. The experience of education with production provides an example of how expertise could flow from South to the North, with lessons to be learned by Western countries about possibilities and disasters. The agricultural and construction bias of Third World initiatives would make it difficult to import them directly, but the most immediate lessons can be drawn from producer cooperatives where members learn skills both of the trade itself and of cooperative management.

Knox and Castles describe side by side Tshwarango Enterprises in Botswana and the five cooperatives set up by the West Glamorgan Common Ownership Development Agency. It is possible to tease out common concerns and problems in whatever part of the world a cooperative is started. A clear advantage is the ownership of the assets, and hence the motivation to maintain the enterprise. Another is the need for whole-group meetings which, while making decisions on such matters as possible products, market outlets, delegation of tasks and budget predictions, give group members practice in participation and articulation. Apart from finance, problems derive from the need for a profound change in attitudes in terms of developing initiative, collective responsibility and a willingness to take one's fate into one's own hands. Gaining confidence in one's own ability is crucial, and continuous training and support may be necessary initially, so that members can successfully 'take over' from development officers.

The suggestion is not that major public schools can be turned overnight into worker cooperatives, but that the identification of the sorts of qualities and skills which will be needed for people to work productively in future might indicate the need for something of a revolution in current teaching styles and objectives.

TVEI, enterprise and capability

The Technical and Vocational Education Initiative (TVEI) in UK was introduced in 1983, significantly with funding from the Manpower Services Commision rather than the Department of Education and Science. In a still decentralized system, it was a way of centralizing, controlling and promoting a technical and vocational emphasis, by using financial incentives to schools. Resourcing is through a 'bid' system by schools — through the LEA — for funds from central government or regional agencies for specific projects. As Saunders (1988) points out, TVEI, although not as overtly ideological as Education for Self-Reliance in Tanzania, has startlingly similar aims:

> In conjunction with LEAs TVEI will explore and test ways of organizing the education of 14–18-year-old people across the ability range so that:
> (i) more of them are attracted to seek the qualifications/skills which will be of direct value to them at work and more of them achieve these qualifications and skills;
> (ii) they are better equipped to enter the world of employment which will await them;
> (iii) they acquire a more direct appreciation of the practical application of the qualifications for which they are working;
> (iv) they become accustomed to using their skills and knowledge to solve the real-world emphasis they will meet at work;
> (v) more emphasis is placed on developing initiative, motivation and enterprise as well as problem-solving skills and other aspects of personal development;

(vi) the construction of the bridge from education to work is begun earlier by giving these young people the opportunity to have direct contact and training/planned work experience with a number of local employers in the relevant specialisms;

(vii) there is close collaboration between local education authorities and industry/commerce/public services etc, so that the curriculum has industry's confidence. (MSC, 1984, p. 34)

The explicit critique in both initiatives is the apparent disassociation between school and other areas of social life.

Alternative areas of activity in UK are the various Enterprise schemes and the Education for Capability movement. The latter emphasizes that

a 'capably' educated person must learn how to exercise creative skills, to develop one of a number of special competencies, the 'know-how' on which modern society depends; and above all to learn how to cope with the problems of life and work. Finally, all these things need to be done, not individually and competitively (as our examination systems demand), but by co-operative effort and joint action. We want our young people to be prepared for a life of responsible action in a world where employers are concerned with what young people can do as well as what they know. (Gorb, 1986)

> A Midlands comprehensive school is trying to boost its first-year intake by offering parents a pack that includes a school tie, stationery and sports insurance, plus a discount on shower units.
>
> A leaflet distributed by the school earlier this term announced: "The shrewed parent now gets our free starter pack for their son or daughter when they take up a place at Manor Park."
>
> This is followed by a list of the educational reasons for choosing the school and a bold claim: "We are national leaders in technology, expressive arts and modern languages."
>
> The leaflet concludes: "And as a little extra the whole family is remembered through the generosity of the school's industrial "twin" – Triton plc, Britain's leading shower manufacturer – which offers a £10 Cash Back for every Triton shower purchased at Payless DIY, Nuneaton – when your child takes up his or her place at Manor Park..."
>
> *(Times Educational Supplement, 3.11.89)*

It is not therefore to be equated with 'understanding industry' schemes, nor with work preparation or work experience. By 1984, 71 recognition awards had been given to programmes which were evaluated by the criteria of: the demonstrated competence of learners developed by the solution to personal problems; the creative abilities of learners expanded; cooperative activity; learners negotiating with teachers what is needed to be learnt; the programme accessible to a wide range of learners; appropriate assessment; demonstrated results; understanding of aims by learners and staff; and coherent programme design (Cantell, 1985).

The Education for Enterprise movement is likewise seen as a contrast to the 'new vocationalism' in curriculum in UK, which acts to prepare young people for working life as employees. The acquisition of qualifications, even signifying vocational experience rather than examination passes, are still designed to impress employers and breed dependency (Gibb, 1984); they breed the idea that a job will be provided for you. The Enterprise movement on the other hand argues the need to encourage and foster self-reliance (as in the Tanzanian model) and 'develop in the minds of young people an image of themselves in the future as employers, or at the very least, self-employed' (Rees, 1988). As such it has been described within the EEC as 'a fundamental criticism of the traditional education system and the traditional curriculum' (IFAPLAN, 1986). Rees describes the working of projects thus:

> Some schools in Britain have begun to develop various kinds of business projects, the most common example of which is 'minicompanies', small replicas of real firms. They raise venture capital (usually by selling shares to friends and family, probably the least realistic aspect of the exercise) and develop a product or service. They constitute a board which makes decisions, and run the business in an attempt to make a profit (and thus be able to pay dividends to share holders) before winding up at the end of the school year. The kinds of pupils involved have tended to be of lower academic ability, partly because of the need to develop a curriculum for them, and partly because the whole exercise is extraordinarily time con-suming: this would create problems for pupils entering for exams . . . .It is difficult to assess the impact of such training and experience on the propen-sity of young people to go out and start a business. However, Young Enter-prise claims to have an annual intake of about 20,000 participants from schools and colleges (known as 'achievers') who have at least been exposed to some experience of running a company. (Rees, 1988, p. 12)

There are indications that education for enterprise will be given a greater emphasis in the State education sector, and the potential profits for schools mean that the inter-sections with local financial management will be interesting ones.

Learning or earning?

It can be seen that most of these programmes involve the notion of 'producing' something which is not just received knowledge. To assess how innovatory they are, the conventional distinction has to be made between education with productive work and education with production. Only in Education with Production (EWP) is there (a) the actual production of goods and/or services which are either marketed or become a subsidy or cost recovery for the school, and (b) radical changes of content, methods and reassessment of education programmes. These definitions exclude, for example, purely vocational schools at one extreme and academic schools with work-experience programmes at the other. Gillespie and Collins (1987) in a thorough international review of 'productive labour in schools' summarize the rationales and strategies for EWP as coming under three headings: financial, pedagogical and political. The financial rationales range from the 'topping up' of state provision through to providing most of the school's income. The pedagogical reasons are the 'real-life experience' which complements abstract learning; the relevance to work; the provision of transition programmes for 'at risk' students in the economic recession; and to improve problem-solving capability and increase self-esteem and empowerment. The political aims are overtly to break down class divisions; to make the curriculum more relevant to industry or agricultural life, and to improve attitudes to these; and to promote cooperative rather than individualistic ethics.

How far these rationales translate into outcomes is clearly problematic, and certain of the elements will take precedence over others, depending both on the economic or political context and the individual school management. In developing countries, for example, cost covering for schools can range from 100 per cent to 5 per cent; in UK a very small proportion of educational resources would be acquired in this way (under 1 per cent of government expenditure). Gillespie and Collins (1987) conclude that the likely success of projects requires:

(a) the collaboration of the local community to be solicited and achieved;
(b) teachers to be convinced of its validity;
(c) teachers receiving massive in-service training in management procedures;
(d) a saleable product with consideration given to distribution;
(e) work activity based in a community with some degree of complexity in its economic life.

When 'the more ambitious' programme is undertaken of integrating the whole curriculum into production this requires:

(a) step-by-step introduction (by age grouping and subject area);
(b) programmes to be devised in relation to local needs; and
(c) the establishment of experimental pilot schools which will gradually influence a neighbourhood (p. 22).

Their most significant comment is 'Above all, the community needs to believe that the childen are learning and not just earning. This, in itself, is a curious paradox.' (p. 24)

Management issues

There are therefore myraid issues for school managers when initiating or maintaining a curriculum or aims which are not purely academic. If productivity is attempted, then we have seen the 'massive' training needed for teachers, which would include basic areas such as accounting, marketing, franchising, investments, credit systems, advertising and so on. Any attempts to site school work in the context of the working base to the community will require equally massive community analysis, relationship forging and consideration of union and parental interpretation. However, we will concentrate on those concerns specific to our focus on the promotion of equity within the school. They are marginalization; assessment; resistance; and contradiction.

Marginalization

The obvious first question is which students participate in which areas of the curriculum. If, unlike Papua New Guinea, the school retains the notion that there is an identifiable difference between academic and practical, then it is likely either that the former will be reserved for those students labelled 'intellectual', or that the latter will come to assume a lower status. Flower (1986) foresees that education for capability may find its wider adoption threatened by three dangers:

> It may be reduced to a feature worthy in its own right but mainly manifested in activities marginal to the main activity of the educational institution. Alternatively, it may exist in parallel with, but without any relation to, what are perceived as the major elements of the curriculum much in the same way as 'general studies' or 'liberal studies' have tended to do in the past. Or in the third case it may through circumstance come to be attached to low status activities within the curriculum and thus itself come to be considered a low status activity inappropriate for inclusion in the timetable of those pursuing mainly academic studies . . . a recognized project has rarely involved the whole institution. Where it has, it has usually been untypical of mainstream education: a highly specialised agency, a non-traditional degree course, an unorthodox school from the private sector or a vocational preparation scheme. (p. 170)

The reality of these dangers is underscored by knowledge of what happened in Tanzania with the self-reliance activities. They were compulsory for all, but accorded low priority by teachers and students alike (Saunders, 1984). Prevocational studies in Sri Lanka suffered the same fate (Wanasinghe, 1982). Vulliamy observed of the practical and agricultural activities engaged in by students in Papua New Guinea that 'while nearly all the students enjoyed their outstation activities, many of them were concerned (as were some teachers) that time spent at the outstation detracted from their 'real' studies. A case-study of the same outstation in 1982 revealed that it had been forced to become more academic and less village-oriented in the intervening period' (Vulliamy 1987a, p. 53).

How then can work — practical or community oriented — studies retain the image of being 'real', that is, a primary function of formal schooling? There were in fact some potentially useful integratory attempts made in Papua New Guinea, whereby 'core' subject work was prepared in a modular way to be tackled through the practical situations the students found themselves in. For example, the Unit 'Decimals and Percentages'

> was rewritten in such a way that all the examples used came from practical situations the students found themselves in during their stay at the out-station. These included operating the tradestore and keeping its daily accounts, which students took turn in doing, and the buying, weighing and selling of copra. The same teacher also taught a one-term outstation social science course. This involved planning and executing a social survey in a local village, analysing the results and presenting them back to the villagers in the form of drama and puppet shows. (Vulliamy, 1987a, p. 54)

This is more than simply using classroom examples 'relevant' to students concerns; it involves the real application in the real and uncertain world. It appears common-sense, and a logical and essential endpoint of learning. There were nonetheless eventually pressures to return to the conventional syllabus topics, after a change in the selection system meant that greater priority was given to syllabus content in the national examination. We see how we must turn once again to assessment in order to fully understand why capabilities become marginalized.

Assessment

Any attempts to raise the status of practical activity, or to integrate manual and mental will involve redefinitions of 'able' and 'less able' and hence new ways of measuring 'ability'. The reasons for the inertia in retaining conventional assessment are obvious enough to warrant no more than a brief reminder: written (hence recordable and static), individual and consensually standardized performance is far easier to assess than fluid, long-term, cooperative endeavour which could be judged differently according to different audiences. How can one assess a puppet play presented to villagers in terms of a ranked set of marks suitable for selection to Higher Education? Houses built by Brigades may look great when completed, but will they last thirty years? No teacher or examination board will hang around long enough to see. Snapshots of a person's capabilities, either frozen in time or futuristic in intent, are all that can be contemplated. Hence the moves towards criterion-referenced, graded assessment and pupil profiling are perhaps as far as can be practically envisaged.

Yet even here there can be tensions: TVEI is designed to be evaluated partly by profiles and character reviews; this now seems to clash with the emphasis in the new National Curriculum proposals on standardized tests at ages 7, 11, 14 and 16. The fate of the character and self-reliance (SR) assessments in Tanzania have been well documented. They were supposed to have equal but independent status to the academic assessments, in that pupils were to gain a satisfactory mark in these non-academic elements in order to achieve a final 'division' or grade. However, teachers tended to be reluctant to designate any student as 'unsatisfactory' in character if they were likely to get a good academic grade. 'Many teachers saw the passing of pupils as good or very good in the assessment of SR as a mere formality. Despite this non-academic component in the assessment system, teachers tended to see pupil success in the academic exams as the most significant aim in their teaching' (Saunders, 1982, p. 46). This was reinforced by the Ministry of National Education's practice of ranking secondary schools on the basis of their academic success in each subject, but with no reference to their ESR performances. It is more likely that the age 7, 11, 14 and 16 tests in UK will similarly be used by government and parents to rank schools; the result will be the concentration on these as the true measure of the school's worth. Profiles will be reserved as indicators to employers of candidates' potential usability in the labour market; they will not be currency for selection into Higher Education.

But if 'enterprise' is the hallmark for achievement at least in a capitalist society, will that start to take over from conventional exams? It is significant that many of the successful mini-companies in UK have been started in the independent sector, where they are not reserved for the 'low achiever' or the working-class child. However, it is unlikely that the ideals espoused in these companies will make much impact on the wider world of large businesses and multinational corporations; small-scale cooperative community endeavours will not necessarily translate into the skills required for progress within a hierarchical, profit-oriented competitive industry. We have to determine not only the implications of 'success' in an enterprise assessment, but also of 'failure'. For students in prestigious schools, and with an assured future, neither may be significant; for pupils and school-leavers for whom it is their only passport, the practical outcome may be critical. Rees calls this 'Blaming the Victim, mark II':

> If, having 'trained' school-leavers in the art of running a small business, some of them duly have a go and fail, inevitably there is the risk of the victim being blamed all the more squarely for that outcome. By mooting

that the responsibility for creating a job lies with the individual, and providing some training in self-employment, the inevitable business failures may be interpreted as personal inadequacies. The targetting of less able pupils, and the more disruptive ones for both work experience in some schools and for exposure to mini-companies and the like means that very often it is exactly those pupils that might be expected to experience the greatest difficulties in raising capital and starting a business that are being encouraged to consider it, and so to perceive their subsequent unemployment as a personal failure. The policy of the MSC deliberately not to include a test of viability when giving people enterprise allowance funds has the effect, it could be argued, of giving encouragement to some young people to pursue ideas that will inevitably fail. (Rees, 1988, p. 18)

Cockburn (1986) had tackled the role of the state in the reproduction of gender inequalities in the labour market through the Youth Training Scheme; work experience has similarly been analyzed as exposing (inuring?) pupils prematurely to the racism and sexism of the workplace (Schilling, 1988). Rees likewise sees little future for a reduction of inequality through self-employment schemes:

girls, non-whites, the working class and the disabled will find it disproportionately difficult to secure investment in the open market. The middle class white young men using Round Table contacts of their parents to fix contracts for their odd-job 'co-ops' clearly have a currency not available to most of the young unemployed . . . younger ones are less likely to survive than older people, and women are both less likely to participate and to succeed. For all the equality potentially possible within co-ops or community businesses, individuals' opportunities to participate in such an enterprise which has even the remotest chance of succeeding are far from equal. (p. 18)

This would explain the rationale behind the recently started Women's Enterprise Development Agency in UK, where stringent planning checks, advice and back-up services try to militate against under-capitalized or insufficiently-prepared schemes by individual women or groups of women.

Such enterprise agencies and ideologies might therefore be interpreted as a fallback position for those 'unsuccessful' in the 'normal' labour or educational market. Self-sufficiency has yet no real transferable currency anywhere in the world, either within education systems or at the transition from school to work. To prevent dualism and the relegation of survival skills and their assessment to a tokenist status, it is self-evident that managers must find a way of redefining 'academic' to incorporate other features than abstracted individualism. Before exploring how, we should first pay keen attention to the resistance to, and subversion of, the attempted solutions to unreal schooling.

Resistance

The potential undermining of integrated or radical ideologies in education stems from three sources: historical biases, current practical difficulties and future markets.

In terms of history, the strong association between the vocational and the under-privileged should never be underestimated. In parts of ex-colonial Africa where black education had been synonymous with preparation for low-paid or manual work, independence was seen to be about bringing quantitative betterment, not radical change.

> Some administrators, teachers and parents . . . welcomed the expansion in secondary and primary schools but did not necessarily want a change in the curriculum, especially the academic secondary curriculum. Independence to them meant having access to those institutions and facilities they had been denied. Education had always been seen as means of escaping from rural poverty; therefore any educational plan that was seen as purporting to keep the young on the land was likely to meet with resistance. Such a plan smacked of vocationalism which had been rejected during the colonial era. To some headmasters, independence did not necessarily mean learning new ways of doing things, but freedom from what was seen as the repressive authority of education officers under colonial rule. . . . If some blacks resisted the suggested ideological changes, it was worse with the white community who regarded such changes as communist inspired. (Maravanyika, 1986, p. 207)

The red-under-the-bed threat is in fact elsewhere usually reserved for areas such as Social Science and Peace Studies; it is more normally the current practicalities rather than ideologies which subvert practical schemes. Van Rensburg (1978) found in Botswana that graduates from the Brigades who had done the necessary manual labour to learn their trade were more productive in their later work than students from conventional trade schools. Yet there was resistance by Brigade trainees to the inevitable tedium of repetitive construction or agricultural work.

> A trainee in the Mechanical Brigade, when learning welding, will be expected to weld several hundred pieces of steel furniture when the brigade has a contract to supply the country's primary schools with classroom furniture. Or a building trainee might be required to lay countless bricks during his three-year course; or to mix concrete or sift river sand. Farm trainees milk cows by hand and clean the dairy shed, for many days on end. A trainee in tanning will be expected to dehair skins that have soaked in lime, to delime them and tan them . . . '

The trainees saw themselves as exploited: 'We have come to learn, not work as labourers'. Interestingly, this resistance does not disappear once in employment: 'Indeed, much in my experience has shown that even when employed, these trainees resent the routine and the work associated with the skill they are supposed to have acquired. They expect all the menial tasks to be carried out by labourers. To this extent, training which responds to such views serves the function of role selection, of ensuring that such people leapfrog others on admission to working life.' (van Rensburg, 1978)

Bunny business on the farm

A LOCAL PAPER called it "Slaughter School." But anyone wanting a blood-thirsty spectacle would hardly think of going to the Margaret Dane School for girls at Bishop's Stortford in Hertfordshire. Its notoriety arises from the fact that, of all the schools in the country which run mini-farms, this seems to have aroused the wrath of vegans — the people who refuse to eat, or use, any meat, fish or egg products.

Particular exception was taken to the killing on the premises of the farm's stock of rabbits and an accusation was made that the school's pupils were forced to watch. But, as one indignant fourth-year girl who has worked on the farm for three years retorted, she has never been forced to watch the slaughter of any animals.

She also reacted strongly to the paper calling the rabbits "pets". The school tries to foster a professional farming attitude amongst the girls who work voluntarily on the farm towards animals.

"We discourage them from giving them names," said head-mistress Jill Dalladay. "This is a very serious attempt to introduce questions of agricultural ethics and to help them come to terms with where their food comes from. It would be wrong to encourage them to treat farm animals as pets."

And, as 14-year-old Danielle Clark, a volunteer responsible for the rabbits, said, nobody likes to think of the animals having to be killed. "I put up with it," she added. "They all have to die sometime."

Besides rabbits, the farm currently has two heifers, two milking goats, two Angora-cross goats, four geese, 40 to 50 chickens (producing some 30 eggs a day) and six turkeys. There are also three ferrets which the teacher in charge, science master Andrew Colebourne (who is also a qualified agricultural specialist), keeps for use in class.

If anything distinguishes the Margaret Dane mini-farm from other school farms, it is the fact that it is run as a self-sufficient business and receives no financial support from the school.

Last year, though, it got a Common Market subsidy for the quality of its beef and lamb. The annual turnover is between £5,000 and £7,000 and any profit is ploughed back into the farm. All the farm's produce — the eggs, rabbits and turkeys, the goat's milk and goat's milk yoghurt — is sold to members of staff and to parents. The small animals are dealt with on site but the larger ones are sent away for slaughter.

The school has introduced certificates for which the girls may qualify. The Level One certificate is for husbanding the smaller animals, whilst Level Two involves an oral examination with a local vet who is the head of the school farm.

"The controversy arose from a vegan who questioned the whole idea," the headmistress said. "We were puzzled as to why we were picked out".

"We do have children who would disagree and staff who are vegetarians. But the whole point of a secondary school is to express your own point of view. The key thing is to base arguments on correct information."

One might want to argue that the academic curriculum is however just another form of tedium management. The repetitive routine nature of much classroom activity in secondary schools throughout the world is not essentially different from brick-laying. Perhaps the objections are fewer, precisely because academic work has no immediate point; one cannot feel exploited by it, merely traumatized.

Academic work is also safe and inexpensive. For those engaged in real production, there are costly mistakes of learning on the job. The alternatives are to learn the skills but not rely on selling the products; or to invest in trying to sell the products and hope they stand the test of time and wear in the available market. Inequalities thus arise through the costs of practical activity: analyses of the Harambee schools in Kenya found that occupationally relevant disciplines such as metalwork, carpentry, mechanics and agriculture, requiring specialized facilities, equipment and staff but teaching the skills most desperately required in the rural areas, were found almost exclusively in the higher grade government schools. The poorer the school the more formalized was the curriculum. Harambee schools were usually unable to offer anything other than a weak academic curriculum (Lillis, 1988).

Everything — costs, history, resistance, assessment problems — seems to point to an inexorable return to the more academic curriculum — whether weak or strong. Are school heads powerless to achieve balance, relevance and integration?

> We learn reading and boredom, writing and boredom, arithmetic and boredom, and so on according to the curriculum, till in the end it is quite certain you can put us to the most boring job there is and we'll endure it.
> (J Common, *Kiddar's Luck*)

Contradictions

Paradoxically, as with all the potential reproduction of inequality, the one site of optimism is the contradictions within the processes of policy formation. While much of vocational training can be viewed as mere preparation for a divided, hierarchical and inequitable workforce, the rhetoric of enterprise supports the notion, at least, of democracy and decision-making for students. The spectacle of working class students learning the skills of problem identification and problem-solving may pose a threat to control, in that eventual autonomy and lateral thinking is not conducive either to a compliant student population nor a compliant labour force. As intimated earlier, it may be that such independence will become channelled into very small-scale and non-threatening industry, as has been the case with women's cooperatives in many parts of the world. Yet it cannot be denied that the potential is there for working class students, girls and ethnic minorities to turn the divided curriculum and its attendant ideologies to their own advantage. In another arena such as China, we can see how political ideologies of decentralized decision-making can be taken up by new groups. People-run schools 'presented new opportunities for the non-professional. Combined with the responsibilities for funding and equipping the schools, working with committees enhanced the peasants' role in educational decision-making and gave them a greater stake in the policy process' (Robinson, 1988, p. 189). Their 'success' resulted in a recentralization of authority in order to impose standardization. The flexibility of the people-run schools, structured to enable pupils to learn as well as to help with their family's agricultural work, were interpreted as allowing students to 'drift'; central and provincial authorities imposed new standards of teaching 'quality'.

Thus while there can be an official rhetoric about people power or even student power, it is clear than an apparent excess of this will provoke strong reactions: heads of schools and colleges will have to tread very carefully in making any real espousal of self-sufficiency and determining their own directions. The most recent study by Saunders (1988) is a very interesting comparative case-study of how headteachers in UK and Tanzania managed the contradictions inherent in the introduction of a practical curriculum. While TVEI and ESR started from very different political régimes and bases, we saw how similar their aims were. Both embodied a critique of conventional schooling, yet the social context of learning remained static. The dilemma faced turned on the lack of congruence with three overlapping characteristics of educational practice in society:

(1) the sifting and distributive function undertaken by schools and the 'backwash' power of its principal mechanism, the leaving exam.
(2) popular assumptions about the operative purposes of the school system, i.e. conventional expectations of school culture and the economic and cultural aspirations of the mass of the people.
(3) the ensemble of working practices that teachers have developed in response to the influence of (1) and (2). (Saunders, 1988)

Saunders points to the need for heads to establish 'cultural bridgeheads' to sustain and nourish the possibilities of the practical curriculum. In Tanzania, he identified three styles of headteacher response to the political orthodoxy which stressed 'application' and 'relevance' and the systematic realities of school practice which did not. The first style was 'creative manipulation', where heads had a sophisticated grasp of getting and using resources, where they juggled school organization and time and increased employed help, and where they generally manipulated teacher involvement. The second style, 'tacit non-compliance', accepted a casual semi-serious attitude to ESR on the part of teachers and pupils as long as teacher strategies were covert or low profile. This increased the likelihood of teachers' abuse of ESR projects and a deterioration of teacher/student relations. A third response, 'literal interpretation' was to adhere literally to ministerial directives and ignore teachers' interpretations. Teachers responded by various strategies ranging from explicit sabotage to covert non-compliance. The UK heads on the other hand had to grapple with 'innovative enclaves', whereby TVEI was to be a pilot process testing different methods within institutions. This had disruptive possibilities, with extra resource allocations going to the 'technical' or 'practical' resource areas, and non-TVEI staff having to support the organizational and professional development demands of TVEI teachers. Again, Saunders distinguished three types of response: 'extension' — whereby TVEI practices were (against the rules) replicated throughout the school, and used as a springboard for internal school change; 'accommodation', whereby selective elements of TVEI, particularly assessment, were replicated; and 'containment', where there was no replication outside the cohort group, and TVEI was used as a palliative to problem areas of school organization. Thus the successful manipulators were able to form the bridgeheads, and 'understood that the degree of control by policy initiators on local institutional expression of policy-in-practice is weak. This understanding enabled them to balance the tension between genuine innovation and systematic inertia' (p. 209).

Such analyses provide the clue to the management of contradiction and duality: the resourcefulness, sophistication and if necessary subversion of official rhetorics by the head or staff of an individual school. Literal acceptance of vocational thrusts or practical activity will only generate teacher sabotage, consumer resistance and ironically, heightened official control if too innovative or democratic. Ways can be found to combine academic and practical in a meaningful way, but they must be subtle and well marketed. Above all, they must take into account teachers' perceptions and interpretations of the functions of schools, as we shall see in the next chapter.

EXERCISE 6:PRODUCTIVE SCHOOLS

The following are examples from different countries of 'productive' schools, programmes or curricula. Which do you think would effectively break down the mental/manual divide? What would be their general effects on other aspects of inequality inside and outside the school?

> Removing the rigid distinction between types of curricular offerings, developing more positive attitudes towards manual work, promoting social cooperation are objectives that feature prominently in EWP programmes. The Democratic Socialist government of Jamaica favoured education with production as a means of fostering its egalitarian ideal of creating a classless society (Manley, 1974), while in Grenada, these types of programmes were linked to the macro-social goals of the Revolution of the early 1980's. Here also the eradication of sex-role stereotyping in the choice of practical work in schools was seen as a means of equalizing opportunities for men and women (Brizan, 1983). Other social objectives include the development of attitudes congenial to the work situation (e.g. punctuality, obedience to authority) and the development of self-reliance at the individual and national levels.
> From Jennings, 1987

THE HENS at Sharnbrook Upper School in Bedfordshire had been laying well. Enough to give a 40p share dividened to the parent–teachers' association and the individual pupils who bought them. One of the Government's most controversial and expensive incursions into the British education system had come home to roost.

Eggs Unlimited, a mini-company run by 14 to 16 year olds at the school, is a product of the Technical and Vocational Education Initiative, a Government-inspired push to shift the 14-plus curriculum towards greater relevance for working life.

In the four years since the first pilot schools started their courses, undreamed-of millions have been pouring quietly into the schools via the Manpower Services Commission.

The number of pupils involved has risen from 4,000 in 1983–4 to 83,500 in 1987–8. Some Labour authorities, such as Inner London, Haringey, Brent and Liverpool, hung back. But this week, the commission announced that the last 12 education authorities outside the scheme had submitted courses for approval; it plans eventually to spread the courses to every maintained school and college in the country catering for the 14–18 age group.

By 1997, the Government will have spent more than £1bn on what is easily the largest-ever investment in the British curriculum. By all accounts it is working, and, in the best schemes, every subject area has been touched both in curriculum content and style.

The teacher at the blackboard has been replaced by the teacher supporting children in assignments that often take them outside the classroom on work experience or residential trips. Modern languages are not dominated by grammar and needless lists of vocabulary. They could involve pupils taking over the local airport, as in Staffordshire, where they become customs officials, announcers or travellers using the language in normal situations.

History need not just be note-taking and listening to teacher. It could be the production of a special newspaper recording the execution of Charles I, treating the event with the vibrancy and shock it would have received at the time.

At Sharnbrook, one of the pilot schools, the scheme has caused a transformation. David Jackson, the head, said: "It gave us resources and it gave us a focus and impetus for change right across the school. It would have been difficult to imagine anything so cohesive as this without TVEI."

The school is now getting its best-ever examination results, and the proportion of children who stay after 16 has increased from 40 per cent pre-TVEI to 60 per cent. All abilities are involved.

Mr Jackson now finds it difficult to separate what is TVEI from the rest of the curriculum because it is so integrated in the whole, despite the pilot scheme being confined to restricted cohorts within year groups. These restrictions quickly became meaningless in such areas as Bedfordshire which insisted that TVEI students should not be picked out as something very different and that all students should be able to benefit from the extra computers, equipment and teaching staff that were flooding in.

The worries are about what will happen when funding ends. The feeling among some teachers is that much will carry on but development work will slow down, teaching groups will grow and some good courses will disappear.

The impact of the proposed national curriculum is almost equally worrying. There are doubts about whether there will be room for the innovative subjects that have emerged despite assurances to the contrary from the Government and the MSC.

Yet, four years ago, the worries were of an entirely different nature. Many local authorities and teachers saw the initiative as an MSC grab for power in the schools and an attempt to impose narrow vocational and technical training on middle or lower-ability children.

It is hard to pinpoint accurately what impact the scheme is having nationally. Some schools have an all-ability spread taking the courses, others have a preponderance of average and lower-ability pupils. Some report improved staying on rates, others have cancelled post-16 courses because of lack of demand.

Research sponsored by the MSC and carried out by the National Foundation for Educational Research has revealed that only a small proportion of the fifth-year pupils involved expect to get A-levels. This suggests that, in most schools, higher ability pupils are not being attracted into the scheme.

The research also showed that more than 75 per cent of the pupils felt that their personal skills — such as learning to work with a team, acting on their own initiative and solving problems — had been greatly enhanced by TVEI.

There is a body of opinion that believes that the MSC has backed off from the vocational part of the scheme and wonders what Mrs Thatcher, Mr Tebbit and Lord Young think about what they have spawned in schools which, at its best, is an enhanced liberal curriculum.

John Woolhouse, Director of the TVEI national steering group, denies that there has been any change in intentions. He points out that the first letter sent about the scheme to local education authorities by Lord Young, when chairman of the MSC, stressed that it was meant to widen and enrich the curriculum.

"Heads would never have responded as they have done had the original intentions of the scheme been narrow and limited," he said. "Many people were somewhat misled by the words 'vocational and technical'. In the English value system, 'vocational' tends to be associated with craft skills and low pay. Many people were projecting anxieties based on the rather low value of those words."

Awareness in industry and commerce varies. Some firms are only dimly aware of the scheme; others have benefited directly. One such is the Bedford branch of Barclays Bank which took on a TVEI pupil from Sharnbrook for work experience. Fortuitously, he arrived at the same time as a batch of personal computers for staff who had little idea how to use them.

He organised training courses and proved such an asset that he was asked back to work there in half-terms and holidays. He had university potential, but he accepted the offer of a job and left at 16.

Mr Jackson, his former head teacher, said: "I don't think rigid vocationalism would have helped industry or fitted its needs. Industry wants and needs youngsters who have skills related to the modern world and a wide range of personal competencies, all of which have come out of TVEI."

(From The Independent 'Success of a Liberal Curriculum', Wendy Berliner, 8 October 1987)

Belize's example is somewhat different. The Rural Education Agricultural Programme (REAP) is a project designed to create the attitudes and provide the skills necessary for young people to contribute to the agricultural development of the country. The schools in which REAP has been implemented cater to the 6–14 + age group, but only those in the final two years of school participate in the programme. The core of REAP are Learning Activity Packs (LAPS) which are outlines of lessons for appropriate grade levels in which teachers are given performance objectives related to a REAP area of study, suggestions for learning activities, instructional materials and reading references. These LAPS are developed around nine areas of study: land and water, soil, health and nutrition, ecology, animals, village study, weather, plants and agricultural practices. These serve as 'threads' to integrate the academic subjects — Language, Arts, Social Studies, Science, Art and Craft and Music. Students are required to spend at least 50 hours per school year doing supervised agricultural practice in school gardens.

(From Jennings, 1987)

Sixth-form pupils work as cleaners at school

AS LESSONS finish at a county high school, some sixth-form pupils are staying behind to clean the classrooms.

The pupils have been recruited as an emergency measure because of a shortage of cleaners at Droitwich High School in Hereford and Worcester.

But the action has been condemned by a union leader as child labour and as the result of cleaners leaving, rather than taking a 23 per cent pay cut.

Droitwich High School is short of eight out of a total cleaning force of 18. "We've tried to get replacements without any success so far and, until we do, as a temporary measure we asked for volunteers from the sixth form" Derek Owen, the head teacher, said. "We have four volunteers working after school from 4pm to 6pm. They will be paid on the same wage scale, but the pay may be lower because of their age."

The crisis has arisen through a 23 per cent pay cut imposed on county council cleaners at 45 schools and colleges to protect their jobs against private competition.

Jerry Bartlett, a Nupe area officer, said employing pupils was hypocritical as, for many years, schools had discouraged students from taking part-time jobs because of studying pressures.

"I'm extremely concerned at the precedent for increasing unemployment by substituting child labour in adult employees' jobs," he added.

But a strong defence came from Dr David Muffett, county education chairman. "If they pay them, that is excellent." he said. "Is it not a good thing for an 18-year-old to grasp the opportunity of beginning to stand on his or her own feet and earn money because there's nobody else willing to take the jobs?"

The Independent,
22 September 1988.

Match-making for profit

Rising inflation and lack of funds have forced thousands of primary and middle schools to open mini-factories in their grounds with pupils providing the labour force. They produce anything from shoe soles to matches, while a few have acquired technical assistance to produce electrical parts.

Profits are ploughed back into the school and, in remote regions, are even used to improve the often substandard living conditions of teachers. In the last few years school-factories have become big business — it is estimated that some 650,000 schools are now involved in such projects. The yearly nation-wide profit is estimated at 1.9 billion yuan (about £300 million) and profits from such ventures now provide more money for research labs and new classrooms than the money from the state.

But there are some concerns. Students are only expected to spend one or two hours a week in the factory, but this is difficult to control, particularly in rural areas.

Neither is it certain how much of the work is dull and repetitive. And a recent report on physical education in Peking was critical of the programme, as factory huts and sheds are often built on already inadequate play and sport areas.

However, with surveys revealing that the new generation of school-leavers are looking down on manual work, preferring instead to seek white-collar office work, the programme will get strong Government support. Favourable tax concessions and priority in obtaining materials are two recent incentives introduced by a Government that is only too relieved to see some of the financial burdens of education removed from its shoulders.

Bob Pateman
Times Educational Supplement,
10 March 1989.

The José Marti Secondary school (JMSS), built by Cubans alongside Jamaican workers, was a gift to Jamaica from the people of Cuba in 1977. Students do agricultural work for two and a half hours per day on a shift system, working on the school farm which occupies 180 acres, housing a piggery, dairy, poultry, agronomy and aquaculture units. Times in between shifts are spent on academic subjects as well as the study of such vocational subjects as Industrial Arts, Farm Management and Business Education. The vocational programme has a work experience component which involves grade 11 students (aged 16–17) spending up to three weeks in work stations or agencies in both the public and private sectors to experience directly a realistic employment situation tied closely to their vocational area of study. A similar Work Experience Programme (WEP) operates in Guyana's Community High Schools where it is referred to as 'Work-Study'. Both the JMSS and the Community High Schools have strong links with the community. Students doing Industrial Arts in both types of institutions, for example, do work such as constructing broiler units for the school farm, making school furniture, repairing household appliances for members of the community and running electrical lines for their own work-shops. Payment received for such services is put back into the running of school programmes. Worth noting is the fact that through the WEP a number of students succeed in getting permanent employment in the situations where they gained work experience.

(From Jennings 1987)

The Crosskeys Islwyn Challenge

Jennifer Rowe, Noel Warkins and Susan Sims

The Crosskeys Islwyn Challenge is in Cwmfelinfach which is in the Sirhowy Valley. It is about fifteen miles from Cardiff and in an industrial unit on an industrial estate.

The unit accommodates not only the Crosskeys Islwyn Challenge but also off-the-job trainees from the Islwyn Borough Council scheme. These trainees spend only two days a week at the unit where they mostly do construction: the other three days of the week are spent on council sites, building walls and fences.

Traditional industry in this area has always relied on coal and steel for its employment. However, over the last twenty years many pits have been closed and the work force in the steel plants at Ebbw Vale, Port Talbot and Llanwern has been dramatically reduced. Job prospects in the coal and steel industries now no longer exist, but it has been anticipated that over the next twenty years industry in South Wales will be based on small units employing twenty to 200 people and covering a wide range of manufacturing industries.

All trainees at the Challenge are aged between sixteen and eighteen and, because the boys and girls work together in mixed groups, the ratio at the Challenge as a whole is 50:50. Trainees are at different levels of education. Some trainees have problems with reading and writing whereas others have obtained some 'O' levels or even one or two 'A' levels.

The Challenge is supported by the local education authority, the Crosskeys Tertiary College, Islwyn Borough Council and the Manpower Services Commission. The Challenge itself is named after the famous poet, Islwyn, who is buried in a small chapel only a few hundred yards away from our unit.

It is possible for trainees to follow a variety of vocational routes. Each route starts with the basic principles and progresses to more complex techniques.

The 'construction route' is made up of several different areas: building, painting, decorating and carpentry. Within this route the trainees built the seminar rooms, the canteen and the dark room. They then fitted the windows and doors and painted the interiors.

The next route is 'engineering and the motor vehicle'. In this route the trainees are taught to maintain and service a motor car. They are also taught how to use a bending machine, a lathe, an oxy-acetylene welder and an arc welder. With these skills they have built a kit car which they call 'The Hustler'.

Another route is 'child care and social welfare'. During their time in this route the trainees learn how to deal with young children, expecially babies. They are taught how to change babies' nappies, how to bathe the baby and also how to sterilize the equipment to be used.

The fourth route is 'catering'. This is split into two separate areas. The first is the provision of a canteen service to trainees, staff and workers from other factories on the estate, and for this they supply a varied and changing menu. The second area is the learning of basic kitchen skills such as following recipes, using machinery and cleaning the kitchen.

The last route is 'office and clerical'. In this route the trainees run the factory by sending out letters, checking goods in and out and filing in-coming information. As well

as this, the trainees are taught office skills such as typing and using the telephone switchboard.

In addition to these five main routes there is also a 'support route' which is printing and photography.

There is no sex stereotyping: all trainees are encouraged to do all the routes. The girls are encouraged to do construction and carpentry and the boys are encouraged to work in the canteen.

As well as the routes there is also a compulsory section called 'core studies'. In this, the trainees get social and life skills, basic numeracy and literacy and also computing, using the computer we have in the office.

Organization and strucutre of the Challenge includes eight important elements. It is a forty-eight week period, involving eight weeks actually on site and eight weeks out on placement, and this pattern is repeated throughout the course.

There is a production element, which currently involves equipment for playgrounds. Revenue from this source finances expeditions and the purchasing of equipment.

Another element is residential: we take two sessions each of two weeks, mainly outdoor activities: for example, canoeing and rock climbing.

Next comes job search. Throughout the course, and really from the first day, the trainee is encouraged to look for a permanent job by taking interviews wherever possible. Last year we had a 60 per cent record of trainees actually getting permanent jobs by the end of the course.

There is a negotiated timetable. It provides trainees with a multi-skill backgound. First, they choose a main vocational route and then follow a balanced timetable. Each day is divided into two sessions, morning and afternoon, thus making ten sessions in all in a five-day week. Within these ten sessions, five are for the main vocational route, two are the computer and core, leaving three sessions with one or more secondary route.

We also have guidance and counselling. Each trainee is allocated to his or her personal tutor. Guidance and counselling takes place at least once a fortnight and any problems that may arise can then be sorted out.

Finally, assessment is of a continuous nature. At the end of every three-hour session the trainees are asked to make a self-assessment. On these assessment sheets the task or activity is broken down into a series of steps and within these steps, six in all, the trainees make a self-assessment varying from 'very easy' to 'very difficult'. With the aid of these assessments, log books or diaries can be kept. The trainees can write comments on the course as well as their own performance.

Of course, the Challenge has had its problems. All trainees are at different educational levels, so it is necessary for lecturers to sub-divide tasks very carefully so that each trainee can gain satisfaction from achieving real objectives. This also requires lecturers to have an intimate knowledge of the educational capability of each trainee.

This is conducted in a classroom split into several sections. Because it is conducted in a classroom many of the trainees resent this as it is too much like a school atmosphere. To remedy this problem, core studies are conducted during the job they are participating in.

Another problem is that of diminishing numbers, since 60 per cent of trainees may leave to take permanent jobs.

(From Burgess, 1986)

Chapter 7

The School as a Workplace:
Teachers' Cultures, Needs and Self-Appraisal

In Chapter 4 gender relations and women teachers were used as an example of ways in which the social divisions within the teaching force could be analyzed and related to the systematic differences in educational outcomes for students. This chapter broadens out to consider teachers' cultures and needs more generally, and to explore how we might think about the commonalities as well as the divisions within the staff of a school.

Some concerns to do with this analysis of the social relations within the work of teaching have already been signalled: the different usages of 'professionalism' (Chapter 1); the effects of centralized appraisal and the potential deskilling of teachers (Chapter 2); vertical and horizontal divisions in the organization of a school staff (Chapters 4 and 6); and the informal language or ethnic groupings which characterize staffrooms (Chapter 5). The patterns of relations within a school staff will both reflect and influence divisions and tensions within the student body; but they should also be explored in the interests of teachers themselves, as well as reviewed as a potential force for school change or continuity.

We start with relatively simple sounding questions: what are schools like to work in? What decides how teachers see their work? Do changes in the work process affect teaching styles? Who should be asking these questions? Given the detailed and delicate ethnographic research needed to unravel such issues, it is perhaps unsurprising that we have not much to go on, especially in rapidly changing circumstances.

> Assessing whether or not the 'essence' or 'heart' of teaching remains intact
> is complicated by the fact that we know so little about teachers' work, and
> what we know is itself fragmented. (Ozga and Lawn, 1988)

Yet if we are to explore the potential for schools of challenging inequality, it is essential to understand the roots of teachers' ideologies and motivations, and how the material conditions of work may militate against innovation.

There are additional problems of deciding who should initiate research into the work of teaching, and for what purpose. There is a strong argument that a sociology of work should be produced by the teachers themselves, as part of critical, reflexive pedagogy. Researchers cannot stand outside as 'critical intellectuals', for they have a moral obligation actively to participate in social movements, if only because of 'the fact that we as researchers and scholars and teacher educators derive certain benefit from an unequally structured, stratified social and economic system (Beyer and Zeichner, 1987). I shall be arguing therefore for the development of teachers' own appraisal of themselves as workers, not just in the interests of 'professional growth', but to generate a collective analysis internationally of the school as a workplace.

The preceding emphasis on 'work' rather than 'teaching' will perhaps have been noted. The identification of teaching as a labour process rather than as a vocation, semi-profession or a craft has been a comparatively recent but important shift in conceptualizing the relationship of teachers to the State. A small but growing body of literature in UK, America and Australia seeks to use teachers' accounts of their life and work to generate a sociology of work which can parallel the occupational analyses within industrial sociology (Ozga and Lawn, 1981; Connell, 1985; Apple, 1986; Ozga, 1988). The careers and biographies of teachers are receiving detailed attention (Ball and Goodson, 1985; Sikes *et al.*, 1985). This can be seen as a reaction both against the predominance of research which regulates teachers to one of a range of 'variables' in the achievement of students, and against some of the more deterministic neo-Marxist accounts which portray teachers as mere transmission agents of State control. Contemporary analyses of teachers' work show teachers not only as active intermediaries between State concerns and students' aspirations, but also show the workplace of school as an immensely variable site of contestation and accommodation by staff.

With regard to Third World countries, the ethnographic* studies to disentangle the complexities of schools as workplaces are sparse. Concentration in educational research has inevitably focused on the students and their careers: access to schools, performance in schools and destinations subsequent to school. Large-scale economic considerations related to manpower planning and to the returns on educational investments appear to lead inexorably to equally large 'tracer' studies of 'cohorts' of students. Alternatively, the analysis has been thematically based, with recurrent hardy annuals such as vocational education or relevance education poking through the educational topsoil at predictable intervals (Davies, 1986a). These may lead to case-study work, but within that, teachers may still be conceptualized in terms of their 'agency' or 'role' in curriculum innovation or in the equitable treatment of different categories of students. Much gender research, for example, has had this focus, paying little attention to the implications of the gender structuring of the teaching profession itself (Davies, 1987a). Dove (1986) in her book, *Teachers and Teacher Education in Developing Countries*, does provide some interesting material on teachers' conditions of work, salaries, status, political organization and responses towards attempted state control such as transfers. Her final appeals for policy and action are inevitably (and perhaps shrewdly) couched, however, in terms of promoting the 'efficiency' or education systems, in enabling curriculum reform — albeit in return for improved career structures and conditions of service. The negotiative aspects of teachers' relationship to the State are nowhere addressed in terms of their own class or race location, of their political critique of state action nor their potential for radical transformation of systems.

Yet I would argue that a focus on teaching as a labour process has wide-spread implications for understanding contemporary change in educational policy. We are not just talking of teachers' 'attitudes', for the attitude studies are nothing new, and are often solicited as a 'factor' in exploring a seemingly more significant issue such as self-reliance or examination reform. That focus is on projects, not on people, and as such is potentially dehumanizing. Teachers' own life histories and occupational cultures are less often seen as important in their own right. Looking at teaching as work, and critically examining ideologies of 'professionalism' should however:

> direct attention to the organization of teachers' work and the workplace context, to teachers' formal and informal groupings and networks, to the division of labour both by function and gender in teaching, to the role of management and supervision, to performance appraisal and efficiency, to strategies of compliance and resistance, and to job design and quality control in education work (Ozga, 1988, p. xii).

This chapter will therefore firstly examine where generalizations can be made internationally about the work of teaching; and secondly where different cultures of work can be found either between countries or within schools. It then uses extracts from a case-study of teachers' work in Botswana which has been published earlier (Davies, 1988) as a partial example of 'outsider' ethnographic research, and what might stem from it. The case study is offered as there is even less Third World material on teacher cultures than there is in the First World. Typical exceptions would be Farrand (1988) for Mexico; Ginsburg and Chaturvedi (1988) for India; and Nwagwu (1977) for Africa. All focus, however, more on professionalism and professional identity rather than on the social relations of the workplace.

Uniform features of the work of teaching

While no-one would suggest that 'teachers' form a homogenous occupational group, there is an argument that teacher culture is characterized by uniformity rather than pluralism (Sachs and Smith, 1988). It does not take an intricate research design to note that traditional authoritarian schools tend to have a certain sameness about them, no matter where they are located. Sachs and Smith claim common constraints for all teachers of the hidden pedagogy, of individualism, of bureaucratic control, and of professional preparation and socialization. Farrand (1988), however, distinguishes uniform features of teaching which apply to all national contexts, and different features relating to national policies, priorities and resources, and to prevailing ideological conditions. I would also want to add to the analysis the different cultures within a school which hinge on divisions such as age, race or gender.

If we examine first these uniform features, the obvious ones are those engendered by 'the teachers' problematic' of time and space; of class size; and of controlling a large cohort of sometimes unwilling participants. Actual 'survival' or 'coping' strategies may vary, but teachers share the necessity to have to develop them. Managing so many students in a small space puts a premium on routine and predictability (Feiman-Nemser and Buchmann, 1985). Class sizes in Third World countries are often even higher than in the First World (Dove, 1986), and over 80 in a class is not unknown. Even with smaller class sizes, it is claimed in UK that teachers spend more time controlling students than teaching them (Sharp and Green, 1975; Denscombe, 1980). Teachers also have little control over the composition or the class or over their timetable and flow of work for the day. The combination of timetables and official syllabuses leads to a fragmented relationship to knowledge for many teachers.

> I dreamed last night I was teaching
> again – that's the only bad dream that
> ever afflicts my sturdy conscience.
> (D. H. Lawrence)

Another common feature often cited is that of isolation. Typical teacher culture emphasizes the autonomy of a teacher in his or her classroom, and the geography of a school sometimes imposes it. Acker (1988) nonetheless argues that while 'isolation' from colleagues is the lot of some teachers most of the time and most teachers some of the time, it is not an inevitable and unalterable feature of schools. 'What is missing is not contact per se, but sufficient specific time set aside for planning and consultation' (p. 317). While there are always staff meetings, such activities as lesson preparation and marking are essentially solitary activities.

With regard to our particular concern for inequality, an important shared value has been identified as the 'culture of individualism' (Hargreaves, 1982), that is, a concern with the cultivation of individual students and their various intellectual and behavioural aptitudes. Acker cites a study where the child-centred ethic came through in a teacher insistence that 'I teach characters, not sexes'. Thus teachers may be selectively 'blind' to social phenomena, and de-emphasize the political contexts of their work. 'The teachers regarded the nature of society as having universal properties that were "commonsense" to all . . . or that the realm of the "political" was removed from the educational sphere' (Acker, 1988). My own experience in teacher education would concur that the combination of consensus sociology and a child-referenced pedagogy during training certainly seems to reinforce a tendency to refer to 'the needs of society' or 'the expectations of society' as if these were homogenous, uncontestable constraints — and of interest only as they impinge on the individual learner. Whether such a culture of individualism is in fact internationally shared is perhaps open to question; Broadfoot and Osborn's comparison found French teachers having a 'universalistic' emphasis on equality and the need to treat all children the same way, rather than demonstrating the 'treating each child as an individual' ideology characteristic of UK teachers (Broadfoot and Osborn, 1988). And even in UK there are some democratic schools. Teachers in countries such as Tanzania and Mozambique, where political education has a high profile may also have a more critical perception of students within a set of social structures. An unreflexive individualism would nonetheless seem to be a common feature of American teacher training, if Ginsburg's (1988) study of college programmes can be generalized.

> Mr Bun has already announced that there will be a magic number which will apply to in-service programmes. The number two will dominate all. For a start the induction courses will last precisely two days. This is based on the contemptuous notion that any fool can teach, so a couple of days for senior people gives sufficient information.
>
> They can then go back to their colleagues and sprinkle it on them in a couple of hours. This was the pattern which turned out to be so inadequate for the GCSE. It was called the cascade method of training, but some people named it the piston model. If the subtlety of that epithet is not apparent, try saying it with a pause before the last two letters.
> Professor Ted Wragg, *Times Educational Supplement*, 9 September 1988.

Yet another highly relevant area of common ground would the 'practicality ethic' (Doyle and Ponder, 1977). Teachers will possess a fund of 'practical' or 'commonsense' knowledge which is formed from the imperatives of the stream of events in daily teaching. The immediacy of the teaching act, and the constant need to make decisions means that teachers rely on 'recipe knowledge' (Esland, 1977) which enables actors to make sense of a situation and to solve problems. Recipes vary from school to school; but innovations may pose a threat to that set of recipes, and to precarious classroom order. Thus Doyle and Ponder explain that teachers' main reactions to a proposed change will be a judgement of its potential as 'practical' or otherwise for classroom use. They suggest that to be 'practical', a proposal must be (a) instrumental (explain what is to be done rather than appeal to principle alone), (b) congruent (fit in reasonably well with the way the teacher normally works and the type of pupils she teaches) and (c) cost effective (expected to produce a return — not necessarily monetary — worth the effort and sacrifice involved). Whether or not teachers' versions of what is 'practical' differ, the effect is to give this ethic higher value than 'theory'. Sachs and Smith (1988) claim 'when faced with a choice between the acceptance of theoretical knowledge and the maintenance of "practical" practice, teachers are likely to reject the former or colonize it . . . teachers reformulate theory into "practical" forms that "work" ' (p. 433). This colonization of innovation or theory has important implications for any establishment of a framework within a school by which a concept such as 'equality' can be tackled.

A final commonality in teachers' cultures would be working within some form of bureaucracy. The time constraints and the lack of control over who and even sometimes what to teach, mean that a teacher rarely feels like an active negotiator within a set of democratic relationships, but like a cog towards the bottom end of a bureaucratic machine. This is expressed by Webb and Ashton (1987) thus:

> for some teachers, the combination of excessive demands, inadequate salary and status panic, lack of recognition and support, uncertainty, and powerlessness engendered attitudes of quiet conformity and unreflective acceptance of the status quo. (p. 30)

They conclude that teachers reified what they called 'the system' and could not see it to be within their power (individually or collectively) to change that system. Any 'unreflective acceptance' of the *status quo* is therefore unlikely to articulate well with a critical analysis of that *status quo* as being racist, sexist, classist or ageist.

> I had reached the point where I hated the very sight of a school. I don't think any boy could have felt more detestation than I did. It's possible, indeed, that this hatred is felt by most novice teachers, simply because they're forcing themselves to go back to an environment they had thankfully left some years before. It's like being crammed back into a playpen. There they are, those dreadful green doors leading off the main hall; the vision, through glass panels, of blackboard and gesturing teacher; the slow ticking of the outsize clock on the wall; the contained murmur; the sudden shriek; the dismal sporting trophies on a shelf.
> Edward Blishen, *Roaring Boys*

These commonalities among teachers — of control problems, of isolation, of individualism, of practicality and of bureaucracy — would seem to point to an inherent conservatism in teacher culture which would not augur well for radical change. Add to this the research findings showing how teachers incline to teach as they were themselves taught, and that continuity, that conservatism becomes more entrenched. As Lortie (1975) points out, teachers have never really left school, and have internalized models of teacher behaviour and role enactment from their early days. Formal training merely activates and legitimates latent knowledge, and initial teaching experience triggers the unconsciously absorbed models in order to survive.

Pluralism within teachers' cultures

This picture of teachers moulded to a uniform shape by the exigencies of past and current 'practical' experience must be offset however against the knowledge that these are only part of the story. All teachers 'cultures' will indeed contain daily survival strategies and preferences for the proven workable, and I would agree that the end result is likely to be more towards conservatism rather than radicalism. Nonetheless, teachers' cultures will also encompass their social and class relations at the workplace, and their differing articulations of responsibility towards whatever national system or ideology is in force.

While in many countries teachers will share a common type of training through the necessity for minimum professional qualifications, in Third World countries the existence of a large proportion of unqualified or untrained teachers means the potential for schisms in a school staff. Seeing teaching as a fallback or temporary job while still hoping for entry to higher status occupations produces a different value system from that possessed by the vocationally inspired. Nwagwu comments of African teachers:

> ... members of the teaching profession in Africa have not been able to identify with one another as people with common interests, objectives, background and training. Those who are professionally qualified are justifiably afraid that the professional bandwagon is overcrowded with inadequate performers and many birds of passage.

Solidarity is complicated by the many different categories of teacher and hence different unions, and the very different status primary and secondary teachers may have.

> The problem for all teachers' unions or associations in African countries is how to bring all these teachers, qualified and unqualified, trained and untrained, together to pursue a common purpose. If all were committed to teaching as a life-long career, the situation would have been easier to control ... there is very little held in common by the various groups who teach in the schools. They would be better described as practitioners and apprentices rather than as members of the teaching profession. (Nwagwu, 1977, p. 534)

The proposals for introducing yet more tiers into the teaching force heightens potential conflict. In UK it is 'licensed teachers', who are to learn on the job; in developing countries it is paraprofessionals drawn in through schemes such as Project IMPACT, which tries to provide low cost basic education utilizing teachers' aides from among the local community, peer learning and self-instructional materials (Dove, 1986). In Indonesia, Liberia and Jamaica, however, there has been little use of teachers' aides within the Project, and primary teachers in Bangladesh have resisted attempts to introduce 'teacher substitutes' into their schools, in spite of, perhaps because of, the considerable saving to the government. Dove comments 'unfortunately, there has been little systematic research in developing countries into the conditions under which paraprofessionals are acceptable and useful' (p. 114). I would add that there has been little systematic research in UK either, and licensed teachers, parent helpers and teachers' aides are likely to meet with varying sorts of opposition from 'professionals'. Among Dove's recommendations is the interesting one that teachers should be trained to manage paraprofessional personnel; this would certainly give credence to the notion of all teachers as 'managers', and help avoid the growing senior management/staff divide.

Qualifications intersect with social origin to provide another area of diversity among school staffs. The social class of teachers has been one longstanding area of interest. The notion that teachers — and schools — are 'middle class' has been evoked to explain working class student failure, because of the mismatch between working class values of immediacy and oracy, and the middle class attachment to deferred gratification and literacy. The basis for such generalizations has always been shaky, especially when examining the social class origins of teachers. Sachs and Smith (1988) cite Australian studies showing that individuals entering teaching are in general from a lower socio-economic class than those entering other professions such as law, medicine and engineering. It must be pointed out, however, that the studies typically look at the occupations of teachers' fathers to locate their class position; Sachs and Smith do not comment on the sexist nature of the research, nor question the validity of the findings — especially when the teaching force in many countries is predominantly a female profession, and the occupation of the mother may be more salient in identifying continuity or change.

Given that the teaching profession is an important arena for social mobility in both directions, it is probably impossible to claim uniformity in social class. In colonial times in many countries, entry to teaching through apprenticeship was one way to assume white collar status and escape manual or agricultural work. Conversely, teaching has been seen as a 'fall-back' position for those high status family products apparently unable to do anything else. The perceived suitability of teaching for women has meant entry by females from the whole class spectrum, with the tendency towards a 'higher' original class position than males. Too much investigation into previous class background may anyway be a fruitless and diversionary pursuit for contemporary

researchers. Ozga and Lawn (1988), in a critique of their own previous 'proletarianization' thesis regarding teachers' work in UK, wonder whether in fact this needs
revision:

> While it is of interest to raise questions based on precise, structural analysis
> of class location, there is little time to spare for such arcane pursuits in the
> face of a government willing to discard decades of negotiated or managed
> consensus to produce policies, each refining earlier versions, which move
> teachers steadily back into their past. (p. 334)

In the face of such erosion of rights, political and social alliances involving teachers dis-
solve or struggle to emerge, and the work relations of the school become partly
determined by union membership. The task is therefore to understand class relations as
subject to historical change, not as static categories. 'Like other forms of work,
teaching should be examined by a thorough study of its practices, struggles, lived
experience and contradictions' (p. 334).

It is such struggles which increasingly mean that it becomes impossible to place
teachers or schools within a unified class or cultural location. Ball (1988) outlines the
effects on schools of the teachers' industrial action in UK 1985–1986, and distinguishes
the 'dispute' between the teacher unions and their employers from the concomitant
'disputes' which arose between teachers themselves as a result of the action. The
changes in working practices 'were mediated differently in different schools and
experienced and interpreted differently by different individual teachers and groups —
men and women teachers, black and white, junior and senior' (p. 297). In some
schools, the action was seen to have a positive effect on staff morale and relationships,
heightening the sense of shared objective interests. Ball surmises this to be a shift from
'professional individualism' to 'collective unionism'. In other schools there was an
inevitable divide between the head or senior management team and the staff, with the
Head's refusal to close a school leading to antipathy and a 'them' and 'us' feeling. 'The
relations between teachers and school management tended to take on the classic
employer-employee form. Any sense of a professional-collegial working relationship
between staff and headteacher was drastically eroded'. The guilt and embarrassment
felt by some teachers over strike action was mirrored by the differing political stand-
points of different teacher unions, whose membership in turn tended to be located in
different levels of seniority in the school. 'Hackles were raised, disgruntlements
focussed and old scores settled. Tensions provoked in relation to issues of race, gender,
promotion, and patterns of influence were laid bare by the dispute. As with other
major organisational events (falling rolls, change of head, amalgamation), industrial
action represents the potential for a restructuring of the established patterns of
advantage and disadvantage and the realisation of new cross-cutting, shared interests'
(p. 301).

Hence Ball (1987) and others such as Hoyle (1986) have argued for a focus on the 'micropolitics' of the school, in order to recognize schools as organizations where individuals and groups compete and manipulate events, using whatever power resources they possess to try to maximize their own interests and satisfactions. Acker, (1988) wryly comments on Ball's book: 'One potential interest group within mixed schools he singles out is women teachers (are men teachers, qua men, an interest group, we might wonder in passing)' (p. 318). While recognizing shifting alliances within schools, we clearly therefore need to see at what point a coalition of interests means that a section of staff become an 'interest group'. This will be an issue for managers of schools as well as teachers themselves in their forging of new networks. The base-line 'common culture' of the work of teaching will be overlaid by different sets of responses to national events and policy formations, as we saw from Ball's account. Redican (1988), in a chapter called 'Subject teachers under stress', describes for example how, because of deskilling in decision-making, subject heads in comprehensive schools in UK have become less powerful than groups of teachers reskilling themselves in pastoral care. While 'stress' appears a potential problem for any teacher, Broadfoot and Osborn (1988) also identify differences in its source as between UK and French teachers. English teachers may experience stress and even 'burn-out' because of the openended and ill-defined nature of their role; but French teachers' principal source of stress is the opposite, in that tight definitions and lack of professional freedom lead to feelings of helplessness and alienation. Similar contrasts will emerge in the Botswana study. The focusing on stress in the West is itself part of the 'intensification' of work that comes with proletarianization, and has unfortunate side effects. As Freedman (1988) argues:

> The coining of the term 'burnout' at the same time that teachers are threatened with the loss of (and loss of control over) their jobs serves to direct the focus of each teacher's growing anger away from a critical analysis of schools (and society) as institutions to a preoccupation with her (or his) own failure. (p. 27)

We should not therefore necessarily see the 'problematic' of teaching, and its concomitant stress, as a unifying force for workers in education. Different interpretations, strategies and coalitions will emerge as 'solutions' to those work conditions, and these may be of more salience in understanding teachers' perceptions of the labour process than the original 'common ground'.

Botswana: contradictions of control[1]

To flesh out these micro-politics in a different context to UK, we should now turn to the Botswana case-study. This was an attempt to explore the work of teaching in a

---

[1] A longer version of this case study has been published in *International Journal of Educational Development* (Davies 1988)

highly centralized economy, yet one where because of its 'emergent' status, central control takes on a very different meaning to UK. Ethnographic work was began in two-case study schools in early 1988, interviewing teachers and attempting to embed their responses within their reactions on self-appraisal schedules, and also within an exploration of the school as a workplace with territories, networks of allegiances and competing definitions of the situation. Emerging themes were: teachers' 'knowledge' in terms of degrees of certainty or uncertainty; staff divisions and cultures; accommodations to control; teachers as storekeepers; and occupational rewards and addictions.

Before beginning this exploration, it is necessary to outline a little background to the situation at the time of the study. Botswana is currently undergoing a massive and sudden increase in educational provision. Education at secondary level was changed from being fee-paying to being 'free' at the beginning of 1988 (the start of the school year), although entry is still selective and based on the primary school leaving results. Books are now loaned instead of bought by students. New junior community secondary schools are being built to serve the rural areas, and some of the previous all-in secondary schools being redesignated as senior secondary schools, that is, taking students only for the last three years before Cambridge O-level (forms Three to Five). Entry to Form Three is again by competitive examination, the Junior Certificate. (A-level is not taken in Botswana state schools; entry to the University is on the results of O-level). The introduction of free secondary education was brought in without a lengthy period or a large degree of consultation, although there would be little political opposition to what was a popular and seemingly egalitarian move. Doubts were expressed by economists, however, about the 'equity' of providing an already élite group with free education: when the majority of children go to secondary school, it does become counter-productive to spend money and effort on fee recovery or means testing; when the minority go (as is still the case in Botswana), it is still economically and socially viable to demand fees from those able to pay.

Of the two case-study schools, one was an urban government school (to be referred to as UGS) with 1190 (mostly day) students, the other a rural(ish) ex-mission all-boarding school with 820 students (to be referred to as RBS). All schools in Botswana are coeducational. Teachers in both institutions were at pains to point out to me that their schools were not 'typical', in that they were prestigious and very well resourced schools compared to the community secondaries; one has to make the usual caveats that ethnography is not necessarily about generalizability. It must be recognized that as high status institutions within an already selective system, the schools occupied a particular class location as preparation for relatively élite positions. RBS in particular had a social mobility function by providing 24-hour socialization into 'modern' living for those children from the remoter cattle posts. Both schools had comparable organizational structures: Head, Deputies, Heads of Department, etc. although RBS had also instigated a number of specialized committees to deal with particular facets such as book loans or staff welfare. Both schools had comprehensive manuals detailing job specifications for all posts of responsibility, organizational procedures, expectations for teachers and duties for students. Both had bursars to deal with finance, and a large support staff almost equal in size to the teaching staff.

The research methodology and limitations are more fully discussed in Davies (1988). The interviews with teachers used a semi-structured format which raised questions of how teachers saw their future careers; how current organizational changes would affect them; the appeals of the work of teaching; what stresses or problems they experienced; their sociality with colleagues; and their perceptions of school management. I observed staff and departmental meetings, which were generally conducted in English. Interview data here is suffixed by codes indicating the gender and origin of the teacher, so that judgements can be made as to where such attributes are significant.

Certainties and uncertainties

The centralization of education provides teachers with paradoxes in terms of the predictability of events. On the one hand, the range of curriculum subjects and their syllabus for each year of schooling are centrally decided, leaving little flexibility in terms of choice of the knowledge base for learning. Secondary schools can design their own schemes of work for the Cambridge examination, but this examination itself acts as an 'intranational' centralizing factor. Choices can be made from prescribed lists in terms of, for example, books for English literature, or topics within Geography, but the degrees of freedom are limited. In neither school was there much room for any activity outside these examination syllabuses during the formal teaching day (6.45am to 1pm); Art, Music, Physical Education, or Drama were not taught except as extracurricular activities or clubs in the afternoon. There are teachers on the national Subject Panels, and draft syllabuses go to schools for consultation, but as the Head of GBS commented: 'I don't know how much thought teachers give to it at this stage . . . only if very conscientious'. The majority of teachers receive the curriculum as given, which, even if the content changes, psychologically provides a stable and non-contestable base for action.

On the other hand, the central control of the teaching force means that local teachers can be posted or transferred at very short notice to any part of the country, on the grounds of manpower needs. They can, of course, also request transfers (and, I was told, married women do occasionally to attempt to escape violent husbands). Transfers can occur for any level of teacher, including Heads, and the subtle ranking of schools will determine whether this is seen as promotion or demotion. While some teachers may stay for a long period in one school, or have the political means to resist unwanted postings, the overall effect is of a very high turnover of teachers, with the staff lists already out of date two weeks into the beginning of the school year. There is clearly unpredictability therefore for individual teachers, either in terms of their own movements and family considerations, or in terms of their potential colleagues, superiors or subordinates. The mitigating factors are the central curriculum, as described above, which means the basic work is the same wherever a teacher goes; and also the small population of Botswana, which means that a teacher is bound to know some members of a 'new' staff, or that a new Head's reputation and ways of working are very well known before he or she arrives. The major problems would be for school management, in terms of monthly uncertainty regarding numbers of staff and in which subjects; and for individual teachers in terms of stressful family and social upheavals.

The logic of central control is clear: a centralized curriculum, whether in Botswana or elsewhere, can enable teachers to be seen by governments as 'resources', to be used wherever need is greatest; the euphemism 'redeployment' in UK has the same principle. It remains to be seen whether the introduction of a national curriculum in UK will permit the same local or national shuffling of the teaching pack. The ideology of central transfer (which is of course not confined to teaching) can be interpreted as a mode of depersonalization; it also prevents the build-up of permanent groupings of organized labour which might challenge government policy.

Staff divisions and cultures

Within the schools themselves, a first significant feature of the staff composition was the large number of expatriate staff — almost half in each school. The British expatriates were a mixture of longstanding and younger short-term volunteers. There were expatriates from other African countries, from Asia, and also Peace Corps volunteers from USA. UGS had fourteen nationalities among the staff. The cosmopolitan nature of the staff, and the high turnover, prevented any deep factions, and seemed to generate easy relationships and a desire to help and advise. Key differences between expatriates and locals would be in terms of type of 'commitment' (Woods, 1981). The expatriates had chosen to come, often under a volunteer ideology if not pay scale, and saw their involvement as catalytic for Botswana schools, but not necessarily 'instrumental' for their own career: 'I think locals should be Heads. We've come to help' (M, Ghana, UGS). A vocational commitment was not always apparent on the other hand in the younger Botswana teachers, who may have been drafted into the job through the sponsorship system for subjects taken at University. 'I had never wanted teaching, never applied for it . . . . I had been programmed for teaching' (F, local, RBS). Ambitions for local teachers lay in gaining a scholarship for further education, or even in escaping to a more lucrative or prestigious job: 'The government doesn't make this profession so attractive . . . '.(F, local, RBS). Older Botswana staff were clearly more settled, and expressed ideologies of 'service' not dissimilar to expatriate views. Teachers in both schools reported getting on well with colleagues, and, apart from the odd clash of individual personality, saw no lasting conflicts, nor any 'racial' tensions. Inevitably, however, sociality tended to go with ethnicity to a certain extent, superficially because of language. English is the official language of secondary schooling, but the Botswana teachers would talk Setswana in the staffroom, while expatriates used mainly English, or perhaps other mother-tongues.

Cultural 'background' factors also intersected with gender to create different staffroom territories. In UGS particularly, men would tend to sit in one group, women in another: my commenting on this generated joking references to 'Kgotla style' — Kgotla being the traditional court in a Botswans village, where men and women are segregated. The alternative explanation I was given by a male teacher was that the men tended to talk about football. Certainly there was a large contingent of UK male teachers interested in sport who would congregate together at break times; the Setswana department was predominantly female anyway and formed their own enclave.

Hierarchical divisions were not greatly in evidence. Heads of Department receive very little financial advantage, and may have to be persuaded to take the job. When an existing HOD leaves, the successor will most often be appointed from within the department, and the high rate of exchange amounts almost to a rota system. While there were almost equal numbers of male and female HODs if both schools were combined, and a female Head in RBS, the rest of the 'senior management' tended however to be male-dominated. A gendered division of labour was apparent in RBS, with women predominating on the social committee, men on the timetable and sports committees; this may have been a temporary and coincidental feature, but the patterns reflected overall gender distributions and discriminations in Botswana, as revealed through my interviews in the Ministry of Education, statistical collection of post-holders, and analysis of the Teachers' Conditions of Service. Within the school, recognition of the potential sexuality of teachers (Hearn and Parkin, 1987) was conveyed by the prohibitions agreed by Heads in 1982 on 'long-slit skirts' and other revealing clothes.

The majority of teachers nonetheless reported having sufficient social contact with colleagues, and a satisfaction with the internal management structure: many teachers in UGS and virtually all in RBS lived on the compound, which led to a community participation feeling rare in UK state schools. 'There's nothing else to do anyway, so you might as well do something with the kids' (M, local, RBS). It would clearly take a long time to unravel whether the career as opposed to the socializing possibilities for teachers were linked to structural divisions such as those discussed above, but expatriate/local and male/female would seem areas for longer term investigation.

Accommodations and resistances

While aspects of central control might appear to depersonalize teachers, it is salutary to reflect on their own interpretations. Many teachers spoke of the physical problems of transfer, but were able to justify it in terms of a 'needs' ideology. They felt personally selected for a job, even in an undesirable area, and thus were able to reinstate their own sense of worth and dignity. They also recognized the 'fairness' of a system which made everyone do their time in a poorer location. Nonetheless, there was an equal recognition that teachers with the right family 'connections' in the government might be able to influence their own lateral if not vertical movements within teaching. These were termed 'inflammables', those who 'cannot be touched'. Yet the small size of Botswana was seen to militate against too efficient nepotism. Mostly there was 'accommodation' to central control of placements, and a frequent interpretation that a posting meant a personal recognition for the contribution a teacher has made and will make to a new situation:

> 'If the job demands that I move, I move. Nobody told me of the situation here. I think the Education Officer knew, she decided not to tell me anything . . . . I went to the Principal and said, who is the Head of Department? I couldn't find any books. The Principal said, one of the reasons you were transferred here was to help us out. Then I realised I couldn't say no [to becoming Head of Department].' (F, local, RBS)

Resistances to bureaucracy came more in terms of issues like the acquisition of resources. A complex 'votehead' system meant a certain allocation of funds for each area; the 'effective' Head was seen as someone who was skilled at 'creative accounting', and the ability to juggle funds around to get what the teachers wanted for their subjects or activities. 'There are finance courses, but they don't want you to know too much' (F, UK, UGS). The poor Head was thus someone who 'did everything by the book' and allowed the red tape to determine priorities for the school. Effective leadership equating with financial pragmatism would not be peculiar to Botswana, but there are some unusual management training implications, to say the least.

These individualized responses to the system have different motivations and effects from concerted resistance. At the time of the study, Forms 3 and 4 were not yet in school as their exam results were delayed because of a teachers' strike over marking. The strike was ostensibly over the payment and the 'appalling' conditions at the Polytechnic where marking was done. Other observers linked the strike to reactions to the Government not recognizing the creation of a new and more radical Teachers' Union than the original (mostly primary teachers') one. The ramifications of this strike are too complex to go into here, but the interface between teaching and micro- or macro-political activity must be noted as a central component of relations and orientations at the workplace. 'You don't have to have an independent mind. It's a passive life, where you don't voice your grievances. Teaching is worse for this. In teaching you're not even allowed to engage in politics . . . so what people do is quit teaching' (F, local, RBS). There is clearly a difference between readiness to engage in private political critique and to engage in public collective action, depending on the perceived effects and effectiveness; the nature of sanctions also articulates with structural divisions between staff such as the expatriate/local one discussed earlier, for expatriate teachers who had joined the strike had later to withdraw, as their contracts would be under threat.

As in any occupation, teachers are thus concerned about recognition, power, and degrees of freedom. 'Teaching is a very good thing as a profession — it becomes a non-sensical thing when the Government doesn't give you the respect that is due. I think the problem might come from some of us . . . and the Ministry . . . changes not to our liking, not consulting teachers.' (M, local, RBS). Questions are therefore raised not about centralized control itself, but about the *use* of power: whether there is sufficient openness, consultation or safe grievance procedures.

Teachers as storekeepers

While few teachers opposed the ideology (if not the practices) of centralized decision-making, it might encourage a technicist approach to the teaching role which could be seen to parallel the 'deskilling' concepts discussed earlier. At the time of the study, the central issue in terms of teachers' activity was the conversion to a book loan scheme. This entailed thousands of books being numbered in three places and stamped ready to give out to students, and registers made to log names against numbers to guard against theft or mutilation. Much time in departmental meetings was given over to deciding the necessary rotas and procedures for this immense but essentially mechanical work. At these points, free education became an administrative issue, or one concerning the 'intensification' (Apple, 1986) of teachers' work load.

> 'We only discuss targets, timings when to have the exams, when we should
> have covered the books. Maybe we share an idea about teaching a book. In
> training, we've done the major aims. We know what we are doing.' (F,
> local, UGS)

Ironically, the introduction of free education had imposed limits on knowledge: with the government paying for books, it had also laid down what those texts were, proscribing 'additional' titles except as staff copies for reference. Many teachers felt that book loan was in fact anti-educational: when students bought their own books, they not only looked after them, but also could retain them for life. A book loan scheme seemed to underline the transience of school knowledge; it was what Postman

148

and Weingartner would have referred to as the 'vaccination' theory of education, that once you have 'had' a subject, you are immune and need not 'have' it again. Teachers were therefore resisting the commodification of knowledge, and its temporal and physical control by institutions rather than the learner. They also felt that returning the books at the end of the year would alter their mode of teaching:

> 'It will affect the way we work — no holiday working. I have been insisting that students should not be given notes, they should make their own during the holidays. But now there's no time, we just have to tell them things.' (F, local, RBS)

The syllabus, too, imposed time constraints, and acted to routinize teaching:

> 'I know the syllabus well, The only thing is, it gets a bit boring. They should change it only for the teachers! But you always learn a little bit more each year — but otherwise routine . . . you have to hurry through the syllabus, therefore it's a strain trying to speed up, and on the other hand you know you shouldn't do it. In one way it makes it easier — you don't have to think about it.' (M, Germany, RBS)

But are teachers then reduced to mechanical purveyors of 'banked' learning, in the Freirian sense? Do the 'deskilling' trends permeate all their occupational culture? It would be dangerous to assume so, and to ignore the creativity, and insistence on personal autonomy that the teachers articulate. 'We are an exam-oriented society — but the way you get through it is your own affair, for O-level. You can use the textbook or not, depending on how you feel . . . . I'd be insulted if anyone gave me a package' (F, exUK local, UGS). Teachers repeatedly talked of how they set their own targets and objectives, did things their own way, in the order they chose, with or without a course book. Many teachers realized the evils of too much 'accommodation' to the system, of teaching 'without having to think about it', of not preparing because you are 'teaching the same material year after year'; the ultimate horror was then to 'realize that you're not as frustrated as you used to be! So it's time for a change'. Whether or not these blows for freedom represent a real challenge to alienated learning, is open to question; the very 'personalization' of teaching methods, the statements such as 'in the classroom, I am me, I am on my own, I can plan my own lesson', mean by definition little collective or orchestrated campaigns. The analogy is perhaps of each teacher a manager of a minimart, where there is little control over the basic goods in stock, but much autonomy about relationships with customers, about display and presentation, and about what stock are simply loss leaders to be got rid of as fast as possible. Another paradox of 'central' control may be that it pushes some teachers into a determined reiteration of their personal decision-making capacity in the classroom. Other teachers are indeed part of the supermarket chain, accepting the 'quality control': 'I like the standardized curriculum. There's no point in branching out, students would have different notes, wondering what the other students are doing.' (F, local, RBS). The point being made is that government attempts at standardization may unintentionally act to polarize teachers into markedly different types of 'coping strategies' (Hargreaves, 1978). These are likely to be linked to the country and culture of a teacher's initial socialization into the profession, but also to personality; I found no clear patterns of difference.

Occupational rewards and addictions

Yet it is important to acknowledge that the work of teaching is more than a series of semi-connected coping or 'survival' strategies (Woods, 1977). My interpretations of the comments of teachers in Botswana about their home and school lives, and about expectations from the community, indicate that it is misleading to see teaching as the site of a number of what were traditionally termed 'role conflicts'. Responses to questions on 'stress' produced very different answers to those that would be elicited in a country of declining rather than expanding budgets for education. Predictable complaints about resources were always suffixed by the acknowledgement that there had been improvements, or that (as indicated earlier) there were innovative ways to get what was needed. The selective nature of secondary schooling meant that in these schools there were no 'non-examination' groups or students destined for unemployment. Strong competition of students to pass the Cambridge exam well, coupled with traditional respect for the teacher and for school learning itself, meant that motivation or its corollary, deviance, were not problematic.

> 'Part of the culture is more respect for adults; respect for school and qualifications. It's not compulsory, so students see it as rewarding ... but here it's for exams. If you sidetrack off the syllabus, they're not so interested .... But the set-up here: anyone could go in and they'd listen.' (M, UK, UGS)

Or as the Head of Department put it, 'Discipline is making sure they've got socks on.' There was an extraordinary congruence in the aims of teachers and students, which was almost exclusively centred around examination results — individually, and in terms of the school's ranking in the published league table. Classrooms were quiet, ordered places, with no challenge to the choice of work set (another benefit to teachers of the external curriculum). I watched a second form double Maths lesson with forty-two pupils last thing on a Friday, where there was not a single rebuke, exhortation or need for comment by the teacher on any aspect of behaviour or attitude to work during the entire eighty minutes. Total compliance sounds unnerving, but such lessons are to an observer not fearful or unhappy; they merely exhibit a strong 'rule frame' which would give support to the research on 'time on task' as one factor in classroom achievement.

The timing of the school day (6.45am–1.00pm) also appears to mitigate against the build-up of stress. While the eight forty-minute periods would be the same amount of teaching time as in a 9.00am–4.00pm day, if not more, and teachers had occasionally to return on a rota basis for some afternoon 'prep' supervision, psychologically they felt that their afternoons were free, and 'time management' or 'dual roles' were rarely seen as a problem. Teachers living on the compound could also return to their house at any time during the school day if they were not teaching.

> 'And from the family point of view, it's maybe the most flexible job according to Botswana standards, because it accommodates the family. You can operate from home . . . . But you have to know how to organize your time — whether to work at home OR help the children with their homework . . . . We have a live-in servant. Most working mothers, most teachers have home help.' (F, local, UGS)

Teacher burnout was thus not a phrase on anyone's lips; and while pay was not high, it was, compared to some countries, regular. Every teacher is entitled to housing, or housing allowance, and transport if posted. Such benefits are expected: 'I thought tea was supplied by the Government,' remarked one new teacher in surprise, on being asked to contribute to the staff tea club. Any stress at the workplace is a product of material conditions, but also of socialization: the expatriate teachers spoke of feeling guilty if they used 'too much chalk and talk'. One Dutch teacher made the interesting comment that 'here it's very unstressful. It's very unfortunate that Europeans try to build in that stress — even do it in Africa. They try to be better. To compete.'

The satisfactions of teaching were the common and predictable ones of seeing children successfully through their school career, interaction in the classroom, and despite or perhaps because of the exam orientation, an interest in 'the whole child' and their welfare:

> 'I like remedial children. I'm able to exert myself more . . . the reimbursement that I have improved somebody, done something for someone's life. Shaping the lives of young people, showing them things . . . intellectually, morally . . . ' (F, local, UGS)

> 'If I were to leave my job, and do something in an office, the thing I would miss would be the interaction with the students. Moulding them, seeing the outcome. Both a qualifications thing and the kind of person they turn out to be. I would say the personal development is the most important thing to me. I get more interested in the ones who don't pass well — what happens to them.' (F, HOD, local, UGS)

The word 'moulding' was a very common one, and it is here we see the real power base to teaching: the sensation of transformation of the inert clay into a satisfactory and visible product: 'You can see it. You can see the kids doing well.' Perhaps the realization is there that control over the curriculum is secondary to the real control over pupils' futures which comes from the 'hidden pedagogy' (Denscombe, 1980), or the 'culture of individualism' we noted earlier. 'I like the Form Ones — you build them up, channel them. It may be selfish, but you see it happen. You are not detached, you are part of the whole thing.' The addiction to the 'selfish' pleasures of such power means a risk of withdrawal symptoms when feedback is missing, or when the students disappoint: 'The joy is that you see different pupils of different years holding positions. You have been part of their development, their career. Conversely I feel unhappy if they are not doing well . . . or in Sri Lanka, killing each other.' (M, Sri Lanka, UGS). But in these Botswana secondary schools, and in a stable polity, the possibilities for pride in students' achievements were still considerable. Whether that will hold in an expanding system when the race for jobs becomes tighter, remains an open question.

Other aspects of the teacher's power and status to be examined are those of responsibility posts, qualifications and wider prestige in the community. In these contexts it was not possible to record a unified view. As indicated, teachers were not in accord about wanting HODs or senior management positions, but once there, they unanimously enjoyed the responsibility and sense of efficacy. Inevitably, personal experiences determined whether promotion, or selection for further education was seen as 'fair' and without nepotism; everything was relative to the procedures in the last school, or the last country one taught in. Disagreements arose too about the overall status of 'being a teacher'; for UK expatriates, with their built-in comparative methodology, teaching was a higher status and more respected profession in Botswana than it was in the UK; for the local teachers, the status was however seen to be declining. A local 'draftee', who nonetheless was now committed to her work, explained:

> 'I've changed my outlook totally about teaching and teaching as a profession. People think teaching is for dumb people. It used to be status in Africa — teachers were everything — they could preach in church, be magistrates, judges. Now the status has gone down . . . that's when I realized that doing teaching didn't mean you'd done badly in school.'

One of the unintended side effects of rapid expansion of the teaching force, and a centralized 'conscription' of not yet highly qualified personnel, is thus interpreted to be a lowering of automatic respect. Parents, too, become more demanding: a large and desperate notice on the Head's door in UGS read

No Form 2 places
No Boarding places
No discussion on any of the above.
(signed)   Headmaster.

While the curriculum remains standard, and students' response is still predictable, status and deference questions are less consistent, and will clearly influence the ambience in which the work of teaching is carried out, and the extent to which greater recognition for teachers is demanded from Government.

Discussion

If we are trying to relate teachers' cultures to types of state control, the above account perhaps only underscores the complexities. Firstly, certain different aspects of 'central' control have been identified: international examinations as deciders of curriculum; national syllabuses as standardizers and 'routinizers' of official practice; the lateral moving of teachers in terms of transfers; and the vertical moving of teachers in terms of designation to senior positions. Each of these requires different forms of 'accommodation' by teachers to establish autonomy and a sense of worth; and such compromises will develop from both individual biographies as well as structural divisions such as nationality. It is difficult to disentangle the threads of what really determines the daily conventions of teaching and learning: is it the Ministry? Cambridge? Or cultural attitudes to work? Van Rensburg (1978) made the interesting comment on the Serowe people that:

> The general atmosphere and the traditional experience are not conducive to a great deal of hard work . . . historically, wealth is not, in any obvious way, the function of harder work and effort, but of social origin, of how many cattle a man inherited. There was little in the colonial experience to suggest that hard, manual work was the key to wealth, and those who went to the mines discovered that the hardest manual work was the least rewarded.

Such concepts surrounding wealth, and distinctions between manual and mental labour, may influence historically both teaching as work and the motivations of students, which then become enmeshed in a single reality in the classroom ethos.

In addition to different aspects of centralized control, certain differences in the meaning of that control have also become apparent. Firstly, 'centralization' is very different in a nation with small population than it would be in a country like France. The possibility of alienation is less when teachers know the individual Education officers, already know colleagues in a new situation, and have possibly shared the same training at the one college. Secondly, centralization is seen differently in a 'developing' country, where ideologies of service, help and even being 'privileged' to teach are expressed without embarrassment. Thirdly, centralization is different when a system is expanding: a transfer to another school in order for them to benefit from one's experience has much more educational logic than arbitrary redeployment because of falling pupil rolls.

Finally, some contradictions have emerged in the exercise of control of teachers and teaching. While teachers did feel limited by certain aspects of central hegemony (the selection function of education; bars on political activity), in other areas it could be argued that central control promotes greater professional freedom. What appears to be a tightly controlled curriculum process could generate an insistence on individual interpretive freedoms around knowledge transmission, and a conviction of the importance of the hidden curriculum in deciding students' futures. Teachers did not feel disenfranchised by external or central direction. Their own sense of power, we saw, comes from their shaping of students, from using the official bureaucracy to their own ends (whether for school finance or personal dignity), from creative interpretations of the set syllabus, and if necessary from industrial action. This, I would argue, is more than the sub-cultural reactive response of a subordinate or proletarianized group: it represents a positive charge which a government would do well to recognize.

Conclusion and management implications

A report of the International Labour Organization on the employment conditions and work of teachers internationally found that stress and sickness were caused when teachers felt they had no control over management decisions regarding promotions and transfer (ILO, 1981); yet we have seen that the question is equally of whether decisions are seen as fair, logical and open, as much as who makes them. Too much secrecy or arbitrariness will only lead teachers to find ways of subverting or opening up the system, and regaining professionality. In the Botswana study nonetheless, there was no recorded desire for complete school autonomy, in terms of schools deciding movements of staff. This supports the views obtained in Morris' (1977) study of the professional freedoms of teachers in 12 countries, for example:

> It is still possible to confuse autonomy and freedom. In capitalist society, the autonomy of the school does not constitute a guarantee of professional freedom but is more generally sensitive to pressure of all kinds. Autonomy means the introduction of competition into the school, the rat race for promotion, open rivalry in the school.

A decade further on from Morris, Demaine (1988) exposes the ideology of the 'new Right' in UK, and its arguments for a 'market' for teacher labour. It wants financial delegation to go a step further and allow every school to employ its own teachers and set whatever salaries it judges to be appropriate. Introducing elements of a free market into education is supposed to make teachers in 'undersubscribed' schools improve their performance; yet of course, as Demaine points out, this presupposes that teachers can control the outcome of their work in the sense of the level of educational performance of the school. This performance is not reducible to the capacities of teachers, and hinges on many other socio-economic factors. As we saw in Chapter 2, market ideologies will lead to greater divisions both within schools and between teachers. In Botswana, Ministry surveillance over the schools meant that any hostility or scape-goating from teachers (both expatriate and local) seemed to be targetted in that direction, rather than turned inward to personnel and groupings within the school. It is the old paradox that if you want internal cooperation you may have to find an external enemy; but the effect can be to make the workplace a relatively collaborative one. However, as we saw from Ball's 1988 study of industrial action in UK, if senior management are also seen in the role of 'employers', in times of crisis or economic cutbacks internal tensions will ensue as well. Responding to market forces may well work in already well-endowed schools in rich areas: the analysis of ruling class private schools in Australia showed a commonality of purpose among parents, teachers and management and a swift response to any changing demands of consumers (Connell, 1985). Yet, as Third World analyses such as those reflected in Bray and Lillis' (1988) collection *Community Financing of Education* show, the ability of communities to pour additional funds into their schools will significantly influence teacher morale and working conditions, and hence, if indirectly, student performance. The poorest communities, even with basic government grants or 'formula funding', are by and large likely to produce the 'poorest' schools — unless a way can be found to mimic the satisfactions and sense of purpose of ruling class or wealthy schools.

The rationale for management — whether authoritarian or democratic — is therefore to provide a non-market structure in a school within which teachers can exercise sufficient freedom to maintain dignity and a sense of personal efficacy, while not being subject in their work to arbitrary fluctuations of competitive market forces. Even in the relatively prestigious schools in Botswana, the 'good head' was the one able to juggle funds to provide a continuity of material support for the teachers. Schools will always have contradictions, tensions and conflicting interest groups; yet the management 'task' for everyone is to recognize and acknowledge these micro-politics while resisting the trends which would metamorphose them into competitive macro-divisions. Lawn (1988) focuses on the labour process of primary headteachers in UK, analyzing how the recent moves by the State toward specifying curriculum, appraising teachers and enhancing the power of parents has made it so that the school is no longer defined as the head's area of policy. 'So, paradoxically, heads assume a real tightened-up role of selecting and organizing teachers to perform (state) defined tasks and of keeping them effective, yet lose control over the whole school as their domain' (p. 165). In Mexico, interestingly, Farrand finds that the professional responsibility of teachers does not come from the Head at all. It comes from personal/professional influences: their own family, their sense of vocation, their own experience as teachers. This would articulate with the research mentioned earlier on how teachers and their styles of work are largely formed by previous experiences and socialization. The significant point is what happens therefore to motivation: 'This would explain, to some extent, the failure of educational innovations decreed at government level . . . the heads, supervisors and education authorities are not the people who influence the teachers' perceptions of their responsibilities' (Farrand, 1988). This failure is fine if the 'innovation' is regressive or divisive, less so if attempting to be progressive or egalitarian.

NO COMMENT

The 'New Era' is the start of a fresh and bright new outlook. What we need to help us promote this image are ideas and suggestions from all employees (apart from teachers) who could have the drive and imagination to help the City Council save money and/or improve efficiency.
From Salford's *Employee Bulletin*, January, on a new education strategy.

Changes in the labour process of teaching in many parts of the world — new technology, intensification, tighter contractual hours or duties, reskilling and deskilling, new divides or negotiating machinery between 'management' and staff — all require a concerted reiteration of the recognition and status needs of teachers and the overall importance of teacher morale. An analysis of teachers' work therefore should not be undertaken in the interest of the control of teachers, nor merely of the performance of schools. It is properly undertaken so that teachers themselves can 'appraise' and critically reflect on the social relations of their workplace and on their overall relation to the labour market. They must develop their own analyses of how the micropolitics of schools articulate with macropolitics of State economies. This implies teachers being involved in (or at least having access to) collective and convincing action research.

EXERCISE 7: SELF APPRAISAL

The following is a career appraisal schedule to enable teachers to reflect on their work and future; on the organization of the school, and how it meets their needs; and on the relation between home and school life. This can be completed as a form of self-assessment.

A. JOB AND CAREER APPRISAL

1. Which of these statements is nearest to your viewpoint on your career in teaching? (TICK ONE):

   ☐ I have no plans for change and am content to continue the work I am doing.
   ☐ I usually wait to see what happens before I plan the next stage of my career.
   ☐ I identify what I want to do in the future and work out the steps needed to get there.
   ☐ I just try to survive from day to day.

2. What do you hope to achieve during the next year at school? ....
   ....
   ....

   What difficulties would prevent you achieving this? ....
   ....
   ....

   What help or guidance would you require from other staff to achieve this? ....
   ....
   ....

3. What have you done best this year? ....
   ....

4. What have you done least well this year? ....
   ....

5. To improve your job satisfaction and your job performance, what could be done by

   Other people in the school? ....
   ....
   ....

   Yourself? ....
   ....
   ....

6. What do you hope to be doing in

   Three years time? ....
   ....

   Ten years time? ....
   ....

   What might prevent you from achieving these desires? ....
   ....

B. THE ORGANIZATION OF THE SCHOOL

7. What do you want from other people in the organization? Here are eight possibilities. Please rank them in order 1–8 according to which is the most important to you (or add others). ([1] would be the most important to you, [8] the least.)

   ☐ I want recognition for doing a good job
   ☐ I want constructive criticism to improve my job performance
   ☐ I want to be left alone to do the job the way I want
   ☐ I want social contact with my colleagues
   ☐ I want colleagues to do their jobs efficiently so I can do mine
   ☐ I want to be listened to
   ☐ I want to be treated with respect
   ☐ I want to be able to say no without feeling guilty or embarassed
   ☐ I want .... (please state)

8. Of those that you marked 1, 2 & 3, how often is that need met?

	very often	often	sometimes	not very often	never
1					
2					
3					

9. Of those that you marked 1, 2 & 3, how often do you meet that need for other people in the school?

	very often	often	sometimes	not very often	never
1					
2					
3					

10. What do you want from the organizational structure of the school? Here are ten possibilities. Please rank them in order 1–10 according to which is most important to you (or add others).

   I want

   ☐ Many opportunities for joint decision-making through meetings etc
   ☐ An efficient administration that makes my work smooth
   ☐ Efficient communication about the goals and running of the school
   ☐ Opportunities for communication between teachers about their problems, needs and suggestions
   ☐ Genuine concern about the personal welfare of the staff
   ☐ Keen monitoring of teachers' work and commitment to the school
   ☐ A feeling that I am working and planning as a member of a team
   ☐ A feeling that the management is setting high professional standards
   ☐ To be continuously involved in aspects of school management myself
   ☐ An opportunity to practise areas of school management myself from time to time
   ☐ I want .... (please state)

11. Of those statements 1, 2 & 3, how often are these needs met by the organization?

	very often	often	sometimes	not very often	never
1					
2					
3					

12. What do you want for yourself within the organization? Here are 9 possibilities. Please rank them 1–9 in order of how important these personal needs are for you.

- ☐ Reasonable financial recognition or reward
- ☐ Holidays and hours to fit in with other parts of my life
- ☐ The feeling I am doing a socially useful job
- ☐ The awareness that I am transmitting knowledge effectively
- ☐ The daily interaction with young people
- ☐ Variety in work
- ☐ Relative independence to use my own judgement and plan work
- ☐ The feeling that I am a professional in the eyes of the community
- ☐ Caring for the personal welfare of the children

13. Of those statements that you marked 1, 2 & 3, how adequately are these needs met for you by the job at present?

	Very adequately	Quite adequately	Sometimes	Not very adequately	Not at all
1					
2					
3					

14. Look at the following list of typical administration duties. Which do you do often, and how well do you, or would you do them? Please put a 1, 2, 3 or 4 against each according to the following:

1. I do this often, and am good at it
2. I do this often, but not particularly well
3. I do this seldom, but would be good at it
4. I do this seldom, and would not be particularly good at it

- ☐ The timetable
- ☐ Curriculum development
- ☐ Relief or cover for absent staff
- ☐ Supervision of new teachers or students
- ☐ Boys' welfare and discipline
- ☐ Girls' welfare and discipline
- ☐ In-service training of other teachers
- ☐ Careers guidance for pupils
- ☐ Examination administration
- ☐ Arrangements for school visits
- ☐ Hospitality for visitors
- ☐ Organization of special events
- ☐ Pupils' personal problems
- ☐ School finance
- ☐ Responsibility for resources/equipment
- ☐ Home/School links
- ☐ Chairing meetings
- ☐ Organizing extra-curricular activities
- ☐ Running the library
- ☐ Taking assembly
- ☐ Other duties .... (please state)

C. YOUR OUT-OF-SCHOOL LIFE

15. What changes, improvements or directions would you like to see in your social or family/home life in the next five years? ....
....
....

    What would prevent you from achieving these changes or directions? ....
....

16. Do you experience any conflicts between the demands of home and work?

    ☐ A lot
    ☐ Some
    ☐ Very few

17. What could be done to reduce this conflict by:

    members of your family? ....
....

    the organization of the school? ....
....

    yourself? ....
....

18. Do you think you plan your use of time effectively?

    ☐ On the whole, no
    ☐ On the whole, yes

19. Here are ten suggestions that have been made for considering the integration of work and personal life. Please rank these in order 1–10 according to which might best help you to tackle your various roles.

    ☐ A life skills or personal development course
    ☐ Time management training
    ☐ Flexible working hours
    ☐ Parental leave for either mother or father when a child is sick
    ☐ Assertiveness training
    ☐ Career counselling
    ☐ Improved child care arrangements, e.g. workplace nurseries
    ☐ Rotational duties in the school so that no-one feels indispensible
    ☐ A clear specification of your school job and duties
    ☐ Responsibility leave for care of relatives

20. Has filing in this questionnaire helped you to think about ways to improve your working and home life?

    ☐ A great deal
    ☐ To some extent
    ☐ Not a lot
    ☐ Not at all

21. Why, or why not? ....
....
....

Chapter 8

Subversion, Corruption and Humour

In the previous chapter, I argued for teachers articulating their needs as workers; the parallel question which cannot be ignored is, what happens when teachers' needs are not met? According to control theory (Glasser, 1986), we do things only because there is a pay-off, because they are satisfying. It is possible for teaching to fulfil all the levels of the various 'hierarchies' of needs identified by psychologists; on the other hand, if we take Glasser's five needs — survival, belonging, power, freedom, fun — it may fulfil only the first, survival need; and if teachers have not been paid for six months, not even that. Glasser suggests that schools may be unsuccessful because they do not have teacher or pupil satisfaction as a major goal; and certainly 'satisfaction' is not an outcome measure on any of the school effectiveness studies mentioned in Chapter 3.

This chapter therefore proposes the reverse of the school effectiveness investigation: the school ineffectiveness survey. It examines the issue of teacher 'deviance' as a particularly underresearched issue. Much, both from psychological and sociological perspectives, has been written about pupil deviance or indiscipline; far less on indiscipline in the teaching force. It is not a comfortable subject for schools, governments or teacher unions. Pupil deviance can be attributed to home background, maladjustment, the peer group, adolescence, television violence, unemployment and a host of other factors extraneous to the school. It is significant that the first researchers (e.g. Phillipson, 1971) to demonstrate differences in pupil deviance and delinquency as between schools with very similar intakes of children were not encouraged by local authorities to continue the comparison. The realization that there could be something in the school itself which was creating truancy or delinquency was not a feature to be relished. Since then, many studies have shown pupil deviance to be directly related to the selective and labelling function of the school, and such research has clearly acted as a critique of both the overall education system and of individual school régimes which create disaffection among their inmates. Any theorizing on teacher deviance, disaffection or disruption has even more political overtones: it is difficult to attribute serious outbreaks of teacher malaise to individual maladjustment, growing pains or poor parenting. There has to be something wrong with a school's management, or the general administration of education, if those who are supposed to be professional gurus exhibit delinquent behaviour.

Much of what follows is therefore impressionistic and anecdotal rather than stemming from a strong or systematic research base. Nonetheless it begins from the conventional labelling theory framework which focuses on the rule-makers as well as the rule-breakers (see Davies, 1984a). What are the 'rules' by which teacher behaviour comes to be defined as 'normal' or 'deviant'? Who has the power to make those rules, and define others as conforming or deviating? Put another way, in whose interests are the norms for teacher behaviour defined? This may seem like a simplistic question: in the interests of the students, of course. We should however unpack this a little and explore how far it is so. Prohibitions on the sexual abuse of pupils would receive, in all likelihood, international support; yet prohibitions on physical abuse are far less widely accepted. In countries where corporal punishment is considered a natural part of discipline and upbringing, it becomes the 'norm' for teachers to beat children, whether officially or informally. Teachers who then refuse to administer violence are seen as deviant — or soft — by students and colleagues alike. There would clearly in this case be disagreement about what is in the real interests of children, and even some admission that 'discipline' is primarily in the interests of the teachers. As with workers in any situation, there will be competing definitions of the situation, and different 'vocabularies of motive'; there will also be official rules or codes of practice sitting side by side with unofficial or uncodified expectations for teacher behaviour.

It is the codified rules which in fact provide the greatest clue to the possibility of teacher deviance; for as with any legal system, the presence of a regulation, rule or instruction signifies the regular possibility of it being broken. In no teacher handbook is it stated: teachers should not murder the inmates of 4C. Yet staff manuals will routinely contain exhortations for teachers to be punctual, dress in certain ways, and keep registers tidy, in a way which suggests regular deviation from such conventions. Handbooks do not suggest those things which should not be dreamt of. If it were stated 'Teachers are expected to be polite to the headteacher', it immediately implies at least a minority who do not live up to expectations. Books of rules, then, curiously provide the biggest clues to the routine deviance of teachers. They do not codify the unspeakable or the inadmissable or the creative, which are possibly the more interesting.

We should first examine what types of 'offences' teachers are committing, and against what or whom. I shall initially classify them into three, albeit, overlapping categories: deviations from 'professional' convention; infringement of the teaching/learning relationship; and abuses of power.

Deviations from convention

Many of these could be perceived as 'victimless' crimes, in that they appear to hurt no-one directly. Conventions on teacher dress fall into this category, although they sometimes, as with student dress, assume monumental proportions. The rationale for insisting on certain dress codes for teachers is on the surface that of acting as a good example to students; of a distancing from ephemeral things such as fashion; and thus of generally enhancing the professional image of the teacher. The question of different definitions of the situation becomes exemplified by this issue. There may firstly be different perceptions by students and staff. My research into deviant pupils found strong reactions by 'difficult' students to what they termed 'scruffy' teachers — yet these were sometimes men wearing suits and ties and appearing to adhere to the professional convention. Students also showed more hostility to any 'show off' male teachers who would parade their new suit or trendy clothes, and also to female teachers who exposed too much leg when sitting down. For the students, the criterion was cleanliness and modesty; a teacher appearing in a stained, crumpled suit was more of an insult to them than one in the clean casual clothes appropriate to their (albeit ancient) years (Davies, 1984a). It is interesting that uncannily parallel pupil perceptions of teachers were found in the West Indies by Payne. Unpopular teachers were rude, unfair and showed lack of respect for pupils by coming to school untidily dressed or insufficiently washed. Students commented: 'They feel they look good (and they look bad) and do not have any manners . . . . The way they treat students, e.g. butting their heads together and throwing chalk and board cleaners at them, and sitting with their legs open' (Payne, 1987, p. 199). Teachers in a position to comment on student posture, dress or uniform codes should themselves be beyond reproach. Thus current decrees by the government of Botswana that male teachers should wear suits and ties or safari suits have understandably provoked strong reactions in the press by teachers realizing, among other things, the impossibility of keeping such garments clean in hot seasons and rural areas (*Botswana Guardian*, 28.2.89).

Codes that imply the potential for irresponsibility among teachers are therefore a double-edged sword. A teacher dress code may make it easier to instil dress codes into pupils, if that is what is desired. But such codes must be instigated and agreed on by teachers if they are not to create and escalate teacher disaffection. In one girls' school where I taught in Mauritius, teachers all wore a 'uniform' grey skirt; but this had been initiated by the staff themselves as a way of showing sisterhood with the girls, of saving decision-making time in the morning, and avoiding irrelevant competition among staff to be 'well-dressed'. As a self-administered, unifying and egalitarian measure in that particular culture, it worked; had it been imposed by the government, the acceptance and outcome would have been less sure.

The conventions surrounding the image of the teacher clearly change enormously over time, but would tend to be related to control rather than just fashion. Strong control over the teaching force is shown in eras when female teachers were not supposed to be married, or had to leave the force on marriage or child-bearing. The conventions around a teacher's role are strongly linked in certain periods to the need for a cheap, feminized teaching force. For Canadian teachers in the 19th century we note that:

> as 'brainworkers' they also at times toiled manually, beautifying their schools, keeping the path to the schoolhouse clear in the winter, and inspecting girls for contagious diseases. (quoted in Ozga and Lawn, 1988)

Tightened prescriptions on the duties and images of teachers may relate to economic strictures; rejection of such deskilling or depersonalization may thus be a political resistance and a different concept of 'professionality' rather than sheer idleness or bloody-mindedness. It is significant here to note the reaction of UK teachers to 'contractual hours' for work. After the tight control of the 19th century, the 20th century concept of the professional teacher became one who could be relied upon to devote the hours of labour necessary to fulfil a role. The open-ended nature of this ensured a maximum output for many teachers based on an internalized notion of duty and responsibility and a strong commitment to relationships with students. As soon as the insult of contractual hours was introduced, there was the predictable response, by some staff, of 'work-to-rule': teachers would make sure they did their hours and no more, and if the hours had all been used up before the end of the year, that was a problem for the management who introduced the idea, not for the individual teacher. What is astonishing is the belief that putting artificial boundaries around the work of teaching would actually enhance performance. 'Deviant' teachers will now be those few who do not fulfil their contractual obligations; the unknown number of teachers who work to rule will not be categorized as deviant, even if their performance is significantly reduced. This underlines the importance in labelling theory of focusing on the rules by which 'deviance' is defined. The management implications are relatively simple: the more teachers are treated like children, the more they will behave like children. Crackdowns which offend their adult sense of responsibility are unfortunately more likely to erode any remaining professional autonomy.

Infringement of the teaching/learning relationship

More effective perhaps than rule enforcement is the display of 'setting a good example'. This percolates every level of an institution. For example, the research shows a significant positive correlation between teacher punctuality and student performance (Rutter *et al.*, 1979), and between staff satisfaction with leadership and the head's attention to her or his own punctuality (Nias, 1980). Thus the head or teacher who consistently infringes the punctuality rule is directly undermining student achievement — not just through the shortened amount of time for learning, but through the hidden message about commitment to the classroom process and respect for the rights and dignity of individuals. Again from my (1984a) research, I have examples of teachers arriving ten minutes late to a lesson, making no apology to the class and then castigating a student who was eleven minutes late. Just as students will rightly perceive teachers smoking but not permitting students to do so as unfair and arbitrary, students are more likely to adhere to punctuality rules if they see staff do so. Such statements seem so self-evident as not to need reiterating; yet it is astonishing how many teachers in all parts of the world feel able to ignore the 'example' principle and assume that the 'do what I say not what I do' authority will still hold weight. Unfortunately the research indicates them to be misguided.

Breaking the rules about timekeeping, attendance, smoking, drinking, politeness and so on, are therefore significant, not just symbolic deviations from the obligation of a teacher to provide a just and fair environment conducive to learning and student satisfaction. Such rule-breaking is more than merely an infringement of convention. It has the hidden message either that (a) there are different rules for teachers and taught, or (b) there are the same rules, but if you are in authority you are permitted to flout them. Acceptance of either of these messages by students is hardly likely to lead to the internalization of 'responsible' adulthood, which the school is supposed to transmit.

Why then do teachers act in ways which in the long term undermine their own effectiveness? It is like shooting yourself in the foot. One could identify a host of reasons, but three particularly spring to mind. The first is the lack of commitment to the teaching profession, and hence to any outcomes of teaching. Brooke and Oxenham (1980), for example, found high staff turnover, unpunctuality and absenteeism in Mexican primary school teachers. They were not strongly committed to the community where they worked, nor even to the job itself. Not feeling pressure from externally set exams, they needed very strong supervision by the Head. In countries therefore where young people are drafted into teaching, it is clearly more difficult to expect an instant sense of purpose. Drafting, or the 'last resortism' we noted in the previous chapter, is more likely to induce a ritualized minimalism which seeks to 'bend' the rules as much as possible in order to reassert individual control. It is exactly the same effect as compulsory universal schooling without compulsory universal high achievement. People will find ways to make sense of a situation and to maximize satisfactions. If teachers are conscripts, mangement has two options: to make the school like an army barracks, or to turn the recruits into professional soldiers. The first involves tight control — teachers clocking in, signing out and generally being kept on parade. Educational institutions in countries as far apart ideologically as Tanzania and Malaysia have instigated such procedures. The second is more difficult, and means teachers identifying their objectives from teaching, and being aware of their own behavioural norms which impinge on those objectives. The notion of 'teacher as researcher' is significant here, for teachers must not only be aware of the link between teacher conduct and student performance, but actively engage in that observation in the classroom and elsewhere. Clearly this activity requires support and training, not just supervision, from school management.

A second reason why teachers act in ways which undermine their official rationale for educating relates to misguided conceptions of the 'authority' of the teacher. An exposure during schooldays to authoritarian, coercive teachers; a teacher training which stresses control, discipline and dominance; the individualistic ethos mentioned in the last chapter which lays stress on the abilities and proclivities of 'the child'; a transmission model of teaching: all these contribute to the image of the teacher as a single expert broadcaster among a collection of potentially faulty radio receivers. The notion of 'first among equals' does not figure here. If the emphasis is on the teacher as arbiter of externalized discipline, commanding automatic respect, then his or her own personal conduct seems to become immaterial. There are teachers — and parents — who genuinely believe that they have the right, even the duty, to insist on behaviour from young people that they themselves need not practise. Transcripts from my deviancy research record teachers insulting pupils, shouting at them, belittling them, and finally berating them for being 'rude'. The irony of this escapes them. It is as if teachers were merely conduits for the transmission of 'accepted values' and not subject to the same analysis. Beating children for beating each other has the same awful and twisted logic. Askew and Ross (1988) have some penetrating insights into the antecedents of male aggression, pinpointing how boys are 'brutalized' by schooling, and given little chance to express or to see from teachers any other roles than competitive, belligerent or dominating ones.

> **Dear Sir/Madam, We are presently providing courses in self-defence for persons in need of advice in handling one-to-one confrontations.**
> **Demand for courses has grown dramatically over the last eight years and we are pleased to design courses to suit any particular group (ie nurses, bus drivers, teachers, etc).**
>
> Letter from Nottingham School of Martial Arts sent to local educational institutions.

The effect of a lack of caring is compounded when the head or senior management take the same views. A third reason for teacher deviance is the direct example of 'leadership'. An interesting case-study provided by a Malaysian teacher read:

> The school was started in 1973. It had a 3 form entry of about 700 students. The head was not a university graduate. He was only trained in teacher training college for six months. The school had 23 teachers and 3 ancillary staff. The problems were that the head always came late (9 or 10am); we rarely had a staff meeting (perhaps twice a year); there was poor control of teachers and students; teachers went out during school hours to have drinks

for hours; there was a high percentage of absenteeism; there were timetable clashes; teachers had a less caring attitude towards needy students; none of the teachers were university graduates; there were low percentage passes every year.

It is difficult to disentangle whether the ineffectiveness of the head stemmed from the teaching staff he found, but it is more than likely that low teacher morale and commitment will be one direct result of low headteacher morale and commitment. Vulliamy (1987b) found in Papua New Guinea that the syle of administration in a school and the levels of staff morale had a considerable effect on the 'quality' of a school. School facilities, desks, teacher housing and student discipline were all important; but 'one was paramount and that was the importance of the headteacher. The only teachers not to view the headteacher as the most important single factor in determining the quality of a school were some headteachers themselves' (p. 209). The 'ideal' head displayed a number of attributes, of which three are significant for our analysis:

(2) setting a good example, especially with relation to punctuality, and having high expectations of staff and students . . .

(6) being scrupulously fair — this applies especially to national headteachers, who are more open to the charge of 'wantokism' (favouring members of their own language grouping or region) . . .

(7) careful handling of problem teachers. National teachers tend not to learn from criticism, but from advice. Difficulties appear to be best handled verbally and informally, with recourse to written memos only if the problem persists. (Vulliamy, 1987b, p. 216)

The importance of the head in this study appears at first sight to conflict with the Mexican evidence mentioned earlier of teachers' sense of professional responsibility having little to do with the headteacher or the educational hierarchy; but whatever the original source of 'responsibility', it would not preclude its operation in day to day practice being heightened or diminished by the overall ethos of the school. Conflicts between teachers and the administration obviously affect teacher morale: in Vulliamy's study, the staff at one school believed that their poorer Grade 10 exam results one year were partly a product of teacher disunity and the expenditure of school effort on an 'investigation' of the headteacher — which failed to substantiate the allegations being made.

It must be admitted however that problems of teacher deviance may also be traced even further up the system. When teachers have not been paid for six months, teacher housing is inadequate or unfairly allocated, teacher transfers are frequent and apparently arbitrary, then it is difficult for even the most enlightened head to maintain teacher commitment and adherence to 'standards'. System inefficiencies trickle all the way down the structure until even the school cat starts to oversleep.

It is at this point that the phenomenon of 'moonlighting' becomes increasingly problematic. Teachers will take on other jobs to supplement (or replace) their income, to the extent that these start to push teaching into second place. In countries where it is traditional for teachers, as all citizens, to own land, grow vegetables or keep cattle, it is difficult to draw a line between 'a productive homestead' and what is a major occupation. 'Natural' extensions of the teaching role in terms of private tutoring and examination coaching also become more attractive and more remunerative — and often less stressful than classroom teaching. A report on Greece indicated:

> To boost their meagre earnings most teachers have two jobs. Some metamorphose to become boozooki singers, jazz musicians, bar attendants and waiters. [The] general secretary of the primary teachers union said, I know many teachers who sing and dance to make ends meet outside school hours . . . it's ridiculous because it prevents them from doing their teaching jobs properly.
>
> Teachers of popular subjects can earn lucrative bonuses giving private lessons in black market crammers. Hundreds of private cram schools or *frontisteria* have sprung up in response to the scramble for places at tertiary institutions.
>
> This year has seen teachers struggle to upgrade their status and salaries. In one of the longest strikes ever taken, high school teachers walked out for six weeks last summer, abandoning children at their desks and delaying end of year and university entrance examinations . . . (Smith, 1988)

When there is an ideology of self-help, the situation becomes even more complicated. A report on China noted teachers selling pickled eggs and working as dancing partners after school to supplement their wages. However, as in UK, institutions in China are being encouraged by government to find cash through entrepreneurial activities and work-study programmes. The Education Minister

> stressed that work-study programmes should cultivate a love of labour and respect for workers and stated that their aim was not financial gain. It is not clear whether he sees Shanghai teachers selling boiled eggs and ice-cream in order to augment their income as part of the government backed policy' (Sampson, 1988).

We return to the question of who makes the rules: one can solve the 'problem' overnight of teachers (and students) who moonlight by turning it into a valued activity.

A YOUNG teacher has been forced to quit his part-time job at a Birmingham kissogram agency.

Languages master Kevin Arthur, 28, has become so popular in his roles, which included a scantily clad Tarzan, that bookings had come in from pupils at Tividale Comprehensive School.

Mr Arthur eventually left the job after Sandwell education bosses heard of his job at Kiss-Line Kissograms U.K. and decided to investigate.

Mr Arthur was unavailable for comment yesterday, but his headmaster, Mr Alan Birch, who had reported him to the education authority, said he was now under investigation.

Interest

''I saw him on a number of occasions and expressed to him that I didn't consider his job was the sort of work a teacher should be doing in his spare time,'' he said.

Night lectures and sports watching were more usual part-time jobs he said.

Relief milkman wanted for three weeks in August (Wetherby area), suit teacher. References required. Further details, Wetherby 66029.
Advertisement in *Harrogate Herald*

As well as State ideology, teachers may also capitalize on State inefficiency to earn more money. It was found in Columbia after the 1975 Nationalization law that with the fusion of state and national financial systems 'large numbers of teachers had been holding full-time teaching positions in both state and national schools, and sometimes in municipal schools as well. Although such practices were strictly illegal, the lack of coordination between the national and state systems had given rise to it, and the generally low salary scales had encouraged it' (Hanson, 1986, p. 99). Retiring teachers were also therefore trying to claim pensions from two or three 'full-time' jobs.

Teaching is not the only occupation where workers have additional jobs, and this discussion is not undertaken in order to imply a moralistic note of disapproval. It would seem nonetheless that there must be a relationship between the degree of commitment and time a teacher gives to his or her supposedly full-time job and the 'performance' of that job. If governments provide only the equivalent of part-time salaries or schools provide only part-time satisfactions for teachers, then a part-time commitment is only to be expected.

Abuses of power

One of the most disturbing and newsworthy types of deviance is however that of real abuses of teachers' position, either in terms of corruption or of physical or sexual offences against students. Harber (1989) in his book *Politics in African Education* has one of the most fascinating and detailed accounts of the types of corruption, bribery and cheating which counteract the attempted implementation of bureaucratic organization. In addition to the absentee teacher who simply 'didn't feel like teaching', there were teachers and Heads in Nigeria who did not have the certificates they claimed to possess, there was certificate forgery, embezzlement of funds and immoral relations with female pupils. 'The [Teaching Service] Commission found that teachers received salaries unrelated to qualifications and experience and that there were fictitious names on the payrolls' (p. 117).

However, the most widespread form of corruption was cheating in examinations. Whole classes with exactly the same answers (and grammatical errors) reveal teachers' foreknowledge of supposedly secret examination questions, and collusion with pupils to achieve passes. Cheating at entry to secondary school then requires underachievers to have to cheat and bribe their way through WASC* examinations five years later. Barley's account of Cameroon examinations is quoted: 'It is impossible not to smile at the sight of question papers being guarded by gendarmes with submachine guns when the envelope they are in has been opened by a man who sold the contents to the highest bidder several days before.' Ishumi and Cooksey (1985) similarly write of Tanzania: 'Stealing and selling of examination papers happens each year with nationally published criminal court cases resulting ... it is frequently alleged that teachers switch examination numbers around, taking a 'bright' child's number and giving it to a relative' (p. 35). Such abuses of the examination system are of course not confined to Africa, and are a worldwide product of the Diploma Disease and the intense competition for valued qualifications. Cheating is now such an accepted form of attaining high marks that Bangladeshi students have recently staged protests over their 'right to cheat' in public examinations (*Guardian*, 18.3.89). Similarly, Allen-Mills describes a New Delhi secondary school examination thus:

> A small crowd gathered outside [the school]. Several people carried books. Shortly after 2pm, a piece of paper was passed out through a window. Those with the books hurriedly consulted them and soon notes were being scribbled and passed inside .... Behind the window 100 or more pupils were sitting the exam. Outside, in a breath-takingly brazen attempt to secure satisfactory grades, parents, friends and private tutors were helping the pupils to cheat. The invigilator did not intervene. (Allen-Mills, 1989)

With teachers accepting bribes and being susceptible to betrayal of trust, examination boards in India now have to have elaborate coding systems; perhaps 15 different versions of each paper, so that no paper-setter knows if the questions he or she devised will eventually be used; and 'flying squads' of inspectors to check examination centres for the use of cribs. Copies of papers still turn up in bazaars before the exam.

> Subsidiary activities were often in some way connected to the formal workplace. Schoolteachers may sell sweets or snacks to the children . . . .
> One teacher who had a freezer in her school campus accommodation sold iced water to pupils . . . .
> (C. Oppong, on Ghanaian teachers)

Whether there is a moral distinction between the teacher who illegally 'coaches' his or her class for an exam in order to enhance reputations and one who sells questions in order to enhance salary, is a moot point. Either way, the effect is the same: to cast doubt on the validity of the public examination as a fair and just selection mechanism. With the combination of qualification inflation and increased pressure on schools to be 'accountable' (in terms of being judged by examination success), various degrees of shady practices are likely only to increase.

> GCSE candidates: No refund will be made except on compassionate grounds (e.g. death of candidate).
> (Letter to examination centres from Cambridge Local Examinations Syndicate)

In the UK, the abuses of power more likely to hit the headlines however are those relating to sexual offences with pupils. A notable case recently involved a music teacher being sent to prison for ten years for fourteen sexual offences against his pupils. One of his victims — raped by him when she was twelve — committed suicide. The awfulness of the situation was compounded by the fact that although a number of complaints had been filed against him over some years, the authority felt that there was never quite enough evidence for dismissal. He was moved by one authority onto the supply staff; in another authority 'a kind of bureaucratic paralysis allowed him to continue teaching, albeit under the extraordinary constraint that he must not be alone with a pupil' (*Times Educational Supplement*, 14.11.88). The weight of the teacher unions, and the known ease by which unfounded allegations against teachers can jeopardize careers, engender a reluctance to accept the word of children in such cases, and a demand for 'proof'. 'The instincts of the system are to back the teacher' (Wilce, 1988). Disciplinary procedures have now been reviewed, and the concerns about sexual abuse generally in UK have meant more weight being given to children's accounts; but the abuse of trust and authority by teachers and even headteachers remains a problem in many countries. A corporate approach has been suggested (Wilce, 1988), whereby a 'consultative forum' including officers from departments other than the employing one, such as police and social services, would consider a case. Certainly in the instance of a headteacher committing offences, it would be wise to broaden out the disciplinary procedures — especially if that headteacher, as can happen in rural areas, carries considerable local power in the community and could intimidate witnesses. The 'corporate' control suggested by Wilce may be fulfilled in some countries by the Board of Management of a school: Bray cites Papua New Guinea Boards as providing 'a check on the behaviour of teachers' through their ability to report to provincial and church authorities' (Bray, 1988a). Dangers can arise nonetheless if there are too many 'outside' bodies monitoring the school, and a confusion if for example both Boards of Management and Parents' Associations see themselves as responsible. As with any forms of complaint about abuse or harassment, there needs to be adequate and well-publicized grievance procedures, with clear points of contact and defined responsibilities for action (see next chapter): this is even more critical when the victim may be in a powerless and unknowledgeable position.

Grievance procedures only work of course if the arbiters of conduct are themselves relatively objective and unimplicated. When corruption goes all up the system, as with examination fraud, then it is difficult to see where to turn. Before the 1968 Reforms in Columbia

> a particularly notorious personnel practice developed in numerous states around election time: hundreds of teachers were hired on the basis of their political loyalty rather than for their teaching ability. In addition, it was not uncommon for a governor to hire hundreds of teachers (sometimes the day before he left office) when there was no money in the budget to pay them . . . there was little fiscal accountability. Phantom schools were even known to exist. Money was sent to pay their teachers' salaries, but in reality, these schools were merely the product of creative bookkeeping. (Hanson, 1986, p. 73)

Such gross abuses will now have been eradicated; but 'creative bookkeeping' remains an ever-present temptation throughout the world. Whether Local Management of Schools in UK will provide greater or lesser opportunity for such 'creative' endeavour will be the subject of interesting research.

Management implications

The mechanisms for dealing with teacher deviance are therefore as varied as the 'crimes' themselves. Preliminary questions by a manager might revolve round

(a) what 'rule' is being broken? Who made the rule? Is it unofficially accepted?
(b) who is the victim?
(c) what teacher need is not being satisfied? Is it a need worth satisfying? Is the school management in a position to satisfy that need?
(d) what 'deviancy' procedures are known and agreed upon by members of the school? At what level can the rule-breaking be dealt with?

In the civil service, when speaking of 'administrative control systems', distinctions are made theoretically between 'performance/motivator' mechanisms and 'detector/corrector' mechanisms (Reeves and Woodward, 1970). The former refer to the means by which an organization motivates and directs staff performance, the latter to the means for ensuring that what should have been done has been done, and identifying discrepancies and taking corrective action. However, in a study of Birmingham City Council, C. Davies (1984a) found the detector/corrector mechanism having limited effectiveness. Section Heads would comment on poor work or on work attitudes perceived as disruptive, but if critical comments failed to bring about an improvement, the next step was the major one of initiating formal disciplinary action. ' "Correction" thus becomes confrontation, a process which may not be suited to all Section Heads' style of supervision and which therefore they may wish to avoid, with a possible consequence of lower work output by the staff members concerned' (Davies, 1984, p. 69). Davies argues that in fact the more essential task is to motivate, and to utilize the self-commitment of employees to shift away from correcting devices to the performance/motivator mechanism — incentives, minimizing hierarchies, participation and acknowledgement of work done. Similarly, in schools and education systems, analyses should be made of what informal and formal mechanisms are available for 'correction' and whether more emphasis can be placed (except in the case of abuse) on 'motivation'. It may not be in the power of Heads to fund salaries, or even to provide a post of responsibility or promotion. Hence Glasser's categories of needs we mentioned at the beginning — survival, power, belonging, freedom and fun — cannot all be met by school management alone. Financial survival and formal power may be outside the Head's remit. Nonetheless, belonging, freedom and fun are free; and so is recognition, whether in terms of informal praise and acknowledgement or in terms of formal appraisal.

> **Trespass on Educational Premises. The notices warning persons against trespass, prepared under the provisions of Section 40 of the Local Government (Miscellaneous Provisions) Act 1982, have now been revised to include specific prohibition of dogs, motorcycles, and golf practice.**
>
> From Humberside Education Bulletin, July 13, 1988.

Fun

The 'fun' element is often overlooked in educational theory and in management literature. Exceptions would be Stebbins (1980) or Woods (1984), and the hints from much of the research on pupils' perceptions of schooling that the 'good' teacher is one you can 'have a laugh with' (Meighan, 1978, Davies, 1984a). Children will use humour as a weapon in the classroom, and woe betide the teacher who over-reacts and is unable to take or return it. Blishen's wonderful account of his first year of teaching bears this out:

> On another occasion, tormented by his class nearly to the point of flight, I saw that Maggs was busy reading something under his desk.
> 'Bring that out here!' I shouted, 'and I'll tear it up!'
> 'Oh Sir!' he said softly, and handed me a New Testament.
> 'You were reading this?'
> He jumped to attention.
> 'Yes, sir! I'm a Christian now, sir. Mr Fish made me one on Sunday.'
> 'Mr Fish?'
> 'At church, sir.'
> And for days after this Maggs trotted round the school with tracts under his arm, where, a week before, comics had been. It gave him great pleasure to have them confiscated in the middle of a lesson.
> 'Don't tear them up, sir', he would say, piously, to one discomfited master after another. (Blishen, 1966, p. 60)

The teacher who cannot take a joke against himself or herself is in the same straits as the humourless headteacher or school manager. The desire by staff to debunk, to deflate and to subvert is very strong if a head pulls rank, is pompous and takes himself or herself too seriously. This is not to say heads should not have serious objectives, views and goals; but there is a distinction between taking issues seriously and taking one's own divine rights seriously — particularly if these are seen as the rights to bore, to waste teachers' precious time, or to tell untruths. At interview for my second teaching job, the Head told me he knew every child in the school by name, and how it was a purposeful musical and artistic community. I was impressed. At my first morning break in the new school, the teachers asked me how I thought I would like it. I explained that my last school was somewhat large and impersonal, and I was pleased that here the Head knew every child in the school by name, The staffroom dissolved. They were beside themselves. Wiping tears from their eyes, they explained that the Head could barely remember his own name, let alone the staffs', and never, ever the childrens'. 'What else did he tell you?' they asked, enthralled. 'Well, about the thriving school orchestra . . . .' I replied, uncertain. That finished them. They could hardly make it back to their classrooms for mirth. Later I was to discover the orchestra — two recorders and a half-size cello — in a cupboard with the equally (thankfully) defunct cane. The point of the story is that in fact that school survived in spite of the Head rather than because of him; but it survived through the teachers' ability to joke their way out of every impasse and frustration. Humour and laughter is a serious business, and should be part of the job specification and appraisal for anyone in the education business — not least for management. Woods (1984) points out the important functions of laughter in the staffroom as a means of neutralizing excessive bureaucracy, of subverting or compromising senior personnel and of promoting solidarity among staff. 'Laughter is an enormous aid to solidarity, and in the harshness of the conditions in which teachers work it is important that they have this support' (p. 193). Staff humour is able to ridicule school rituals of assembly, sports days, fire drills, and expose their pretentiousness. Long-standing jokes are sometimes developed out of nothing in particular, and are not always just a release of tension, but an act of creativity. Woods also identifies the 'laughter inhibitors':

> Thus the psychological and physiological state of the teacher, perceived injustices, the undermining of status, threats to equilibrium, interdepartmental and interpersonal rivalry or hatred, and the obstruction of routes to secondary adjustments, all work as blockages to laughter, either dispelling its efficacy or pre-empting its use. But these all imply breakdown or non-survival. They represent cracks in the system. Invariably they are repaired by humour, or at least humour is a sign of its repair. Laughter is the coping mechanism *par excellence*. Lack of it might suggest non-survival. Its presence is a sure indication of managing. (p. 202)

The implication is that the effective manager might 'appraise' the extent of school effectiveness through a 'laughter quotient'; or at least that she or he might find cause for concern if days passed without significant laughs from the staff. Humour *by* management is a risky business if staff do not find their jokes funny, or have heard them before; but as Stebbins points out:

> Any form of humour with a subject or audience communicates the message that those people are worthy of some sort of attention, favourable or

unfavourable. Humour that works to promote consensus indicates to the audience (and perhaps the subject) that they are worthy of sharing an atmosphere of good cheer with the humorist. Moreover, such humour tends to convey, albeit only temporarily, a degree of equality between humorist and audience. While they are laughing together at something, status differences are momentarily forgotten. (Stebbins, 1980 p. 95).

Stebbins is referring primarily to teachers' use of humour with students; but the same principles apply to management and staff. Humour is the great equalizer, and should feature prominently in any school or institution.

The problem however is deciding what can be dealt with lightly and what requires heavy treatment, what can be joked about and what offends. Sexist and racist jokes are invariably offensive to someone; and jokes made by teachers at pupils' expense backfire as much as jokes made by superiors at subordinates' expense. Humour in management terms involves laughing at yourself; and not turning potentially serious issues such as harassment into occasions for ribaldry.

A nice example from Lesotho of 'fun' treatment for deviance might nonetheless conclude this section:

One day we discovered that many students and staff were eating fruit from the orchard. I was told by the offenders that they were not stealing because 'they were picking the fruit in broad daylight, so that everybody could see them'. The local farm manager and I decided to spray the whole orchard with clean water, while covering ourselves in heavy protective clothing, masks, gloves etc. Afterwards we let it be known that the trees had been sprayed with an unusually high dose of metasystox, an extremely dangerous poison. Everybody was warned not to eat any of the lethal fruits. In fact, nobody did for quite some time. The manager and I had a lot of fun and this helped bridge the many cultural differences between us. (Zijp, 1983)

Conclusion

It is self-evident that the different levels of deviance outlined earlier require different levels of response. Some are behaviours directed at meaningless rules and are best left alone. Some are 'fun' attempts at subversion, and can be contained at the 'fun' level without escalation. Deviance which affects student learning and hence student satis-factions (such as absenteeism or inadequate preparation) might be tackled by the same principles as with children: persuasion; behaviour modification (rewarding instances of 'good' behaviour to build up effective habits); sliding scales of reprimands and warnings. Teacher deviance is both an efficiency and an equity issue. It is clearly inefficient by any performance standards if teachers do not do the job for which they are paid. It is also inequitable, in that some teachers will be working harder than others, or gaining more school or community resources than others. Inequality arises also in that at least part of what I would construe as teacher deviance will be infringements of some pupils' basic right to a humane, non-violent, non-sexist, non-racist environment. In a democratic school, where decision-making is shared, it should however, not fall to the Head to be the sole arbiter of behaviour. Teachers themselves should be deciding their norms of conduct and how extreme deviations might be sanctioned. What you do if the whole staff is corrupt is, however, anyone's guess.

The concluding exercise is designed to see if what works for seven-year-olds works for adults — taking responsibility for one's own behaviour, and using group solutions to decide 'normality' and its permitted standard deviations.

EXERCISE 8: CONCEPTS OF 'DISCIPLINE'

1. Read these two extracts.
2. Summarize the main principles involved in deciding discipline in the first.
3. How far could these be applied in other instances, such as the second?

Those of us unfamiliar with infant and primary schools cannot grasp the importance of toilets to the smooth running of the institutions.

Take the proclivity of small boys to make puddles on the floor — what would you do if a seven-year-old complained ''there's wee all over the place, Miss''?

I would summon the caretaker and issue an edict to all the little boys in my charge: ''Thou shall not wee on the floor — or else!'' And if I caught the culprits, I fear that they might receive a thick ear.

That, apparently, is not the way to do it and I am grateful to Joan Webster, head of the Cavell First and Nursery School in Norwich, for putting me right.

She had two youngsters coming to her a few years ago upset about the loos. They used a less polite word than ''wee'' and asked Miss to do something.

Mrs Webster declined and suggested they spent the weekend discussing the problem before coming to see her again on the Monday morning.

Monday arrived and youngster number one announced that he and his friend were going to make a notice: ''Please do not wee on the toilet floor, thank you, signed . . . ''

The notice went up and all was well for a couple of weeks but, alas, the puddles returned and the two boys asked the head if they could have some time in assembly.

Permission was granted and the entire school was lectured by the two. To this day the toilets have remained dry.

It all sounds a little too good to be true but Mrs Webster insists that the

most effective way to run a school is to give pupils as many opportunities as possible to make decisions for themselves. She calls it ''talking out'' and *The TES* was at her school to see it in action.

It was an encouraging start to the day for a journalist. Scrawled on the school wall the message: ''I love you''. What to do with the culprit?

The spelling was correct so no need for remedial attention for the young Romeo, but graffiti is frowned upon so action had to be taken. Congratulate him on his grammar while reprimanding the breach of rules? Ask who the lucky lady is?

Mrs Webster explains: ''I had a word in assembly explaining that I didn't want to find the culprit, only ensure that it didn't happen again.''

The theory is that the kids will listen and then ''talk out'' the problem among themselves before coming up with a solution.

So it was that poor old Leon had to face up to the consequences of his crime and with his classmates take action to cleanse the offending slogan.

There would have been no point, insists, Mrs Webster, in any adult laying down the law. That's the way to produce automatons — children so unused to thinking that they have to ask: ''Please Miss, can I sharpen my pencil?''

After toilets, ''to sharpen or not to sharpen'' is the major issue at the lower end of the primary school. Gill Coathup, deputy to Mrs Webster, and ''talking out'' co-theorist, says that boys and girls with blunted pencils tugging at teacher's skirt is an everyday occurrence. And an unnecessary one if only teachers would trust the young to

take decisions.

Mrs Webster arrived at Cavell school four years ago and discovered 150 five to eight-year-olds running around the playground knocking each other over. A noisy place and sometimes violent one. This is not to make it sound like the Red Lion at chucking out time but to emphasize that there was a lot of aggression in the air.

A lot of aggro and a traditional attitude towards it, especially from the dads — ''If he kicks you, kick him back.'' The teachers patrolled, issued orders — NO FIGHTING — and did their best. But their best, says Mrs Webster, was not enough because as long as the restraint was external (teachers) rather than internal (pupils) the aggression could at best be contained, but never eradicated.

The key was to convince the children that they were responsible for their own behaviour. They had to be taught to take decisions.

But first, decisions were taken for them: ''We scrapped lining up and sitting in rows.'' Think about it and you will see why. If teacher instructs ''line up'' the pupil is freed from responsibility for taking a decision as to when and how he, or she, should enter the class.

So. They have no formal opening time at Cavell, no formal playtime either. A break, yes. But pupils decide whether they go out, stay in the class, visit the library. And they go to the toilet when they wish and sharpen their pencils when they need to do so.

It could be the Cavell First and Nursery School Teacher and Pupil Co-operative — Bennism alive and well in the middle of a Norwich council estate.

From Hugill, B. ''Peeved Peers and Puddles'' *Times Educational Supplement*, 17 February, 1989.

THE DISCIPLINE MASTER

Mr Syed, the new principal of the high school, was seated in his office waiting for Mr Lim to keep his appointment. As he waited, the principal recalled the problems he had encountered with Mr Lim, the school's discipline master, and pondered about how he should deal with the situation.

At first, Mr Syed recalled, he had been pleased to allow Mr Lim, an experienced teacher, to organise the school discipline, but later a number of incidents gave him cause to be concerned. Although students were not allowed to leave the school premises during school hours — 7.15 a.m. to 1.00 p.m., without permission of the principal, Mr Syed had met a student leaving the school. On investigating, the principal found that Mr Lim had sent the student to the Union's office on an errand concerning Union affairs. When Mr Syed discussed the incident with Mr Lim he was assured that there would no recurrence of the breach of regulations.

In another instance students complained that Mr Lim consistently came late to classes and at other times never came at all. Teachers too complained that Mr Lim's class was extremely noisy when they were teaching next door. The principal's investigation resulted in him teaching the class in Mr Lim's absence. The discussion with Mr Lim concerning his unsatisfactory behaviour produced the desired outcome and Mr Lim had been on time to all his class since.

A few days ago Mr Lim had requested permission to go home during school hours to care for his son who was ill and home alone. However, the principal now knew that instead of going home Mr Lim went to have his car serviced at a garage and had not spent the remainder of his time at his home. And, yesterday, a form five student, Ahmad had complained that Mr Lim had slapped him because his hair was longer than the specified length. Mr Lim, an experienced discipline master, should have known that the regulations did not permit him to slap a student. Today, Ahmad's father had complained about the slapping of his son, whose conduct over the years had always been reported as good.

A knock on the door signalled the principal that Mr Lim had arrived and he drew a deep breath before calling ''Please come in!''

DISCUSSION

As Mr Syed, the principal, what would you do?

(From: *The Commonwealth Casebook for School Administrators: Case Studies in Theory and Practice*, Commonwealth Secretariat, 1982)

Chapter 9

The Management of Equity Policies in the School

Notice spotted on a school noticeboard: 'If you think you have a problem, you should see the headteacher'.

This chapter argues that it is not in fact enough for heads or senior management to react to equity problems as they arise. More systematic and forward-looking policies are necessary to counter the inexorable tendencies for social inequalities to be reproduced in the education system. It must be acknowledged from the outset that there are dissenting voices, based on the doubt as to whether we should 'dump' problems of equity on the school. Is this equal opportunities on the cheap? Does focusing on the school's role draw attention away from the real culprits in the uneven distribution of resources — extremes of capitalism, patriarchy or colonialism? Are teachers already overloaded, with their work increasingly intensified? Does equity provision become yet another guilt-inducing duty of the teacher to add to the current academic, pastoral, technical, extra-curricular and accountability pressures?

It might well be all these things. Our survey of equal opportunity provision in higher education in UK (Williams, Davies and Cocking, 1989) indicated that those institutions that had effectively implemented any policy and made any change had developed quite formalized structures — an equal opportunities committee or working party, or a designated officer. It would seem that equal opportunities cannot be left to goodwill or interested individuals, but requires participatory structures and constant monitoring. This means meetings. And work. And discussion. And work. And vigilance. And work. Teachers already soon reach what has been termed 'decisional saturation', whereby they cannot cope with any more participatory meetings on top of the daily decision-making of their 'normal' role. We should therefore examine the various possible structures for equity work in a school in the light of this concern for the burden of the teacher. It will be argued nonetheless that an equity concern is not just an 'add-on' sprinkling for the top-soil, but should permeate the deep layers of school life. It should also create a richer loam and better quality growth, not just because of reducing inequalities among teachers, but because, if taken to its logical conclusion, it makes school a more 'satisfying' place for all members. Initially, however, until a concern for equal rights becomes automatic for all, the specific efforts of determined people will probably be required.

Titles for the base

Does it matter what we call the person or group mandated to promote equity? I once saw a spoof 'Instant Jargon Generator' which gave three columns of words and suggested picking three numbers at random to come up with combinations such as 'Instructional Simulation Subsystems' or 'Programmed Implementation Module'. In like vein, here are the common possibilities: try picking any number from each column:

1. Equal	Opportunities	Committee
2. Race	Equality	Unit
3. Women's	Affairs	Coordinator
4. Gender	Awareness	Working Party
5. Multicultural	Policy	Programme
6. Anti-racist	Rights	Group
7. Disadvantage	Concerns	Sub-committee
8. Minority	Education	Task force
9. Social Divisions	Value	Convenor

However, this exercise is not to trivialize the issue. Names are important, and the most crucial column is in fact the central one, which indicates less who is to do what to whom, but the philosophies and political underpinnings of the action. While I have worked in activities labelled 'equal opportunities' for more than a decade, I am increasingly aware that the notion of 'opportunity' can be used as a justification for continuing inequality of the grossest kind. The old joke that equal opportunity is simply the opportunity to become unequal is never more true than when arguing the access versus outcomes debate: given people's 'natural' inequalities, is not all we can aim for the genuine opportunity to reach their 'potential' (whatever that might mean)? The notion of 'opportunity' derives from the competitive, aspirational materialism of many cultures, not just western ones. It implies that the central function of the school is to provide chances, nor satisfactions. It assumes a context of limited openings, not inalienable rights. It devolves responsibility onto those who should take up the 'opportunities' preferred to them. We get a different picture if we argue for equal value or equal rights; the fact that this is seen as much more political and contentious shows how bland and unthreatening equal 'opportunity' can be. It is, of course, just for this reason that it may be advisable initially to depict one's work in this manner. I shall to begin with retain the term 'equal opportunities', or the shorthand 'EO', to describe current endeavours, as this is how provision is commonly named in schools and workplaces. In the long term, however, it may not solve the dilemmas around equity provision which we shall look at later.

Composition

Once it is decided to instigate an EO focal point or structure in a school, what should decide its composition? Possibilities are usually some combination of:

— self-selected interested individuals
— senior representatives from each of the major groupings (e.g. heads of department or heads of house)
— voluntary representatives from each of the major groupings
— a quota representing the gender/ethnic/disabled etc. balance on the staff
— the existing senior management team plus interested individuals
— one coordinator with power to coopt or ask support
— a balance of academic and support staff, or balance of mental and manual workers in the organization
— representatives from the Unions
— community representatives
— equal representatives from staff and student body

We can see the usual tensions between voluntarism and compulsion, between grass-roots and authority status. It might be thought on the one hand that people really interested in the work will do a better job than those drafted in because of their position. On the other hand, it could be argued that the way to get people interested and committed is to coopt them and give them jobs to do. Similarly, there is the argument that equity work in particular needs to stem from the 'popular' level, an argument matched by the knowledge that such grass-roots initiatives may falter unless commitment from 'the top' is built in.

My view and experience is that such bodies must be 'representative' at the broadest level, even if this generates varying degrees of commitment by participants. Anyone who has studied feminist strategy for influencing meetings will know that the mathematics of committees means that a group as small as three can swing a committee of ten if the three are united and the rest undecided or unorganized. Assuming enough faintly knowledgeable people in the team, they should be able to 'educate' the rest. For both ideological and experiential reasons it is clearly particularly crucial that students are represented — and at more than a token level.

Terms of reference

A committee or officer will then have to specify their terms of reference, for consultation and agreement by the whole staff. This will include some of the following:

1. *Formulating a policy statement.* At the beginning of equal value work usually comes some statement of intent. It involves a pledge, or commitment or reiteration of basic philosophy. Examples are 'X institution is an Equal Opportunities Employer. It undertakes not to discriminate on the basis of (sex, race, class, political views, sexual orientation, disability, marital status, family responsibilities, etc.)'. More realistic are perhaps those statements that admit 'X institution is striving to be an Equal Opportunities Employer', recognizing that the process towards equal value is a long and slow one, and premature claims to purity should not be made.

Other statements will at the outset specify that not only will the institution not discriminate in future, but that it will undertake a programme of positive action to rectify previous imbalances or injustices. It is important to get these statements both as full as possible and agreed by preferably a majority: they should form the basic reference point for all the activities that follow. They can of course in themselves be counterproductive, in that having spent many hours thrashing out the policy statement, and publicizing it, there can then arise complacency that everyone's heart is

in the right place, and nothing more need ensue. It should be acknowledged that they are not merely descriptions of a present stance, but indications of an active future.

2. *Translating pre-determined policy.* Single institutions may of course be operating within a wider set of policy initiatives. In UK, state schools and colleges (not higher education) will generally be working in the framework of the Local Authority policy, and may have to adhere to their guidelines. Thus an institution may simply reiterate an Authority policy on equal opportunities, or add riders to suit local conditions. Teacher unions may suggest 'Model Guidelines' for members to follow. In centralized systems, governments may issue directives about equity work or policy, although, as indicated in Chapter 3, these can be vague statements of a commitment to equality rather than guidelines to individual schools for positive action. Conversely, government statements can be absolute directives to schools, in terms of making curricula compulsory for all, or determining quotas or differentiated pass marks for entry to a particular level of education. I know of no Third World government that has issued a set of guidelines to all schools in terms of action they themselves might take to work for equity within their own institution.

3. *Monitoring.* A first task of any EO group is to start to keep track of who is where and who gets what. Thus statistics must be kept of the proportions of male/female and of different ethnic groupings in terms of:

(a) students: (i) in applications, if appropriate
(ii) at entry
(iii) at exit (including drop-out rates)
(iv) in subjects/courses/options
(v) in examination results
(vi) in destinations (jobs, further education)

(b) staff: (i) in applications
(ii) in interviews
(iii) in acceptances
(iv) in transfers
(v) on roll
(vi) in different curriculum areas
(vii) in levels of seniority

Monitoring is of course fraught with difficulty. While it is relatively easy to ensure gender information on records, and to extract it, ethnic monitoring is complicated by the number of categories needed, the elusive boundaries around these categories, and the sensitivity attached to asking and stating ethnic or national identity. As with debates on whether ethnic origin should be asked for on census forms, there are suspicions by ethnic minority communities as to what this information will be used for, and by whom. It seems contradictory to insist that race and sex will not be taken into consideration for jobs or study and then to insist on this information on application forms and records for monitoring purposes. The conventional solution is to have application forms in two parts: the first, which goes on to the selection panels, contains only the information relevant to the job or course: name, qualifications, experience, and reasons for applying. The other part contains the information for monitoring, and is removed and kept in separate records. This would contain gender, ethnic origin, age, marital status, nationality, number of dependents and so on — all the information needed to check in a general way as to whether people with particular attributes are being over- or under-represented in certain areas. It will be noted that I put 'age' into this section on dimensions normally irrelevant to the job or study course: as we saw in Chapter 1, the use of maximum levels of age as a selection factor can act as indirect discrimination if certain groups of candidates are likely to be older (because of marriage, child-rearing, teenage pregnancy, etc.). It is important that precise requirements for acceptance are thought through — if necessary such as physical fitness or mental alertness — rather than inaccurate proxies such as 'age', which can exclude potentially suitable candidates. For jobs, insisting on youth is of course a way of depressing salary levels; but it perhaps ought to be up to the candidate to decide whether or not to accept a salary 'commensurate' with age.

The negotiation around the information on these monitoring records will, however, occur mostly around ethnic origin. In UK, the ethnic categories and identifications which have been tested for the 1991 Census are: White; Black Caribbean; Black African; Black Other (please describe); Indian; Pakistani; Bangladeshi; Chinese; Any other ethnic group (please describe). The country of birth is also asked. Educational institutions have taken similar divisions, acknowledging that they are far from perfect, and will inevitably cause a degree of confusion, inaccuracy or offence. Of crucial importance in any country is to have consultations where possible with representatives of different ethnic communities to determine what categories are acceptable and meaningful to them, and to explain the positive purposes behind asking the questions.

Even more ill-defined categories such as 'social class' are virtually impossible to include on monitoring, unless one records father's or mother's occupation. The elusiveness of 'class' as a category is one reason why, as discussed in Chapter 3, the focus in actual policy and monitoring has been on gender and race, in spite of the bracketing of gender, race and class, and of the initial sociological concern in the 1960s and 1970s with social class outcomes. Thus the official monitoring may well not include all the categories of potential discrimination mentioned in the policy statement, and it is important to make that clear.

4. *Research.* In addition to quantitative data, the other form of monitoring is qualitative research and espionage. If the statistics reveal discrepancies in gender

achievement or ethnic minority access to the next level, a deeper analysis is required of the hidden processes in schools and classrooms which may contribute to such unevenness. This may take the form of observational research or of action research, even if the boundaries between them become blurred. Observational research might involve a teacher being invited to watch another teacher's class in order to trace the gender or racial dynamics of that class in terms of interactions between students, or between teachers and students; the way space is used; who asks and answers questions of whom; who is praised, criticized or ignored. Action research involves a more directly interventionist approach. It requires trying to change a situation while researching the effects of that intervention. An example would be the interventionist research is of course a bit like trying to push the bus you're riding in; but it relies on programme in a school designed to encourage more girls to think about non-traditional careers. The most instructive and unexpected part of the research was noting the changes in attitude necessary from the (male) teachers who had to use the new curriculum materials with the girls; action research can uncover barriers and causations in a way that conventional 'attitude' questionnaires never can. Action research is of course a bit like trying to push the bus you're riding in; but it relies on the cooperative ideal in terms either of collaboration between 'teacher' and 'researcher', or the notion of 'teachers-as-researchers'. If more than one is involved, at least one person can hop out of the bus at intervals to record and reflect. Action research can of course include 'students-as-researchers', and children as young as 8 or 9 can act as interviewers and generate their own data (Pollard, 1985). Students investigating inequality in their institution will be seen as even more threatening than teachers doing the same thing; but it is possibly the most direct way to create 'awareness' and to challenge outdated restrictive practices.

5. *Rolling Programmes.* As with any programme requiring a feedback loop, equity prgrammes can never be anything other than provisional, dependent on the next

One last thought. Whatever has happened to the women footballers? You can't make an excuse like this anymore.

round of monitoring, evaluation and review. Nonetheless it has been found important to put names to procedures. It is not enough to say 'everyone must be watchful about discrimination' or 'government should make sure enough women are appointed'. An action column on the committee minutes plus a 'sell-by' date will put the spotlight on the responsible bodies for particular activities under the programme. A mythical example would be:

Item 4: *EO Policy*	*Person*	*By (date)*
Library to check number of books written in mother tongue, and provide list for purchase	Mrs Jones	Jan 30th
EO Committee to provide definitions of sexual harassment for next meeting	Convenor	Feb 5th
Report on liaison with college re access course for mature learners	Dep. Head	Feb 1st

We see the reason why formal structures become necessary: committees need to have to report to higher committees, and/or to have powers and preferably a budget delegated to them. The actual activities around equity will not all be spelled out in the rolling programmes, but may include curriculum review; new curriculum initiatives such as Black Studies, Gender Studies or mother-tongue teaching; staff training; new clubs/activities; careers advice; staff seminars; or assertiveness training.

6. *Setting targets.* A way to galvanize action is to decide where you want to be and work backwards from there. Quotas involve positive discrimination in favour of a particular group, and override 'normal' criteria for treatment. Targets involve positive action to enable certain figures to become reality, which may include helping people to meet those 'normal' criteria, rather than to bypass them. The Borough of Southwark for example has set recruitment targets for its education service of 50 per cent women, 30 per cent black or ethnic minority membership and 6 per cent with disabilities by 1995. This is a long lead time, but represents a realistic effort to match the existing dynamics of the community with future representation in the service. Targets arouse less backlash and less labelling of 'substandard' or 'remedial' than quotas; they also have a hidden message of conviction that there are or will be sufficient 'able' people in particular groups to fill suitable slots. Targets permit debate on the possibility of ethnic or gender membership being a criterion for selection in itself, in addition to regular qualifications: hence if one is aiming at a certain proportion of women headteachers, just being a woman may give you certain brownie points to compensate for perhaps less formal managerial experience. To justify this, it is essential to have established firm benefits (perhaps for students' perceptions of authority) of having women headteachers, in addition to the 'equal rights for women' argument. Otherwise it smacks of quotas. The point is that targets should be less rigid, arbitrary and divisive

than quotas, in that the real reasons for wanting to change a balance are always kept in the forefront and reviewed.

7. *Giving Advice.* It is significant how soon an EO Committee can become a counselling service: all sorts of related — and unrelated — problems and anxieties start to be brought to their attention. I do not think it is just 'problem creation' in the way that the establishment of a remedial department or a sin bin will overnight have to find previously unsuspecting students to put into them. It is more that sanctioning equal value as a worthwhile activity can bring to the surface very deep concerns that teachers have about their dealings with students, dealings that relate to the 'warming up' and 'cooling out' dilemmas mentioned in Chapter 1. In sensitive times, the need for reassurance about when discrimination is positive and when negative, or even when particular nomenclatures (such as Black) are acceptable or not, is very strong. Designated EO people may find themselves confronted with people's unnamed fears, as well as their old grouses. Unsatisfactory phenomena that previously were not even seen as able to be groused about, such as sexual harassment, will also start coming to the surface. There should be a government warning on all cartons of EO policies: this policy can seriously damage your time. I recently received a serious memo complaining of the lack of left-handed writing chairs in a seminar room. To be honest, I had not thought of this as an EO concern. Yet it clearly is — whose else? Like the lager advertisements, equal opportunities reaches the parts other policies cannot reach.

8. *Defining and clarifying areas of ambiguity.* The need for advice is linked to the need for clarity about both boundaries of jurisdiction and definitions of acceptable and unacceptable behaviour. One initial task of an EO structure is to define terms such as sexism, racism, harassment, or disability as they apply to the organization. Some standard definitions will be found in the glossary to this book; they would need adaptation and perhaps examples as they pertain to different cultures and different institutions.

9. *Building up a Resource Unit.* One is of course not always alone in this endeavour. In UK at least, a mass of material can be collected which will facilitate work, and which staff or students can refer to directly. There is no shortage of guidelines or checklists for looking at bias in curriculum. There are model guidelines and codes of practice from the unions, the Equal Opportunities Commission, the Commission for Racial Equality, as well as all the research literature on race and class in education. In Third World countries, this facility is more sparse, and even the term 'Equal Opportunity' may meet with some puzzlement. When basic textbooks for students are in short supply, it is difficult to argue for expenditure on EO materials. Some British Councils may be able to help; and it may be a role for teacher training institutions or curriculum development agencies to house and develop guidelines for schools.

10. *Supporting Staff in their Initiatives.* While targets and broad objectives will be

defined in the policy statement for the institution, staff may need support in their particular implementation of EO. At the higher education level, a recent example where we had some involvement was a department proposing to run a women-only management course. This in UK needs special dispensation under the Sex Discrimination Act, but the application is usually a formality for an activity proposed by what can be designated a 'training institution' and which seeks merely to compensate for previous imbalances in such training. However, the institution's own lawyers objected to the course on the grounds that the Charter stipulated that courses should be open to men and women alike, and they refused to apply for the waiver. The task of the EO committee was to investigate the legal niceties and explore precedents from other institutions which had mounted similar courses.

At a more mundane level, support might be given to those on the staff concerned with marketing; an interesting reason for schools or colleges operating in a competitive market for students to focus on imbalances in student population is the perception that sex, race and class represent 'untapped market segments' (Scribbens and Davies, 1988). When the scramble for students becomes intense, we can capitalize on institutional self-interest to lend support for ventures that try to attract more students from under-represented groups. One would have to weigh up the ethical doubts about seeing women, blacks and the underprivileged merely as targets for advertising and a source of potential revenue, against the pragmatic knowledge that the fastest way forward is often the judicious use of people's economic self-interest.

11. *Repositories for complaints.* While the notion of 'complaints' sounds negative, support and analysis must also be provided for those instances when the EO policy does not appear to be working, or when behaviour continues which is in direct contrast to the ideals expressed. Part of monitoring will be the recording of reported instances of a boy or a girl failing to get on a course of their choice; sexual or racial harassment of staff or students; sexist or racist remarks made wittingly or unwittingly by staff or students; difficulties with obtaining maternity leave provision; a female student made to leave school because of pregnancy while the student father is allowed to continue; students reporting discrimination or racism/sexism in their dealings with employers on interviews, work experience or community work; curriculum biases and gaps in resources; and discrimination for staff in getting a responsibility post. Publicizing the general outlines of the complaint, if this can be done without breaching confidentiality, permits the staff or even students to respond and participate in decisions about what should be done. A bank of such instances can provide useful case-study material for in-service training courses and staff development within the school. Complaints are not always negative and are another form of action research to build up a picture of institutional reality. An example of a particular 'multicultural' policy, with its procedures for recording every adverse incident, was given in Chapter 5; as we saw there, the temptation to 'play things down' must be resisted if victims are to be protected and consistent messages about acceptable behaviour transmitted.

12. *Developing Grievance Procedures.* Together with this collection of incidents, there needs to be a developed, formal and well-publicized set of grievance procedures. There is little point in having an expressed commitment to equity if members of an institution do not quite know where to go if these ideals are not met. Built into the policy should be clear instructions on where to take a grievance in the first instance, or a set of alternatives if that proves unsatisfactory. There may be a recognized chain of information, while retaining the confidentiality of the original complaint. For example, it might be stated that a student or staff member could report initially to a tutor, who would then report to the EO committee; or to a member of the committee, who would in formal, written cases, automatically report to the head. Much depends on the nature of the grievance, and whether it is directed against an individual or more generally against institutional policy. Such grievance procedures are clearly linked to the 'definitions' and 'policy' role of EO work, so that people know if they have a genuine cause for grievance according to those parameters.

13. *Wider links.* A final but important term of reference may be the formal responsibility to the wider community outside the institution. This may involve parental contacts to explain or negotiate the policy, or links with ethnic minority communities and women's organizations who can advise, provide visiting speakers, be invited to the school to see its work, and generally be made to feel that the school is attempting to be responsive to their needs. It can also involve work with future employers to persuade them to accept more girls or more boys into non-traditional occupations and to search for role models in their own organizations who can come to the school to provide careers advice. Organizations and agencies providing assistance in self-employment or income-generating activities may be a very important resource equal to the formal employment sector. Links with any official organizations concerned with equity can also be instigated, so that an institution is aware of the current activities and resources from a government Women's Unit, Community Development Unit, or a Rural Women's Programme; or from designated Commissions or Councils such as Racial Equality, Equal Opportunities or Civil Liberties.

Problems

While the above list seems long and prescriptive, drawing up the Terms of Reference may in fact be the easy part, at least conceptually. The day-to-day attempts at change are the hardest part, and underscore how deep-rooted is the potential for inequality in schools and society. The major problems relate to the intersections between the various dimensions of inequality, and the differing principles attached to conflicting notions of 'equal rights'. An example would be the clash between anti-sexism and multiculturalism in terms of religious belief. A home-school liaison teacher recounts:

Some feminists disapprove of challenging ethnically based cultural differences, but over some issues I feel it is necessary. I am angry when Jewish males pray 'Blessed art Thou that I was not born a woman,' when a Catholic male denies a woman access to birth control, when Muslims say 'Men are superior to women on account of the qualities in which God has given them pre-eminence.' I am not ambivalent. I am angry about female circumcision, about male oppression and violence towards females being excused as an aspect of cultural tradition; I am angry that such violence occurs in most societies. (Preston, 1986, p. 155)

The difficulty is, as Walkling and Brannigan (1986) point out:

Sexism can be, in theory, rooted in beliefs which are among the most strongly held and which are crucial to cultural identity. That is, they can be the very sort of belief which those of us who value a multicultural society think that minorities have a right to preserve. (p. 22)

A similar tension can emerge in official policy. One case involved a London head who saw himself caught between the council's policies on racism and sexism. He wanted to appoint a white woman, married to an Asian, to one of the school's four head-of-year posts, because the other three were held by men. He contacted Ealing's equal opportunities unit to confirm that that was in line with their policy. The school was 99 per cent ethnic minority, (mainly Sikh and Hindu) and he also felt that Asian girls would be happier going to a female for pastoral concerns than to a male. The majority of the governors however wanted a Muslim schoolmaster to have the job, and the head expressed his disquiet about the eventual interview procedures. He was accused of making a racist remark, and although the allegations were unfounded, eventually left the job ('Head: I was caught in equality trap', *Sunday Times*, 13 September, 1987).

Yet another dilemma revolves around the segregation/integration debate. Should one support some ethnic minority groups' demand for separate Muslim schools — particularly for the 'protection' of their girls — or is that socially divisive and in the long term limiting rather than enriching for pupils' potential? Can one be against separate Muslim schools but support single-sex education or single-sex groups in general because it provides a space for girls to experience an educative environment free from male domination? If there are voluntary-aided Roman Catholic and Jewish schools, logically there must be permitted Muslim and Sikh schools. The question is how far sectarian schools use their interpretations of religion and culture to generate both open minds and open job opportunities — for both sexes. A female Muslim vice-principal of a state community college made an interesting personal statement recently:

Personally, education means opening up and having a wider perspective on life; not having a blinkered one-dimensional view . . . . Contrary to some popular myths in western circulation, Islam does not forbid you to do any of the things that I have done professionally. A lot of the things, so called 'injustices', that people pick up are things which come from a patriarchal (male dominated) social order. With our society being basically patriarchal, a lot of the norms are dictated by that social order. I believe people tend to confuse Islam with the social order and many things which exist in Muslim society are really cultural laws rather than Islamic laws and you really need to understand Islam to appreciate this. (Hussain, 1989, pp. 37–38).

One could not perhaps generalize about future 'Muslim schools' therefore. Just as with so-called secular schools, each institution would have to be examined independently to see how its particular version of culture, or freedom of speech, freedom of worship or (importantly) freedom not to worship, fitted with the notion of an open society.

Such criteria regarding freedom and openness begin to dig into issues of how we understand terms like 'liberty' and 'choice'. The freedom to be racist or sexist may not be an unalienable right; nor may be the freedom to 'choose' a school for one's children. The Government of Jamaica tried to break the dominance which upper socio-economic level groups, mostly with 'fair' skins, had in terms of their children's access to secondary education — which was achieved through private or 'prep' education. It allocated 70 per cent of secondary school places to government primary schools, attended mainly by the more economically disadvantaged black families. Substantial numbers of the higher socio-economic groups reacted by sending their children to state schools for a year or so before the selection examination, thus maintaining their advantage, and still releasing 30 per cent of places to those remaining in the private sector (Bacchus, 1986). People will find ways to bend quota systems and equity policies, and 'freedom of choice' is one of the biggest levers in such bending.

"I've no wish to take the chairperson's job. But since you ask for frankness, I must say I do not feel comfortable about being her deputy!"

'Equality' is therefore, as we have seen, another word to be interpreted differently by different interest groups. A headline last year in the *Times Educational Supplement* ran 'When equal does not mean fair', and the article referred to the Belfast High Court's decision that the current system of awarding selective school places to 27 per cent of boys and 27 per cent of girls contravened the sex discrimination laws. Since girls do better in the tests, the system meant that some girls who had gained higher scores than boys who passed, failed the test. The results for that year were to be re-assessed to identify the top 27 per cent of the entire transfer age group, and 305 girls got letters saying they 'passed' after all (*Times Educational Supplement*, 15 July, 1988). However, the Northern Ireland Department of Education refused to withdraw grammar school places from those boys who by the new system now failed to qualify. The Northern Ireland Equal Opportunities Commission objected to that decision, on the grounds that 555 girls who obtained an identical or higher mark than these boys would still be denied a grammar school place. The Lord Chief Justice, in another hearing, agreed, and these girls had then also to be offered places. It is interesting finding women arguing the pure meritocracy principle, when so much EO work has defended compensatory policies, as we saw in Chapter 3.

We have therefore to find workable criteria to tackle dilemmas and contradictions as they arise in our EO work. In terms of the culture versus gender issue, Walkling and Brannigan's (1986) solution is to keep in the forefront the notion of children's rights:

> Cultures are not the kinds of entity which can be accorded rights which transcend those of the individual members of the cultural group . . . . Good education is always both anti-racist and anti-sexist. The possibility of conflict occurs only when we forget who our clients are and, out of a mis-guided sense of tolerance forget that the ultimate bearers of educational rights are individual children and not their parents or their parents' representatives. (pp. 23–24)

That still leaves open the question of rights to what, and who decides the rights of the child. As I argued in a chapter on 'Racism and Sexism' for a book on *The Primary School Teacher* (Davies, 1987b):

> It seems to me that we need an overarching principle on both a personal and school level which would if necessary determine whether a gender or ethnicity claim took precedence. For me that principle is the humanistic one, that education should be about opening rather than closing or limiting possibilities for individuals and groups. If the motives for adherence to faith, or for segregation, are liberating ones, then they should be supported. If they deny the pupil the right to be able to make choices later on, they should be resisted. The dilemma . . . between acknowledgment or playing down a child's ethnic/gender identity is again resolved in identifying how

far this opens up the interaction: it may be that the acknowledgment permits the fuller expression or realisation of his or her cultural experience; but if I label him/her as 'passive' or even 'conscientious' solely on the basis of ethnic/gender membership, then I close off other possibilities for behaviour, or shut my eyes to different manifestations which might need my attention. (p. 175)

There will always be tensions in education between the acknowledgment of individual difference, or group difference, and the 'fairness' implied by a definition of equality which equates with 'sameness'. Our EO policy and implementation should not paradoxically promote the notion of the *different* needs of the sexes, of ethnic minorities, of the economically disadvantaged, to the detriment of a declaration of the basic needs which we all share. The policy therefore needs to have underpinning it the institutions's view of basic, common, shared rights so that the day-to-day pragmatism and solving of dilemmas becomes less arbitrary and less individualistic.

A bill of rights

As philosophers have pointed out for centuries, 'rights' and 'freedoms' do not exist in a vacuum, but must always be suffixed by precision as to the right to do what, or the freedom from what or to have what. 'Rights' do not exist in a social vacuum either: if we expect certain rights, we must be prepared to accord those rights to others. A suggested 'Bill of Rights', drawn from various parts of this book, would look something like this:

1. A right to dignity and respect, and a responsibility to accord dignity and respect to others.
2. A right to recognition, and a responsibility to give recognition to others.
3. A right to an environment free from bias or discrimination, and a responsibility to create that environment for others.
4. A right to an awareness that one's own culture is changeable, and a responsibility to try to understand and evaluate others' cultures.
5. A right to personal growth in terms of a range of skills, and a responsibility to help the growth of others.
6. A right to satisfaction and sense of achievement, and a responsibility not to allow this satisfaction to be bought at the expense of others' sense of underachievement.
7. A right to fun, stimulation, interest and laughs, and a responsibility not to deny this to others.
8. A right to participation in decision-making, and a responsibility for the decisions that are made.

These rights are not absolute. The point of juxtaposing them with responsibility is that the claiming of these rights depends on the willingness to accord them to others. For the first right, for example, as we noted in the chapter on teacher deviance, teachers who are disrespectful or brutal towards children forfeit their right to respect and gentleness in return. 'Recognition', secondly, refers to a whole range of possibilities, in that it is at the base line simply the opposite of being ignored or marginalized. I recall with admiration the head who tried to give every child in the school a specific role to play, so that 'no child can be absent without being missed'. Teachers, as we saw in Chapter 7, equally need recognition, and, as I am finding from my research, rate 'constructive criticism' high on their list of needs from management. Recognition does not therefore just mean praise, but can include criticism: the point is that in a large, sometimes anonymous institution, it is important to ensure that someone knows you are there and is aware of what you can do.

Rights 3 and 4 refer to the problems of cultural 'freedoms'. As we saw, one person's anti-sexism is another person's racism. My view is that 'culture', or even religion, should not be seen as a fixed or unchallengeable entity. A culture is a collection of social inventions, which like any invention, can be overtaken when more appropriate methods come to light. We are more than happy to devise new management cultures — why not new sex role cultures, new authority cultures, new family cultures? The responsibility is to challenge the inbuilt resistance or inertia that is symbolized by the sad reply 'it is our culture', when apparent injustices are exposed. The right is to a vision of a 'culture' being a ragbag of shared views and practices, and to an awareness that altering one aspect does not necessarily bring the whole edifice down. The right is to the skills for critical analysis of culture or religion so that students and teachers can evaluate where it can be transcended and where best left intact, and in whose interests.

Rights 5 and 6 refer to the more traditional objectives of schooling, although 'satisfaction', as we noted Glasser pointing out, has not been seen as a major goal. Again, the purpose of juxtaposing 'responsibility' is to attempt to portray 'satisfaction' as non-competitive. 'Achievement' is often sought at the expense of the non-achievement of someone else; but our EO policy has to work out radical ways to provide and monitor some sense of achievement for all.

Rights 7 and 8 denote our social rights and responsibilities. As indicated in Chapter 8, laughter is a serious business, and we have a basic responsibility not to make life any more miserable for others than it has to be. The final right underpins all the rest: in the end, we have the right to take part in decisions about the things that effect us, and ultimately about what our other rights are and how they should be implemented. But we also have to learn the equally important responsibility for the results of those decisions. The decision to be deviant or disruptive, to be racist or sexist, is in the end a personal one, and students should not learn to project responsibility for behaviour on to the 'discipline' of the teacher, or the 'culture' of the group.

It will be obvious that these 'basic rights' represent a personal 'decision' for the author, and cannot and should not be accepted as self-evident. They are presented merely as an example of how an EO committee might begin firstly to decide on the practical implementation of its terms of reference, and secondly to resolve tensions and dilemmas arising from what is in effect an attempt to change the culture of the school or even the education system.

What I hope becomes apparent is that 'school effectiveness' starts to have a much broader remit than 'performance indicators' such as examination results. It goes deeper than the measures such as 'numbers present' (the 'bottoms-on-seats' ideology which characterizes the efficacy of learning as counting up students in terms of 'Full-Time Equivalents'). We see that 'equal opportunities' is not just about the opportunity to gain qualifications. It will be the attempt to measure school 'effectiveness' by the extent to which these eight basic rights have been accorded. The evaluation is qualitative rather than quantitative, and not necessarily open to comparative ranking of schools. It is the attempt to measure rather than the actual measurement which is possibly the more important. Sometimes the evaluation will be done through absence rather than presence: the right to dignity might be measured by the absence of humiliation. The right to a bias-free environment may be measured by a decrease in racist/sexist incidents. Other rights may need periodic questionnaires or interviews to probe students' perceptions of themselves, of schooling or of teachers. Yet other rights can be monitored in conventional 'performance' ways, to assess skills that have been learned. It will be noted that selective examinations are never a good measure for the school effective in according common rights, as they are rationed. Graded, criterion-referenced assessment demonstrating visible progress is the only feasible way of seeing whether growth in skills has been possible for all.

Many equity programmes, whether nationally or institutionally, have been a nonsense because they have attempted to use the inappropriate end of the scale for measurement. If we conceive of the 'resources' or 'gifts' within a school as on a spectrum ranging from scarce to freely available, then they might be arranged thus:

Figure 9.1

SCARCE						FREELY AVAILABLE
selective entry qualifications	'high' performance on norm-referenced tests	power	progress on criterion-referenced assessment	ability to critically evaluate culture	decision-making	recognition dignity fun

There appears a reluctance to use the right hand end for evaluation of school effectiveness, or equity, simply because those resources can be available without cost, and seem therefore not worth considering. Only scarce things appear worth concentrating on. This is like measuring the success of a shoe-shop by the number of size 11 shoes it sells, instead of how many customers go away with comfortable footwear. It would be possible marginally to increase the number of size 11s sold, by aggressive marketing or special attention paid to large-footed customers; but given the rationed number of size 11 people in the market, this would have to be at the expense of other shoe shops. It would possibly be at the expense of the rest of the shoe-buying public, who would be deprived of attention. No retailer would dream of concentrating all its attention on an inelastic market segment; yet this is just what knowledge retailers do when they focus on scarce commodities such as exams as indicators of educational 'success'.

Yet just because some things can be freely available, does not of course mean that they are. The 'efficient' school is therefore one that concentrates first on those things which are not finite, and which can in theory be distributed freely. Efficiency merges with equality to ensure that free 'goods' are not withheld. To focus on the size 11s is to warp the vision. To conceive of 'equality' in terms of redistributing examination achievement leads — because of competitiveness and streaming — to greater inequalities in the distribution of rights and responsibilities. The defence is usually that it is because exams are so scarce, because they are the key to all future openings, that we must target our redistribution there; but it is just this short-sightedness which has led to our schools being such inefficient and inequitable places. To pander to the diploma disease is to undermine EO work. Only by asserting basic and non-rationed rights, can an EO policy give all people the tools and the footwear to march into the future with a degree of confidence.

EXERCISE 9: EQUAL RIGHTS

1. Firstly draw up a 'bill of rights' for members of your institution (or adapt the set given above).
2. Then decide an 'EO' structure or body which would be efficient in ensuring that everyone has an 'equal opportunity' both to be accorded those rights and to take responsibility for according those rights to others.
3. How would each 'right' be measured or monitored?

Chapter 10

Conclusion: Management as Distributive Politics

... although schools and universities may be excellent places to continue the struggle for a better world, such institutions are not generally equipped to recreate the world in the image of their teachings. They cannot guarantee their graduates a fair distribution of jobs nor equal access to anything but ideas. (Rothermund and Simon, 1986, *Education and the Integration of Ethnic Minorities*)

This book has tried to explore how far the above statement is generally true; if true, why; and whether the internal management of schools can have any impact on social equality and the distribution of social goods. The introduction argued that school management should be seen against a backcloth of apparent dilemmas between demands of equity and efficiency; of a breakdown in the acceptance of a fair meritocracy because of shifts in the relationship between schooling and employment; and of changes in state control of education in many parts of the world. Concepts of the 'professional' teacher are forged within this quest for control, that is within the struggle for power between educational institutions and government, or church, or parents. Dilemmas in teaching and management were argued also to relate to the tensions between those definitions of 'equal' which refer to rationed opportunity within the competitive, selective function of formal schooling (with the need to differentiate and discourage the unsuccessful); and those definitions which imply common treatment and satisfactory experiences for all (with the need to provide encouragement for everyone).

The examination of centralization and decentralization policies found that current economic imperatives in many parts of the world were likely to encourage greater inequalities. The areas explored — 'rational' management, accountability, national curricula, financial devolution, consumer choice — seemed to give legitimacy to an ideology of the survival of the fittest. It was hinted that the school would have to exercise considerable ingenuity if inequality was not to become entrenched. The further exploration of the particular dimensions of social class, gender and ethnicity established that disparities in educational outcomes did appear international, and required forceful policies to even begin to challenge the school's successful role in perpetuating income differentials, sexism and racism. Trying to narrow the gap between the eventual mental and manual workers in a country was also seen to be doomed to failure, unless creative ways were found to use the contradictions in state policy and to harness people's self-interest. In Chapter 7 it was argued that ignoring teachers' interests and cultures was also undertaken at one's peril: school management had to bear in mind both the common experiences or problems of teachers and the individual and group strategies arising from different social and political positions. A further exploration of deviance and corruption by teacher added the complication that even the supposedly 'impartial' features of school such as examinations were open to manipulation and monetary or power interests.

However, the reverse side of the coin is the potential benefit of self-interest, creativity and strategic resistance. Inequalities are not inexorable social forces: they, like cultures, are social creations acting to the advantage of particular groups. The way to challenge social inequalities is not through appeals to charity but through the creative use of self- and national interest. It has to be shown that inequality is inefficient. It has to be shown that sexism and patriarchy are bad for men. It has to be shown that lack of recognition for everyone in the end breeds deviance. It has to be shown that trying to get more ethnic minorities, women or the poor through exam-ination or selection hurdles is to focus on the inefficient end of things. The book has argued that 'equal opportunity' (as often defined) is a high cost, low return policy.

It was thus proposed in the last chapter that we should begin by ensuring equal access not just to ideas (although that in itself could be nicely subversive), but to some notion of basic human rights. The proposals were that we all had a claim to dignity, recognition, a bias-free environment, political awareness, personal growth, a sense of satisfaction, fun and participation in decisions that affect us. These rights, unlike opportunities, are not rationed, and do not necessarily need additional monetary resources. They are contingent on people's responsibility to accord those rights to others. The fact that they can be distributed by 'management' and by all school part-icipants will make the school into a more efficient operation. Equal rights is a low-cost, high return policy.

Yet it implies a radical shake-up of the conventional relations of schooling. One cannot in the end merely tell people to share, to cooperate, to respect, to tolerate diversity. Those relationships must be built into the structure of the institution. One cannot order people not to be racist or sexist; for that is the lunacy of using a power position to tell people not to use a power position. The authoritarian head angrily preaching brotherly love while wielding a cane is a recognizable parody; but it is not far from the ideology behind much dominance-oriented management. When student and staff control rather than student and staff satisfaction is the primary goal, then any equal opportunities policy is likely to be a sham.

It is the contemporary fashion to describe schools as 'loosely-coupled systems', with the departments, houses, units and so on indicating the existence of multiple and overlapping areas of interest and jurisdiction (Weick, 1976). There is no necessarily clear connection between the structure of a school and the outcomes of its work, no real formal attempts at 'quality control'. Bell (1980) even talks of school as an 'anarchic organization' — not formless or unpredictable, but anarchic in the sense that the relationship between its goals, its members and its technology is not as clear as conventional organization theory would have us believe. People in school have, as we have seen, different goals, different socialization experiences, and different political affiliations; they are confronted with contradictory demands from the state and from their clients. The response to this has been to portray 'effective' school management as the elimination or preemption of conflict. There results a tension between such attempted domination, or enforced harmony, and the different interests of members; this forges the 'micropolitics' of the school (Ball, 1987). Micropolitics may operate to inhibit change, to maintain the *status quo*; they also highlight the degree of 'tenuousness, dysfunction, interruption and possibility' inherent in educational contexts.

There appears a contradiction here: 'good' schools are supposed to evidence a consensus and consistency on goals; yet all the ethnographic research will show this to be impossible. I suspect the apparent consensus relates ironically to the differentiating function of the school — much as everyone on the Titanic was agreed on wanting to get a place on the inadequate lifeboats. Yet a focus on equity could begin to outline a structure which builds on the possibilities for an equal stake in the organization, and which begins from our commonalities rather than our conflicts and struggles. Much traditional school structure is built on the things that can be used to divide us: age, expertise, 'ability', gender, subject aptitude. The 'best' assessment is seen to be that which makes fine discriminations between people — the ideology of 'find out what people can't do and then test them on it'. This explains the centrality of maths in school, as one of the great potential social dividers, and the one easy way to sort sheep from goats. There is a curious inverted logic in trying to find a consensus on goals and yet working within structures which openly build on or celebrate difference. It is no wonder that schools are arenas of contest over material advantage, and that the micropolitics of segments, coalitions and alliances militate against radical change. If instead we conceive of a structure which builds on what we have in common and not what divides us, then the possibilities for both equity and efficiency begin to come into focus.

Let us see what happens when we reject the dividers and build on the commonalities.

Dividers to be rejected

There are various sorts of potential entrenched discriminators which clearly should not be present in an institution professing a care for equity and a concern for efficiency. However, they can be part of established 'tradition', and their suggested removal may meet with resistance. I present four in order of the degree to which their removal constitutes a form of heresy.

(a)*Authoritarian or coercive relationships.* Many equal opportunities policies or legal frameworks appear quite 'coercive' in the sense that they forbid certain behaviours and insist on others. 'Contract compliance', as we saw in Chapter 5, is a practice used by some authorities whereby firms are not awarded contracts unless they are demonstrably equal opportunities employers or have a positive action programme. Similarly, an equal opportunities policy of guidelines in a school may state that it does not tolerate racist or sexist conduct, and that there are recognized sanctions which can be applied. Yet it is important not to confuse this framework for defining acceptable limits of behaviour for all with the use of power to insist on non-universal behaviour. This latter refers to the problem raised in the chapter on teacher 'deviance', the problem of teachers attempting to insist on behavioural standards which they themselves do not practise. I would term this 'inconsistent coercion'. A heretical proposition which I put to beginning teachers, who elsewhere get messages such as 'start tough and soften up later', or 'never smile before Christmas' is the proposition 'never treat, speak to or expect behaviour of a child in a way that you would not treat, speak to or expect behaviour of an adult'. If one of the functions of schooling is to socialize children into

adult behaviour, it is counterproductive to enforce rules which no adults then have to follow. Adults do not line up in playgrounds, in sex-divided ranks. They do not ask permission to use the toilet. They do not have to sit still, sit up straight, focus on one adult for hours, or have to stay in when someone else infringes a social rule. Things that adults are expected to do are to be polite, say please, look welcoming, explain our actions and tolerate fallibility. If a colleague did not hear something in a meeting, we would not snap 'pay attention'. Yet much of so-called 'discipline' is founded on unusual and extraordinary behaviour patterns which prepare children for nothing much. The result is either a rejection of all adult authority as meaningless, or a blind acceptance that it is adults or others who tell you what to do, and you need not work it out for yourself. Neither of these positions is likely to produce the internally responsible grown-up that the school is supposed to cast into the world.

> In a first year art class at a South London secondary school, the topic was a local street scene. Studying the work of a West Indian girl, the art teacher asked 'Why don't you draw any black people in the picture?' 'Miss, are we allowed to?' came the reply.
> (Arora & Duncan *Multicultural Education* 1986)

There is a clear link between authoritarian relationships, racism, sexism and other forms of power abuse. We know that children from violent homes are more likely to act in violent ways towards their own children. We know that sexual abusers are more likely to have been sexually abused themselves. Similarly, children who have been subjected for a number of years to teachers who abuse power by dominating, bullying, humiliating and ordering unreasonable behaviour are more likely to see no reason not to abuse power themselves. Racism or sexism are attempts to denigrate or belittle others, and can be direct transfers from the experience of being denigrated or belittled — at school, home or work.

The difficulty is making democratic relationships part of whole school policy. One teacher on his or her own being courteous, considerate, according children respect, refusing to administer physical or verbal violence, may be seen as 'soft' by students and colleagues alike. That is why any equity programme in school has also, by discussion and negotiation among teachers, to arrive at a reasonable consensus on teacher/pupil relationships. In this instance, it is not good management to tolerate too much diversity if this means brutality or externally imposed and arbitrary 'discipline'.

(b)*Streaming, ranking, tracking.* Any organization which permanently groups its inmates on the basis of their perceived possession of something valued, in this case ability, cannot be equitable. It precludes the basic rights of recognition and dignity. We know enough from all the labelling and expectations research to be aware that members of a 'low' stream underperform, have lower self-esteem and are more likely to be disruptive. They are more likely to be ethnic minority students or from lower income groups. Permanent remedial groups show the same effects. Streaming is also therefore inefficient. It undermines any notion of a common, or national curriculum, for as Holt (1987) points out 'any suggestion that we use knowledge to differentiate between pupils is incompatible with the notion of a shared practice' (p. 140). Ranking people on their perceived overall orientation to knowledge is saying to low-stream students 'We value sharpness, speed, memory, concentration; but you haven't got much of those. Your fate is to stay with others like you'. Dividing students according to some notion of generalized 'ability' also acts to divide and rank the staff who teach them. It is indicative that we can talk of 'remedial teachers'; and see them as a race apart. Streaming creates, not solves, management problems.

Setting, that is having different groups available in different curriculum areas, is not necessarily so divisive. To avoid the possibility that certain students will find themselves in the bottom set for everything, and implicitly form a stream, three things are important. Firstly, the reasons for their existence must be clear. Why have sets for Maths if students are working through individualized workbooks? Secondly, students must be able to negotiate their membership of a set; and thirdly, 'progress' through the sets must be a desirable end-goal. This year I shall willingly place myself in the bottom set for skiing, because we have to stay as a group, and I want a slow pace. But I know that next year I should be able to elect for the intermediate group — otherwise I shall ask for my money back. Sets should be a reference point for a level of skill at a particular curriculum area; and they would probably contain a mixture of ages. Sets only work if they are geared to interaction between students, with support and conviviality. If they are geared only to the interests of the teacher who wants to feel she or he needs prepare only for a homogenous group with unalterable levels of intelligence, they are no improvement on streaming.

(c)*Hierarchies.* Contrary to current 'line management' fashion, schools do better without multiple tiers of power. Inserting extra management teams, appraisers, and finely graded posts with 'administrative responsibility', all act to remove choices about teaching and learning even further from the real practitioners. Excessive hierarchies militate against the rights of participation in decision-making and self-determination. Handy summed it up so well in his examination of schools from an organisation point of view:

> Complicated structures and many-layered hierarchies do not produce excellence . . . . If the Roman Catholic Church needs no more than five levels in its hierarchy, most organisations should be able to manage with

fewer. Clear lines of command, clear divisions of responsibility and as few staff at the centre as possible: this seems to be the recipe for effectiveness . . . .Schools have more grades for staff than they need for their operational hierarchy. From the child to the head there are seldom more than five operation levels. On that count they do well. However secondary schools have often pursued the purely functional route (in their case 'departments' are the functions), complicated by the academic/pastoral divide, resulting in an unbalanced matrix with the academic subjects across the head or the grid and house groups or year groups down the side. The result can be a diffusion of responsibility. Who is actually responsible for the education of each pupil? In the net of the matrix it is easy to slip through. (Handy, 1984, p. 32)

While it can be argued that hierarchies provide avenues for promotion and therefore status and motivation for teachers, other professions manage without them. In UK, 'solicitors and accountants expect to be partners (three grades up from entry) by the time they are 40 at the latest. They do not then give up and retire, but they are geared into the success of the whole enterprise. How might schools work the same trick?' We might answer Handy's question by testing our notions of 'success': for if success is the equitable and efficient take-up of basic rights, then it is counterproductive if some are seen as more responsible and hence more remunerated for this than others. I have always thought it inequitable that school 'managers' should be paid more than classroom teachers. The Tanzanian model of democratic education means in contrast that staff are paid on seniority and years of service, and heads may earn less than some of their teachers. I am also interested in the suggestion of teachers employing administrators, rather than the other way round. Some private schools in Hong Kong do this, with the teaching team deciding curriculum and policy, doing without a head and employing administrative and finance people to cover the organizational needs of the school. The cry may come, this may work with small outfits, but what of large comprehensives? To which the answer is, do we have to have large schools? Efficiencies of scale and 'viable' sixth forms are counteracted by the expense of seemingly necessary complex and highly remunerated hierarchies of management, and by inefficiencies through the anonymity which induces lack of individual recognition and satisfaction. We must find structures which minimize hierarchies, not generate them.

(d)*Leadership*. More heretical still than the argument for minimizing vertical divisions is the questioning of our deeply ingrained desire for 'leadership'. Bennis long ago listed nicely the endless proliferation of terms:

As we survey the path leadership theory has taken, we spot the wreckage of 'trait theory', the 'great man' theory, and 'the situationist critique', leadership styles, functional leadership and finally, leaderless leadership; to say nothing of bureaucratic leadership, charismatic leadership, democratic-autocratic-laissez-faire leadership, group-centred leadership, reality-centred leadership, leadership by objective, and so on. The dialectic and reversals of emphases in this area very nearly rival the tortuous twists and turns of child-rearing practices. (Bennis, 1959, p. 259)

In an argument for an 'educative and empowering notion of leadership', Smyth (1985) quotes this and Greenfield's 'anti-leadership' view:

It is one that recognizes a plurality of values in human society and that denies ultimate legitimacy to any action. What we are left with, therefore, is contention among values or, more accurately, among those who espouse different values. In this view we are leaders in some degree. We all have legitimacy in the degree to which we act out of our own values and can involve others in them. This view rejects the idea of a simple, unitary value structure as the foundation for any large, complex social order. In this view, all social orders are pluralistic and there will always be struggle and contention among those who represent the conflicting values within the structure. Those who represent the contending values are the leaders and they are in all respects human, fallible, self-interested, perverse, dogged, changeable, and ephemeral. In social possibility, we are all leaders. Certainly none of us can claim the ultimate right to leadership. (Greenfield, 1981, p. 27)

I think that Smyth backtracks from this position, and while I endorse his notion of empowerment as 'enabling' teachers to develop ways of framing their own problems, involving 'working' towards obtaining resources for them, it is unfortunate that the term 'leadership' is still retained for the language of 'helping', 'enabling' and 'working'. The reason why we have such a proliferation of preferred types of leadership for schools is that all of them are predicated on the wrong assumption. If you cannot find the solution to a question, it is because you are asking the wrong question. We are asking 'what style of leadership' instead of 'why do we want to be led?'. The obsession with leadership for schools goes back to the militaristic philosophy which underpins so much school organization. When an aim is to kill as many people as possible, then the need for blind obedience and unquestioning acceptance of authority does require identifiable bodies in charge. Heads will still talk of 'steering a tight ship' and 'marshalling the troops'. I argued in the chapter on gender and management that our notions of leadership are masculinist and not women-friendly or indeed, user-friendly. I am further arguing here that 'leadership' has been a counterproductive blind alley for school organization, and that we would be better off without it. It will always imply an authority, a sole organizer whose claims to knowledge, expertise and rightness are ultimately superior to anyone else's. Equitable organizations such as cooperatives or large General Practitioners groups do not have 'leaders'. The notion that you can 'lead' people into equality is a contradiction in terms.

Equity promoters

The replacements for coercion, streaming, hierarcies and leadership are not, however, their obvious or polar opposites. The espousal of 'mixed ability' can be a dangerous one, for it still acts to convey the message that 'ability' is the key determinant of teacher orientations towards students, and that ability is a unitary phenomenon which the presenting children have varying amounts of. The replacement for coercion is not a laissez-faire attitude, nor relativism* with regard to behaviour standards. On the contrary, there must be, particularly with regard to equity, an emphasis on standards, but it is how these norms are decided and monitored that distinguishes a coercive from a democratic régime. The questioning of hierarchies and leadership does not imply an anarchic organization, an 'everyone for themselves' scramble; it implies a flatter, less rigid profile, but one which requires in some ways a more complex set of organizational relationships.

(a) *Federalism and mini-schools.* Small is beautiful, but it is also efficient. Toogood describes his 'human scale' minischools within a large comprehensive in UK as an attempt to reduce the impact of institutionalization and to build bridges between the classroom and the surrounding environment. Important questions were realized about the ownership of territory and the ownership of time: 'Nobody learns to manage time without the opportunity to do so. Where it is all laid out for the person the initiative in creative learning has already been withdrawn. This is a particularly important reason why small learning units having long blocks of time available for decisions by small teams of people should be the basic and normal way a secondary school is run' (Toogood, 1989, p. 109). Children in Madeley Court had a sense of belonging and of responsibility for their 'base'. Theft was almost as absent 'as it is in a submarine'. Parents, teachers and children felt passionately about 'their' minischool, and raised in one year more than the annual *per capita* allocation from the local education authority. Children with special needs could find a place in such an environment, saving the county's special schools bill, it was estimated, £157,000 a year. 'It enabled teachers to meet the needs, rather than to pass on the problem to a hierarchy of pastoral specialists. Toogood's phrase 'learning home' for the bases is a significant one, which we shall return to when looking at management images.

(b)*Power sharing and small-group decision making.* It is by no means self-evident that delegation of power leads automatically to greater equity — Chapter 2 indicated how the nature of 'delegation' and the various possibilities for 'decentralization' may simply lead to different concentrations of power rather than a greater sharing of it. The minischool response however is often for small groups of teachers convened for particular purposes to solve specific problems, rather than permanent concentrations. People gain in management experience and share the burden of decision-making. Handy suggests:

> ... schools, which cannot suddenly start having bursars, might consider splitting the administrative functions off from the professional hierarchy. If a professional has to do the timetabling, the examination schedules, look after the school numbers and arrange parents' meetings, does it have to be the senior professional? Why not share the jobs around the junior professionals, so that a little administration could enlarge their view of the world without interfering too much with their teaching. It might even be that some turn out to be better administrators than teachers — future bursars perhaps. (1984, p. 36)

Sharing tasks is a more democratic political process in general, but also militates against entrenched inequalities among the teaching staff. A recent education management course for black and Asian teachers in London was an attempt to break down the vicious circle by which black teachers did not get senior jobs because they had no experience of management, and yet without promotion there was no opportunity of management experience (*Times Educational Supplement,* 3 March 1989, 'Learning skills to move off the bottom rungs'). One black teacher on the course commented: 'This course is improving my confidence. *You never get a chance to see management at work when you are in a school*' (my italics). This is a serious indictment of school management, if it remains invisible and apart from that which it is supposedly coordinating.

(c)*Organizational responsiveness.* As well as 'democratic structures', another platitude needs restating: that the organization should fit the needs of its members rather than the other way round. Again, certain management theories have much to answer for in their reification of 'the organization' or 'organizational needs' as something apart from the people in it. The bureaucratic — and sociological — emphasis on 'role' has also dehumanized institutions. As Holt points out:

> Systems approaches to curriculum change, like organization development (O.D.) and 'GRIDS' ... are animated by a concept of the teacher as role-player rather than person: one exists not by virtue of living a life but as a member of an organization. People remain strangers: professional discourse deals with function rather than ... humaneness. In this, such devices reflect the technocratic culture of managerialism. (Holt, 1987, p. 71)

The alternative is to provide a flexible enough structure to meet people's needs as they emerge. For teachers, this may mean job-sharing; flexi-time; paternity leave; acknowledgment of the benefits of different out-of-school experiences (child-rearing, fostering, caring for relatives, agricultural sufficiency). For the students, the equivalent of flexi-time is flexi-schooling itself. The philosophy is that students can select school components and sessions to put together a package which suits their needs or future career ideas (see Meighan, 1989). This is a relatively new notion for UK, but is, or could be applied in many parts of the world. Girls in India have been helped to attend school by flexible school hours which fit into their domestic responsibilities (Kelly, 1987). Bacchus (1986) cites however the more typical reaction of school authorities to nomadic peoples or even settled populations who are unable to send their children to school with any degree of regularity:

> In fact administrators have always tended to take existing organisational structures and sometimes even the current administrative arrangements as given and expect the local population to reorganize their ways of living to fit in with these patterns . . . .For example, they are more likely to see the answer to the problem of irregular attendance as the introduction of a compulsory education ordinance which allows them to specify the hours and the times of the year when schools would be open and then expect the population to adapt their life-styles in order to conform to these regulations. The point here is that if equity in education is to be made a more attainable goal then administrators and policymakers have to be prepared to be more flexible in the kind of practices and organisational structures which they develop in order to provide education, especially for these marginalised groups. (p. 68)

Flexi-schooling not only helps marginalized groups, but is able to respond to a broad range of consumer choice. There could be a fear that it might thus be taken over by the right wing and converted into a voucher system — which in the end would serve only to increase inequalities. But the idea of learners negotiating curriculum and time is at root a radical movement which would do much to militate against excessive teacher dominance and autocracy. It may also act to break down the mental/manual divide in a way that imposed vocational curricula never will (see Chapter 6): for students put together their own 'applied' package with specific options in mind.

Job-sharing among teachers can act in the same way to break down divisive practical/academic images. A study of teacher job-sharers showed not only that it benefitted women who had other responsibilities, but that an interesting group of job-sharers, including several men, wanted to combine teaching with other interests or jobs: artists, craftsmen or women, a journalist, voluntary workers, and a few husband-and-wife teams who wanted to share child-rearing. Linguists could thus combine teaching with translation work; crafts experts could offer more to pupils if they were still practising their skills (*Times Educational Supplement*, 27 January, 1989). As we saw in Chapter 8, the problem of moonlighting and second jobs by teachers can be solved at a stroke by making 'alternative' activities a recognized part of official ideology for educators.

(d)*Student-directed learning*. An alternative (or an addition) to students negotiating their way in and out of school is for them to direct their own learning within even such potentially rigid structures as national curricula. An example in UK would be Knowle High School's 'success-based' curriculum. This is a direct attempt to ensure the equivalent of the equal rights to satisfaction and recognition I argued for in the last chapter. In their ICA (Integrated Curriculum Assessment, but dubbed 'I Can Achieve') curriculum units are broken down into graded modules accessible to all abilities, with clearly defined objectives, intermittent assessments and merit awards. This may sound highly curriculum-led and teacher-directed, but the following extracts from Harrison (1989) seem to point to a basically democratic process occurring:

> Fundamental to ICA is the direct responsibility pupils have for directing their own learning . . . . Twice a year each pupil negotiates with his or her form tutor an overall profile of achievements which is jointly signed before going in the pupil's Record of Personal Achievement — a substantial ring file . . . the RPA is owned and kept by the pupil. Nobody has access to it without his or her permission. But because the contents are so positive, pupils regard them with pride and are eager for them to be looked at . . . .

> Truancy — a major summertime problem in seaside resorts — has been drastically reduced. Pupils can now see exactly where they are going within school and all chidren, many of whom would have been classified as failures under the old [streamed] regime, are experiencing continual success. Ian [Pike, the Head] believes that success breeds success: 'The perception used to be, that it's too easy to tell people what they can do and that the only way of producing progress is to slap them with what they can't'.

> Styles of teaching have had to change. Assistant head Bob Johnson says 'Because children are all working individually and assessment is going on all the time in lessons, teachers can no longer chalk and talk. Teachers are not at their desks anymore. What seems to have gone in lessons is the confrontation that the desk between teacher and class used to symbolise' . . . .

> 'I know there are similar schemes. But ICA is ours. It's owned by staff and students and we're proud of it. Bolt-on models never seem to work. They produce the right paperwork in the end. But it's the process that matters, not the product'.

The key words in this account are 'success', 'negotiation' and 'ownership'. Just as in Madeley Court's minischools, where students and staff felt they 'owned' the learning bases, here people 'own' the curriculum scheme, and students 'own' their achievement records. An equal rights manifesto would not be hard to draw up in these contexts; but significantly, it may not be needed.

(e) *Student-directed behaviour.* The one problem with individualized work, negotiated curricula and flexi-hours could be the difficulty of maintaining a corporate, cooperative ethic. Built into graded assessments therefore could be the criterion that the knowledge gained has been used to help or teach someone else; or (as we saw in Papua New Guinea, Chapter 6) has been used in the service of the community. Like so many other aspects of democratic schooling, sharing knowledge is not only equitable, but efficient: peer tutoring has been demonstrated not only to help the person being taught, but to improve the skills and insights of the 'teacher' in the pair. Building in and legitimating cooperation avoids the double messages otherwise so pervasive of formal schooling. In Australia, Connell *et al.* (1982) noted the contradiction between the working-class families' 'practices of cooperative coping' and the schools' demands for individual achievement. Similarly, Dunn *et al.* (1989) quote a UK student:

> He's always on about help thy neighbour and that you try and do that in his lessons and you're out. He's always on at us for talkin'. I mean they're all hypocrites. I mean you go to the staffroom for somat and they don't even open the door. They leave you standin' there for ages, they're so busy talkin'. (p. 186)

A truly educational reversal of the normal teacher directive 'don't talk, don't listen to each other, listen to me' would be 'talk to each other, listen to each other, talk to me'. Askew and Ross (1988) found male pupils in UK never really listening to each other. 'Conversations' were more collections of statements. Years of listening to the teacher had not transferred to an interest in others' views and feelings. A 'peer mediation' experiment in US found that the use of trained 'peer counsellors' could however resolve tensions such as ethnic disputes far better than recourse to the school's security guards. 'Research shows that kids watch an average of thirty hours of TV a week. But the average time of two-way conversation — kids being listened to — is fifteen minutes a week.' (*Education Now,* 1989). One great resource in large institutions such as schools is the potentiality for an audience; yet the obsession with silent work, with control, ignores that potential for children talking out their fears and prejudices and experiences of injustice.

Essential to the business of removing hypocrisy and double messages is listening to students and insisting on their participation in deciding the rules of the school and the social conventions of the teaching/learning relationship. In schools where the rules are decided by a student council, or a Moot, or some other representative body, students approve rules rather than see themselves as passive recipients of them. A primary school head writing on democratic practice comments 'As most school rules are concerned with their own safety, the children articulate them for themselves to the group before they approve them. "Everyone is equal in feelings" is an important part of democratic practice. We encourage children to express their feelings' (Acton, 1989, p. 162).

School management as a family concern

Put simply, then, to achieve equity and efficiency, out go coercion, streaming, hierarchies and leadership; and in come federalism, power-sharing, organizational responsiveness, student-directed learning and student-directed conduct. There is nothing new in these suggestions. They sound naive, 'woolly liberal' and antithetical to teacher professionalism. The encouraging aspect is that they are starting to emerge and prove themselves viable in a variety of contexts all over the world. They can, and do, act as a mode of resistance to Hunt's 'incorporation' of education into the big business ethic, and to provide alternative scenarios for who might 'control' education — and who might benefit from it.

It remains to ask, what sort of management images would be generated by such emphases? Here the term 'image' is used, not model. The notion of a management 'model' is for schools a hazardous one. The implication of a blueprint for action leads to the rigidity, inflexibility and inappropriateness which characterize inhumane and inefficient organizations. One can have principles in school; and I have outlined principles of equity in the last chapter. But one cannot have management principles — except insofar as an acceptance of the basic management principle being to ensure the maintenance of the educational principles. Management is only a means to an end. There can be no model for management until we know what that end is. The flow charts, the neat boxes with the little arrows between 'goals' and 'implementation', the grids of roles, tasks, styles, functions — none of these even begin to capture the essence of what heads or teachers do and why. They cannot be prescriptions in a vacuum, without knowing the ends; they are not even descriptions of the messy realities of school life.

What we can have however is images. If the end result of the school is indeed to be an equitable sharing of satisfactions, then we need an image in our minds of small-scale distribution, not of manufacturing. When schools appear to reproduce inequalities through their non-accidental 'correspondence' with the hierarchies and divisions of the workplace, then it does not help to have management images which also correspond to stratified organizations.

The final heresy of this book is therefore to replace the one-person 'leadership' model with a family-derived picture. If small, collective and humane organizations are the best way forward to our goals of equity and efficiency, then we should look to a domestic/parenting/family business analogy rather than the technical/industrial one. This of course is not prestigious or selective and will therefore not be popular with the presenters (or recipients) of 'expert' management training courses. Yet it is my premise that 'effective' home management is much more akin in style to schools than is 'effective' management of Shell International. Much of the mystification surrounding management courses and activity is what Lauffer terms 'artificially produced uncertainty':

In the guise of providing clarity, some consultants have mystified organisational processes so as to increase the demand for their services. Attorneys have mystified divorce, thereby artificially creating an area of uncertainty over which they exercise considerable control. Whether by accident or collusion, accountants have created such complexity in the tax laws as to make their services (to some of us, at least) indispensible. (Lauffer, 1985)

A head, like a parent, who is permanently indispensible is a dangerous phenomenon that does not allow others to grow. Schools need 'effective' management: but the practices should be revealed as commonsense and available to all. Let us therefore examine some of the typical management dimensions of an institution with an image in our minds of parents or a small family business rather than directors of the World Bank. Families may be sites for disasters as much as any other institution; but because most of us have grown up in them, it is easier to envisage a 'successful' family, and to conceptualize parenting 'mistakes' than it is to envisage the boardroom of ICI. Put at its most crude level, the management of schools or families is about who gets what, who does what and who says what to whom about that getting and doing. The more upmarket labels would be resource distribution; task and time allocation; and communication.

(a)*Resource Distribution.* This refers to the basis on which both equal and unequal allocations of available goods are made to members. Much school management, like domestic management, is about sharing goods between competing claimants, knowing when the cake should be shared equally or distributed according to age or need or yesterday's consumption. If resources are scarce, it may be decided to share them exactly: to divide an orange equally between two children, the family principle is often 'one to cut, one to choose'. Never is an orange cut so equally, and cries of 'unfair' averted. Delegation of resource allocation is relatively simple when the basis is one of parity between claimants. One of the reasons for Margaret Thatcher's popularity with women voters is apparently her household analogies. She is prone to liken running the country to organizing the family budget. Homilies like 'what you haven't got you can't spend' will justify no end of cutbacks and economies. Whatever we might think about State policies, it is significant that no great claims are made to understanding the imperatives of cash flow.

However, what the Thatcherite position fails to highlight sufficiently is that scarce resources generate a highly debatable value position on their disproportionate allocation — whether more to defence, health, education or subsidies to agriculture. We should remember that the 'formula funding' that may decide educational resourcing also disguises value positions about who 'deserves' what. In families, the basis for unequal allocations would relate to the survival need: taller people need more calories, younger people more sleep. But this is only up to a point: a wife or husband does not go to bed fifteen minutes later than their partner because they are three months older. Formulae for funding and budget allocations cannot be hard rules: they must be constantly open to review and discussion, and linked to the equal opportunities monitoring. If targets have been reached, the 'compensatory' funding for disadvantaged groups no longer holds.

(b)*People's task and time allocation.* The management courses and books which neatly divide 'management of people', 'management of tasks' and 'management of time' miss a crucial point. These three things are inseparable. People do tasks, and it takes them a certain amount of time to do them; one cannot conceive of tasks and time outside the people who are involved and what it means to them. While divisions of labour are to be found in most families, over-permanent or over-rigid divisions (like over-rigid budgets) create difficulties as people grow, change or fall ill. Delegation of duties to children or to the other parent is the common solution, with elder siblings responsible for younger ones or having tasks in the family business. The key to family delegation is the acceptance that people do things in different ways. You do not delegate preparation of the evening meal and then hang around nervously making suggestions and comments. Tasks must be fully given away: if the responsibility is then yours, there is a degree of satisfaction, however tedious. Family stereotyping occurs when there is over-personalization of tasks, the 'I've got your coal in for you' syndrome. A person or group needs to own a task, so as not to imply or claim imposition.

Job specifications and responsibilities are usually provided for teachers in schools; the management duty is therefore to enable these to be drawn up for and by the students. As indicated earlier when talking of federalism, it is important for people to feel integral to a community, so that their absence will be missed. This is more difficult to achieve in a school than in a family business, but it is actually more efficient than having sleeping partners. If people have insufficient to do, or have got insufficient recognition, they will either withdraw from the family firm, or claim constant attention. Hence the syndrome which a colleague called 'Daddy's Right Arm'. 'Our father would cut off his right arm for you', she explained, 'but then he would spend the next ten years saying "Was that arm all right? How are you getting on with that arm? Do bring the arm back if it's no good" '. Efficient and equitable delegation tries to obviate the need for amputations of people's best assets.

Having tasks shared out does not of course solve the problem of when to do them, and how often. School management is indeed more akin to housework than it is to car manufacturing. The objectives are there, but they are achieved spasmodically and in the face of conflicting needs. As fast as one set is achieved, they will get messed up again. The executive literature on time management stresses doing only one thing at a time, and compartmentalizing activity. Anyone running a home and family knows this is a nonsense: the true management skill is doing at least three things at once, as you prepare supper, answer the 'phone, forward plan the next day, supervise the homework and mediate the arguments. Given the similarly conflicting demands and dilemmas of schooling, an ability to tackle issues simultaneously, and shift priorities around, is a much under-estimated technique. The connection with gender-inclusive management and the valuation of female learned aptitudes is, one hopes, clear at this point.

(c)*Communication*. Another misleading image in management literature is of 'lines of communication'. The implication is that there can be more than one stage between an expression of need or information and its recipient. Yet Equal Opportunities Committees in local authorities have been found to falter unless there is direct access to the levers of power and the decision-making procedures. Large centralized bureaucracies become both inefficient and alienating if members do not know what has happened to requests and who makes final decisions. While in a family, 'go and ask your mother' might be an acceptable delegation of responsibility, we can see that a reply of 'I will ask your mother for you' leaves a wealth of uncertainty about what negotiations and message changes would be happening in the interim. Federalism and mini-schools should be there to enable one-stage communication in both or all directions.

If we were running a small family business, we would constantly need local market research on consumer demand and preferences. Similarly, direct communication of needs and wants is basic to family relationships. Marriage counsellors will point to 'breakdowns of communication' whereby partners do not talk or listen to each other, or whereby expression of need is done through hinting, nagging, martyrdom or attempted putdowns. The message from assertiveness training is 'knowing what you want and saying what you want'. If schools went to arbitration, many would end up in the divorce courts because of poor communication. One of the reasons, apparently, why education is linked to fertility patterns and smaller family size in Third World countries is that 'educated' husbands and wives talk to each other. Thinking about communication in school is therefore to be concerned about what people want, and telling them where you are going. The benefits of the research on students' perceptions of schooling are not just the academic ones of 'insights' into pupils' needs, but the direct spin-off of pupils feeling consulted about the organization, and feeling more involved. The implications for management are the obvious ones of space for statements of people's wants and needs; and negotiation and compromise when wants and opinions differ.

Disasters and crisis management also come under the heading of communication. This is the acknowledgment that what can go wrong, will; and that fall-back positions are crucial if children are not to be left stranded, delegated shopping not forgotten, tricky relationships with relatives not soured. Networks, extended family, babysitters, transport rotas all need to be cultivated and reciprocated. In a family business, one is heavily reliant on individual people and their caprices. The neat organizational charts with role functions and channels of communication imply the possibility of a perfect bureaucracy; yet management is a messy, unpredictable, disaster-prone activity. It involves very much knowing who your friends are. We saw in Chapter 2 the calamities in assuming there can be a perfectly functioning people-proof organizational system. If there is going to be any management training, it should be in spinning webs of communication and working out lines of retreat.

Particularly in any increased autonomy for schools, communication should be viewed politically as encompassing the possibility for debate, conflict and argument. Children learn negotiative strategies at their parents' knee; teachers and students, as intimated in the first chapter, will also develop through the overt politicization and creative use of communicative competencies.

Management as politics

Clearly, the family analogy can be overstretched, and becomes tortuous at times; but it is introduced in this book firstly to demystify school management and secondly to argue that management in its broadest sense is about distribution, not leadership. It is about the processes of deciding who gets what, where, when and at whose cost. Communication and resource or task allocation are political activities, not organizational 'skills'. The politics of the family and the politics of the school are both highly complex arenas for activity, and the management of them revolves around the delicate sharing of care, work, time, and material resources. Some goods can be distributed freely; others will be contested and competed for. But effective distribution cannot in the long term be resolved by charismatic or any other sort of leadership: it is resolved by the basic commonalities of the members of the political unit. A family or clan is a selfish unit. It will organize in its own interests, and if it wants to avoid break-up, it will distribute fairly among its members. The equitable school, ironically, also acknowledges the self-seeking nature of its members, and builds on desires for satisfaction and stimulation to ensure at least a basic level of common outcomes.

The major difference between the family and the school is not just that of scale, but of the outside struggle for control. Families are not directly required to be efficient, to be monitored, to show value for money. Schools on the other hand may be expected to subsume their members' interests to some 'greater good' — whether this is national growth, national identity, manpower planning, the enterprise economy, or calls for law and order. A school may successfully and democratically generate its own criteria for efficient outcomes. In terms of organizational features, it may outlaw the dividers and stress the equity promoters. But however successful it is on its own terms, it will have to face the constant pressures of State intervention or vested economic interests.

In addition to domestic management, that is the inner distribution of goods, the further management dimensions for a school are therefore those of outward manoeuvre and marketing. Change has to be gradual, stealthy, considered, and always, as the previous head of the innovative Countesthorpe College puts it, aware of the 'sticking point of society'. Experimentation in education is tolerated only 'up to a point'. Radical schools have foundered therefore because of a refusal to recognize 'The Point'. 'It is possible to push right up to the boundaries of acceptability, but after that a restructuring of society would be necessary, and the place to accomplish that is certainly not from within a school' (Watts, 1989, p. 18). The traditions around ideologies of work, of gender relations, of race or tribal affiliations, are not to be blown open by appeals to reason. The capital owners' desire for a conformist, authority-accepting workforce will not go away. The international, multinational, monetarist order is unlikely to tolerate schools which emit brash challenges to that order, schools who fire salvoes at social inequality.

The final management concern is therefore to turn out school products — teachers and students — who apparently have the skills required; who are not averse to a little enterprise; who are aware of social conventions and norms; but who are politically astute, committed to equal rights and who are prepared to acknowledge their future responsibility for the rights of others. A summary term for this might be 'utilitarian democracy'; and it requires marketing. This is marketing not in the current sense of 'selling' the school in order to recruit both money and students, but in the sense of promoting a viable image of the school to parents, local power holders, the teaching profession and the media, in order to resist incorporation or closure. The management knack is making a school operate in the interests of all its members, while appearing to operate in the interests of the national or local economy. The truly equitable school, I hope this book has shown, will in the long term demonstrate that these interests are in fact convergent. The basic political function of school management is to show that equity *is* efficiency.

Bibliography

ABBOTT, P. and SAPSFORD, R. (1988) *Women and Social Class*, London, Tavistock.

ACKER, S. (1988) 'Teachers, Gender and Resistance'. *British Journal of Sociology of Education*, 9, 3 pp. 307–322.

ACTON, A. (1989) 'Democratic Practice in a Primary School', in Harber and Meighan (*op. cit*), pp. 157–162.

ADAMS, J. (1981) 'The Contribution of Education for Self-Reliance to Manpower Development in Tanzania: a Critical Appraisal', *International Journal of Educational Development*, 2, 1, pp. 67–86.

AL-KHALIFA, E. (1987) *School Management Development and Women Teachers' Project: Summary Report* Birmingham City Council Mimeo, Slough: NFER/EMIE.

ALLEN-MILLS, T. (1987) 'Banda makes Latin a must at Africa's Eton', *The Independent*. 8 October.

ALLEN-MILLS, T. (1989) 'Mass cheating puts India's examiners to the test'. *The Independent*, 15 April.

AMMA. (1987) *Multicultural and Anti-Racist Education Today*, London, Assistant Masters and Mistresses Association.

APPLE, M. (1986) *Teachers and Texts: a Political Economy of Class and Gender Relations in Education*, London, Routledge and Kegan Paul.

ARCHER, J. and LLOYD, B. (1985) *Sex and Gender*, Cambridge, Cambridge University Press.

ASKEW, S. and ROSS, C. (1988) *Boys Don't Cry: boys and sexism in education*, Milton Keynes, Open University Press.

AVALOS, B. (1986) *Teaching The Children of the Poor: An Ethnograpahic Study in Latin America*, Ottowa, International Development Research Centre.

BACCHUS, M. (1986) 'The Role of Education in Achieving Equity and Maintaining Cultural Diversity', in *'Plural' Societies' Conference Proceedings: Equity and Diversity: Challenges for Educational Administrators*, 6th International Intervisitation Programme in Educational Administration, Hawaii, Fiji, New Zealand.

BAINS REPORT (1972) *The new local authorities: management and structure*, London, HMSO.

BAKER, C. (1988) *Key Issues in Bilingualism and Bilingual Education Development*, Clevedon Multilingual Matters.

BALL, S. (1984) (Ed.) *Comprehensive Schooling: A Reader*, Lewes, Falmer Press.

BALL, S. (1987) *The Micro-politics of the School: Towards a Sociology of School Organisation*, London, Methuen.

BALL, S. (1988) 'Staff Relations During the Teachers' Industrial Action: context, conflict and proletarianization', *British Journal of Sociology of Education*, 9, 3, pp. 289–306.

BALL, S. and GOODSON, I. (Eds.) (1985) *Teachers' Lives and Careers*, Lewes, Falmer Press.

BANKS, J. and LYNCH, J. (Eds.) (1986) *Multicultural Education in Western Societies*, London, Holt, Rinehart and Winston.

BARNES, D. (1985) Review of Hargreaves Report. *British Journal of Sociology of Education*, 6, 3, pp. 328–331.

BATES, R. (Ed.) (1983) *Educational Administration and the Management of Knowledge*, Australia, Deakin University.

BATES, R. (1984) 'Educational versus Managerial Evaluation in Schools', in Broadfoot, *op. cit*, pp. 127–144.

BELL, L. (1980) 'The School as an Organisation: A Re-appraisal, *British Journal of Sociology of Education*, 1, 2, pp. 183–192.

BENNIS, V. (1959) 'Leadership Theory and administrative behaviour: the problem of authority', *Administrative Science Quarterly*, 4, pp. 259–260.

BERG, L. (1968) *Risinghill: Death of a Comprehensive School*, London, Penguin Books.

BEYER, L. and ZEICHNER, K. (1987) 'Teacher Education in Cultural Context', in POPKEWITZ, T. (Ed.) *Critical Studies in Teacher Education*, New York, Falmer Press.

BEYNON, J. and MACKAY, H. (1989) 'Information Technology into Education: Towards a Critical Perspective', *Journal of Education Policy*, 4, 3 (forthcoming).

BLISHEN, E. (1966) *Roaring Boys*, London, Panther.

BOLAM, R. (1986) 'The National Development Centre for School Management Training', in HOYLE, E. and MCMAHON, A., *op.cit*, pp. 252–271.

BOWLES, H. and GINTIS, S. (1976) *Schooling in Capitalist America*, London, Routledge and Kegan Paul.

BRAY, M. (1985) 'Decentralization and equality of educational opportunity in Papua New Guinea', in LAUGLO, J. and MCLEAN, M. *op.cit.*, pp.142–158.

BRAY, M. (1988a) 'Community Management and Financing of Schools in Papua New Guinea', in BRAY, M. with LILLIS, K., *op.cit*, pp. 155–170.

BRAY, M., (1988b) 'School Fees-Philosophical and Operational Issues', in BRAY, M. and LILLIS, K., *op.cit.*, pp. 55–66.

BRAY, M., CLARKE, P. and STEPHENS, D. (1986) *Education and Society in Africa*, London, Edward Arnold.

BRAY, M. and COOPER, G. (1979) 'Education and Nation-building in Nigeria since the Civil War', *Comparative Education*, 15, pp. 33–42.

BRAY, M. and LILLIS, K. (1988) (Eds.) *Community Financing of Education: Issues and Policy Implications in Less Developed Countries*, Oxford, Pergamon.

BRITE, (1989) *Evidence to the English Working Group*, University of Birmingham: Bilingualism and its Role in the Teaching of English Project.

BROADFOOT, P. (Ed.) (1984) *Selection, Certification and Control*, Lewes, Falmer Press.

BROADFOOT, P. (1985) 'Towards conformity: educational control and the growth of corporate management in England and France', in LAUGLO, J. and MCLEAN, M. *op.cit.*, pp. 105–118.

BROADFOOT, P., OSBORN, M., GILLY, M. and PAILLOT, A. (1987) 'Teachers' Conceptions of their Professional Responsibility: some international comparisons', *Comparative Education*, 23, 3, pp. 287–301.

BROADFOOT, P. and OSBORN, M. (1988) 'What Professional responsibility means to Teachers: national contexts and classroom constraints' *British Journal of Sociology of Education*, 9, 3, pp. 265–288.

BROOKE, N. and OXENHAM, J. (1980) *The Quality of Education in Mexican Primary Schools*, Brighton, Institute of Development Studies, University of Sussex.

BRUNEI DEPARTMENT OF EDUCATION (1983) *Education Statistics,* Department of Education, State of Brunei, June 1983, pp. 24–27.

BURGESS, T. (Ed.) (1985) *Education for Capability*, Windsor, NFER/Nelson.

BYRNE, E. (1978) *Women and Education*, London, Tavistock.

CAMPBELL, J., LITTLE, V. and TOMLINSON, J. (1987) 'Multiplying the Divisions? Intimations of educational policy post-1987', *Journal of Educational Policy*, 2, 4, pp. 360–378.

CANTELL, T. (1985) 'The Scheme in Operation', in BURGESS, T., *op.cit.*, pp. 114–124.

CARNOY, M. and LEVIN, H. (1985) *Schooling and Work in the Democratic State*, Stanford, Stanford University Press.

CARRINGTON, B. and SHORT, G. (1987) 'Breakthrough to Political literacy: political education, anti-racist teaching and the primary school', *Journal of Education Policy*, 2, 1, pp. 1–13.

CHEW TOW YOW (1986) 'The National Institue of Educational Management, Malaysia', in HOYLE, E. and MCMAHON, A. *op.cit.* pp. 283–294.

CHISHOLM, L. and HOLLAND, J. (1986) 'Girls and Occupational Choice: anti-sexism in Action in a Curriculum Development Project', *British Journal of Sociology of Education*, 7,4, pp. 353–365.

COARD, B. (1971) *How the West Indian Child is made Educationally Subnormal in the British School System*, London, New Beacon Books.

COCKBURN, C. (1986) *Training for 'Her' Job and for 'His': Tackling Occupational Segregation by Sex in the Youth Training Scheme*, Manchester, Equal Opportunities Commission.

COHN, T. (1987) *Multicultural Teaching*, Staffs, Trentham Books.

COLE, M. (1986) 'Teaching and Learning about Racism; a Critique of multicultural education in Britain', in MODGIL, S. *et al* (Eds.) *Multicultural Education: the Interminable Debate*, Lewes, Falmer Press.

COMMONWEALTH SECRETARIAT (1982) *The Commonwealth casebook for School Administrators*, HARRIS, A. (Ed.), London, Commonwealth Secretariat.

COMMONWEALTH SECRETARIAT (1986) *Towards a Policy for Women Overseas Students in the UK*, Proceedings of a Seminar, London, June 1986.

CONNELL, R. (1985) *Teachers' Work*, Sydney, George Allen and Unwin.

CONNELL, R., ASHENDEN, D., KESSLER, S., DOWSETT, G. (1982) *Making The Difference: Schools, Families and Social Division*, Sydney, George Allen and Unwin.

CUMMINS, J. (1977) 'Cognitive Factors associated with the attainment of intermediate levels of bilingual status', *The Modern Language Journal*, 16, pp. 3–10.

DAVEY, A. (1983) *Learning to be Prejudiced*, London, Edward Arnold.

DAVIDSON, J. (1987) *Essential Management Checklists*, London: Kogan Page.

DAVIES, C. (1984) 'Administrative Staff Control Systems: The Case of Birmingham City Council', *Local Government Studies*, July/August.

DAVIES, L. (1984a) *Pupil Power: Deviance and Gender in School*, Lewes, Falmer Press.

DAVIES, L. (1984b) 'Gender and Comprehensive Schooling', in BALL, S. (Ed.) *op.cit.*, pp. 47–66.

DAVIES, L. (1986a) 'Policies on Inequality in the Third World: dependency or autonomy?', *British Journal of Sociology of Education*, 7, 2, pp. 191–204.

DAVIES, L. (1986b) 'Women, Educational Administration and the Third World: A Comparative Framework for Analysis', *International Journal of Educational Development*, 6, 1, pp. 61–75.

DAVIES, L. (1987a) 'Research Dilemmas Concerning Gender and the Management of Education in Third World Countries', *Comparative Education*, 23, 1, pp. 87–96.

DAVIES, L. (1987b) 'Racism and Sexism', in DELAMONT, S. (Ed.) *The Primary School Teacher*, Lewes, Falmer Press, pp. 162–176.

DAVIES, L. (1988) 'Contradictions of Control: Lessons from Exploring Teachers' Work in Botswana', *International Journal of Educational Development*, 8, 4, pp. 293–303.

DAVIES, L. (1989) 'Gender and Educational Administration in Third World Countries', *International Encyclopedia of Education, Supplementary Volume I*, (Eds.) HUSEN, T. and NEVILLE, T., POSTLETHWAITE, pp. 367–371.

DAVIES, L. and ORAM, R. (Eds.) (1988) *Education and National Development Special Issue (20), Educational Review*, 40, 2.

DEMAINE, J. (1988) 'Teachers' Work, Curriculum and the New Right', *British Journal of Sociology of Education*, 9, 3, pp. 247–264.

DENSCOMBE, M. (1980) 'The Work content of teaching: an analytic framework for the study of teachers in classrooms', *British Journal of Sociology of Education*, 1, pp. 279–292.

DERRECK, V. (1979) *The Comparative Functionality of Formal and non-formal Education for Women — Final Report*, Washington, USAID.

DIXON, B. (1977) *Catching Them Young Vol. 1: Sex, Race and Class in Children's Fiction*, London, Pluto Press.

DORE, R. (1976) *The Diploma Disease*, Berkeley, University of California Press.

DOVE, L. (1986) *Teachers and Teacher Education in Developing Countries*, London, Croom Helm.

DOYLE, W. and PONDER, G. (1977) 'The Practicality Ethic in Teacher Decision-making', *Interchange*, 8, pp. 1–12.

DUNN, K., RUDDUCK, J. and COWIE, H. (1989) 'Developing group work in the secondary school and cooperation and the ideology of individualism in schools', in HARBER, C. and MEIGHAN, R. (Eds.), *op.cit*, pp. 183–193.

DUPONT, B. (1981) *Unequal Education: Study of Sex Differences in Secondary School Curricula*, Paris, UNESCO.

EDUCATION NOW, 'Peer Mediators in conflict resolution in the Bronx', p. 29, March/April 1989. (No author given).

EJIOGU, A. (1982) 'Sex Differences in the Leader Behaviour of Nigerian College Principals', *Journal of Educational and Administrative History*, 14, 1, pp. 55–61.

ESLAND, G. (1977) *Schooling and Pedagogy*, Milton Keynes, Open University Press.

EVETTS, J. (1988) 'Assessment and appraisal of primary teaching: the consequences for primary teachers' careers'. Paper presented at *International Sociology of Education Conference*, Westhill, Birmingham, January 1988.

FARRAND, J. (1988) 'Mexican Primary School Teachers' Sense of Professional Responsibility', *Comparative Education*, 24, 1, pp. 103–124.

FEIMAN-NEMSER, S. and BUCHMANN, M. (1985) 'Pitfalls of experience in teacher preparation'; *Teachers' College Record*, 87, pp. 53–65.

FLOWER, F. (1986) 'Towards Capability', in BURGESS, T. *op.cit.*, pp. 167–176.

FOSTER, P. (1965) 'The Vocational School Fallacy in development planning', in ANDERSON, C. and BOWMAN, M. (Eds.) *Education and Economic Development*, Chicago, Aldine, pp. 142–166.

FRASHER, J. and FRASHER, R. (1979) 'Educational Administration: a Feminine Profession', *Educational Administration Quarterly*, 15, 2, pp. 1–13.

FREEDMAN, S. (1988) 'Teacher burnout and institutional stress', in OZGA, J. *op.cit.*, pp. 133–145.

FULLAN, M. (1985) 'Change processes and strategies at the local level', *Elementary School Journal*, 85, 3, pp. 391–421.

GAMBIA MINISTRY (1982) *The Republic of the Gambia Education Statistics*, Ministry and Department of Education.

GIBB, A. (1984) 'Factors Fostering Entrepreneurship: the role of Education', in WATTS, A. and MORAN, P. (Eds.) *Education for Enterprise*, Cambridge, Careers Research and Advisory Service, pp. 13–18.

GILLBORN, D. (1988) 'Ethnicity and Educational Opportunity: case studies of West Indian male-white teacher relationships', *British Journal of Sociology of Education*, 9, 4, pp. 371–385.

GILLESPIE, R. and COLLINS, C. (1987) 'Productive Labour in Schools: An international evaluation', *Prospects*, 17, 1, pp. 11–26.

GINSBURG, M. (1988) '*Contradictions in Teacher Education and Society*' Lewes, Falmer Press.

GINSBURG, M. and CHATURVEDI, V. (1988) 'Teachers and the ideology of professionalism in India and England', *Comparative Education Review*, 4, pp. 4–32.

GLASSER, V. (1985) *Control Theory in the Classroom*, New York, Harper and Row.

GOLDSMITH, J. and SHAWCROSS, V. (1985) *It ain't half sexist, Mum: Women as Overseas Students in the UK*, London, WUS/UKCOSA.

GORB, P. (1986) 'Education for Capability', in BURGESS, T. *op.cit.*, pp. 109–113.

GREENFIELD, T. (1973) 'Organizations as Social Inventions: Rethinking assumptions about change', *Journal of Applied Behavioural Science*, 9, 5, pp. 551–574.

GREENFIELD, T. (1978) 'Reflections on Organizational Theory and the Truths of Irreconcilable realities', *Educational Administration Quarterly*, 14, 2, pp. 1–73.

GREENFIELD, T. (1981) 'Understanding educational organizations as cultural entities: some ideas, methods and metaphors'. Paper to a conference on *Administrative Leadership: New Perspectives on Theory and Practice*, University of Illinois, Urbana Champaign.

GREENLAND, J. (Ed.) (1983) *In-service Training of Primary Teachers in Africa*, London, Macmillan.

GREENWOOD, C., HININGS, B. and RANSON, S. (1975) 'Contingency Theory and the organization of local authorities', *Public Administration*, 53, pp. 1–23.

GREY, C. (1982) 'Corporate Planning and Management: A Survey' *Public Administration*, Vol. 60, Autumn, pp. 349–355.

HAFFENDEN, I. (1986) 'Issues in Curriculum Innovation and Implementation: The Seychelles National Youth Service 1981–86', Paper presented at *British Educational Research Association* conference, Bristol, September 1986.

HALL, V., MACKAY, H. and MORGAN, C. (1986) *Headteachers at Work*, Milton Keynes, Open University Press.

HANDY, C. (1984) *Taken for Granted? Understanding Schools as Organisations*, Schools Council Programme 1, Longman.

HANSON, E. (1986) *Educational Reform and Administrative Development: The Cases of Colombia and Venezuela*, Stanford, Hoover Press.

HARBER, C. (1989) *Politics in African Education*, Basingstoke, Macmillan.

HARBER, C. and MEIGHAN, R. (1989) *The Democratic School*, Ticknall, Education Now Books.

HARDING, J., HILDEBRAND, G. and KLAININ, S. (1988) 'Recent International Concerns in Gender and Science/Technology', in DAVIES, L. and ORAM, R. *op.cit.*, pp. 185–194.

HARGREAVES, A. (1978) 'The Significance of classroom coping strategies', in BARTON, L. and MEIGHAN, R. (Eds.) *Sociological Interpretations of Schools and Classrooms*, Driffield, Nafferton.

HARGREAVES, D. (1982) *The Challenge of the Comprehensive School*, London, Routledge and Kegan Paul.

HARRISON, P. (1989) 'Outstanding achievement', *Times Educational Supplement*, 3 February.

HARTLEY, L. and BROADFOOT, P. (1988) 'Assessing teacher performance', *Journal of Educational Policy*, 3, 1, pp. 39–50.

HATTON, E. (1985) 'Equality, Class and Power: a case study', *British Journal of Sociology of Education*, 6, pp. 255–272.

HEARN, J. and PARKIN, W. (1987) *'Sex' at 'work': The Power and Paradox of Organisation Sexuality*, Sussex, Wheatsheaf Books.

HEATH, A. and CLIFFORD, P. (1981) 'The Measurement and Evaluation of School Differences', *Oxford Review of Education*, 7, 1, pp. 33–40.

HEYNEMANN, S. and LOXLEY, W. (1983) 'The effect of primary-school quality on academic achievement across 29 high- and low-income countries', *American Journal of Sociology*, 88, 6, pp. 1162–1194.

HMSO (1985) *Education For All: Report of the Committee of Inquiry into the Education of Children from Ethnic Minority Groups (The Swann Report)*, London, HMSO Cmnd 9453.

HOLMES, J. (1984) *The Position of Women in the Senior Management of Secondary Schools*, Unpublished M.Ed. thesis, University of Birmingham.

HOLT, M. (1987) *Judgement, Planning and Educational Change*, London, Harper and Row.

HOPKINS, D. (Ed.) (1987) *Improving the Quality of Schooling: Lessons from the OECD International School Improvement Project*, Lewes, Falmer Press.

HOPPER, E. (Ed.) (1971) *Readings in the Theory of Education Systems*, London, Hutchinson.

HOROWITZ, T. (1988) 'Awareness without legitimation: the Israeli educational system's response to cultural differences', *Journal of Education Policy*, 3, 1, pp. 1–8.

HOYLE, E. (1986) *The Politics of School Management*, London, Hodder and Stoughton.

HOYLE, E. and MCMAHON, A. (Eds.) (1986) *World Yearbook of Education 1986: The Management of Schools*, London, Kogan Page.

HSRC (1981) Report of the Main Committee of the Human Sciences Research Council, *Investigation into Education: Education Provision in the RSA. The de Lange Report*, Pretoria: Dept. of National Education, Republic of South Africa.

HUNT, F. (1987) *The Incorporation of Education*, London, Routledge and Kegan Paul.

HUSSAIN, F. (Ed.) *Muslim Women*, London, Croom Helm.

HUSSAIN, F. (1989) 'A Moment in Time', *Education Impact*, 5, pp. 36–38.

IFAPLAN (1986) *Education for Enterprise: an interim report*, Brussels, IFAPLAN Project Office.

ILEA (1981) *Education in a multiethnic society: An aide-mémoire for the Inspectorate*, Inner London Education Authority.

ILEA (1983) *Race, Sex and Class, 1. Achievement in School*, Inner London Education Authority.

ILEA (1985) *Improving Secondary Schools* (The Hargreaves Report), Inner London Education Authority.

ILO (1981) *Employment and conditions of work of teachers*, Geneva, International Labour Organization.

ISHUMI, A. and COOKSEY, B. (1985) 'Policy and Practice in Tanzanian Secondary Education Since 1967', quoted in Harber (1989), *op.cit.* pp. 118.

JEFFCOATE, R. (1985) 'Anti-racism as an educational ideology' in ARNOT, M. (Ed.) *Race and Gender: Equal Opportunities Policies in Education*, Oxford, Pergamon.

JENCKS, C., SMITH, M., ACLAND, H., BANE, M., COHEN, D., GINTIS, G., HEYNS, B. and MICHELSON, S. (1972) *Inequality: A Reassessment of the Affects of Family and Schooling in America*, New York: Basic Books.

JENNINGS, Z. (1987) 'Preparation of the youth for the world of work: the effectiveness of programmes linking education with production in the Commonwealth Caribbean', *International Journal of Educational Development*, 7, 4, pp. 265–276.

JIMENEZ, E. and TAN, J. (1987) 'Decentralised and Private Education: The Case of Pakistan', *Comparative Education*, 23, 2, pp. 173–189.

KELLER, E. (1980) *Education, Manpower and Development: The Impact of Educational Policy in Kenya*, Nairobi, Kenya Literature Bureau.

KELLY, G. (1987) 'Setting State Policy on Women's Education in the Third World: perspectives from comparative research', *Comparative Education*, 32, 1, pp. 95–102.

KESSLER, S., ASHENDEN, D., CONNELL, R. and DOWSETT, G. (1985) 'Gender Relations in secondary school', *Sociology of Education*, 58, 1, pp. 34–48.

KINGDON, M. and STOBART, G. (1988) *GCSE Examined*, Lewes, Falmer Press.

KIRP, D. (1979) *Doing Good By Doing Little*, Berkeley, California, University of Californian Press.

KNOX, D. and CASTLES, S. (1982) 'Education with Production: Learning from the Third World', *International Journal of Educational Development*, 2, 1, pp. 1–14.

LACEY, C. (1988) 'Towards a relevant curriculum in today's world', *Education Now*, No.2, pp. 20–23.

LAUFFER, A. (1985) *Careers, Colleagues and Conflicts: Understanding Gender, Race and Ethnicity at the Workplace*, Beverley Hills, Sage.

LAUGLO, J. and LILLIS, K. (Eds.) (1988) *Vocationalising Education: An International Perspective*, Oxford, Pergamon Press.

LAUGLO, J. and MCLEAN, M. (Eds.) (1985) *The Control of Education*, London, Heinemann.

LAWN, M. (1988) 'Skill in Schoolwork: work relations in the Primary School', in OZGA, J. *op.cit.* pp. 161–175.

LILLIS, K. (1987) 'Community Financing of Education: issues from Kenya', *Journal of Education Policy*, 2, 2, pp. 99–118.

LILLIS, K. (1988) 'Issues of Quality', in BRAY, M. and LILLIS, K. *op.cit.* pp. 75–84.

LINN, P. (1985) 'Microcomputers in Education: living and dead labour', in SOLOMONIDOS, T. and LEVIDOW, L. (Eds.) *Compulsive Technology: computers as culture*, London, Free Association.

LITTLE, A. (1986) 'Educational Inequalities: Race and Class', in ROGERS, R. (Ed.) *Education and Social Class*, Lewes, Falmer Press.

LORTIE, D. (1975) *Schoolteacher: A sociological Analysis*, Chicago, University of Chicago Press.

LOUW, W. (1988) 'In-service Upgrading of Black Teachers' Qualifications', in SHARPES, D. (Ed.) *International Perspectives on Teacher Education*, London, Routledge and Kegan Paul.

MACKAY, H. (1987) 'Information Technology into Education: Towards a Critical Perspective', Paper presented at the British Educational Research Association Conference, Manchester, September, 1987.

MAHONY, P. (1985) *Schools for the Boys?*, London, Hutchinson.

MALAYSIA (1982) *The New Primary School Curriculum*, Kuala Lumpur, Ministry of Education.

MARAVANYIKA, O. (1986) 'School Management and nation building in a newly independent state', in HOYLE, E. and MCMAHON, A. (Eds.) *op.cit.*, pp. 199–210.

MARLAND, M. (1982) 'Staffing for Sexism: educational leadership and role models', *Westminster Studies in Education*, 5, pp. 11–26.

MARTIN, V. (1983) 'Gender Differentiation in Secondary Education in Zambia', Unpublished BPhil (Ed) dissertation, University of Birmingham.

MCNAMARA, V. (1982) 'The Long-term effect of 'carrots': the secondary school extension project in Papua New Guinea', *International Journal of Educational Development*, 1, 3, pp. 49–60.

MEIGHAN, R. (1978) 'A Pupil's Eye View of Teaching Performance', *The Learners' Viewpoint*, Educational Review Special Number 10, pp. 125–138.

MEIGHAN, R. (1989) *Flexischooling*, Ticknall, Education Now.

MORRIS, B. (1977) *Some Aspects of the Professional Freedom of Teachers: an international pilot enquiry*, Paris, UNESCO.

MULLER, J. (1987) 'Much Ado: 'manpower shortages' and educational policy reform in South Africa', *Journal of Educational Policy*, 2, 2, pp. 83–98.

MWIRIA, K. (1985) *The Kenya Harambee Movement: A Historical Perspective*, Unpublished PhD thesis, Stanford University.

NATIONAL CURRICULUM COUNCIL, (1989) *An Introduction to the National Curriculum*, in association with The Open University.

NEWSAM, P. (1986) 'Equity and Diversity — Learning to Live together', 6th International Intervisitation Programme Conference, *Equity and Diversity: Challenges for Educational Administrators*, Hawai, Fiji, New Zealand.

NIAS, J. (1980) 'Leadership Styles and Job-Satisfaction in Primary Schools', in BUSH, T. *et al.*, (Eds.) *Approaches to School Management*, London, Harper and Row, pp. 255–273.

NUTTGENS, P. (1986) 'The Educational Failure', in BURGESS, T. *op.cit.*, pp. 24–32.

NWAGWU, N. (1977) 'Problems of professional identity among African school teachers', *Journal of Educational Administration and History*, 9, 2, pp. 49–54.

O'CALLAGHAN, M. (1977) *Namibia: the effects of apartheid on culture and education*, Paris, UNESCO.

OPPONG, C. and ABU, K. (1987) *Seven Roles of Women: Impact of education, migration and employment on Ghanaian mothers*, Geneva, International Labour Office.

OXENHAM, J. (Ed.) (1984) *Education versus Qualifications*, London, George Allen and Unwin.

OZGA, J. (Ed.) (1988) *Schoolwork: Approaches to the Labour Process of Teaching*, Milton Keynes, Open University Press.

OZGA, J. and LAWN, M. (1981) *Teachers, Professionalism and Class: a study of organized teachers*, Lewes, Falmer Press.

OZGA, J. and LAWN, M. (1988) 'Interpreting the Labour Process of Teaching', *British Journal of Sociology of Education*, 9, 3, pp. 323–336.

PASCAL, C. (1987) 'Democratic Primary School Government: Conflicts and Dichotomies', *Educational Management and Administration*, 15, 3, pp. 193–202.

PAYNE, M. (1987) 'Determinants of Teacher Popularity and Unpopularity: A West Indian Perspective', *Journal of Education for Teaching*, 13, 3, pp. 193–206.

PHILLIPSON, M. (1971) 'Juvenile Delinquency and the school', in CARSON, W. and WILES, P. (Eds.) *Crime and Delinquency in Britain*, London, Martin Robertson.

POLAN, A. (1989) 'School: The Inevitable Democracy?', in HARBER, C. and MEIGHAN, R. *op.cit.*, pp. 28–47.

POLLARD, A. (1985) 'Opportunities and Difficulties of a teacher-ethnographer: A personal account', in BURGESS, R. (Ed.) *Field Methods in the Study of Education*, Lewes, Falmer Press.

POSTMAN, N. and WEINGARTNER, C. (1971) *Teaching as a Subversive Activity*, Harmondsworth: Penguin.

PRESTON, A. (1986) 'Propaganda in the Nursery', in BROWNE, N. and FRANCE, P. (Eds.) *Untying the Apron Strings: anti-sexist provision for the under-fives*, Milton Keynes, Open University Press.

PRING, R. (1987) 'Privatisation in Education', *Journal of Educational Policy*, 2, 4, pp. 289–300.

PSACHAROPOULOS, G. and WOODHALL, M. (1985) *Education and Development: Analysis of Investment Choices*, New York, Oxford University Press.

PURKEY, S. and SMITH, M. (1983) 'Effective schools: A Review'; *Elementary School Journal*, 83, pp. 427–452.

RAIKES, K. (1978) 'Rural differentiation and class formation in Tanzania', *Journal of Peasant Societies*, 5, 3, pp. 285–325.

REDICAN, B. (1988) 'Subject Teachers under Stress', in OZGA, J. *op.cit.*, pp. 146–158.

REES, T. (1988) 'Education for Enterprise: the state and alternative employment for young people', *Journal of Educational Policy*, 3, 1, pp. 9–22.

REEVES, T. and WOODWARD, J. (1970) 'The Study of Managerial Control', in WOODWARD, J. (Ed.) *Industrial Organization Behaviour and Control*, Oxford, Oxford University Press.

REPUBLIC OF SOUTH AFRICA (1984) *Central Statistical Services*, Pretoria, Human Sciences Research Council.

REYNOLDS, D. (1976) 'The Delinquent School', in HAMMERSLEY, M. and WOODS, P. (Eds.) *The Process of Schooling*, London, Routledge and Kegan Paul.

REYNOLDS, D. and SULLIVAN, M. (1987) *The Comprehensive Experiment: a comparison of the selective and non-selective school organization*, Lewes, Falmer Press.

ROBINSON, J. (1988) 'State Control and Local Financing of Schools in China', in BRAY, M. and LILLIS, K. *op.cit.*, pp. 181–196.

ROTHERMUND, D. and SIMON, J. (1986) *Education and the Integration of Ethnic Minorities*, London, Frances Pinter.

RUTTER, M., MAUGHAM, B., MORTIMORE, P. and OUSTEN, J. (1979) *Fifteen Thousand Hours: Secondary Schools and their effects on Children*, London, Open Books.

SACHS, J. and SMITH, R. (1988) 'Constructing Teacher Culture', *British Journal of Sociology of Education*, 9, 4, pp. 423–436.

SAMPSON, C. (1988) 'Where self-help means selling pickled eggs', *Times Educational Supplement*, 2.9.88.

SAUNDERS, M. (1982) 'Productive activity in the curriculum: changing the literate bias of secondary schools in Tanzania', *British Journal of Sociology of Education*, 3, pp. 39–55.

SAUNDERS, M. (1984) *Implementing a 'practical action' curriculum policy: a case-study of 'Education for Self-reliance' in Tanzanian secondary schools*, University of Lancaster, PhD thesis.

SAUNDERS, M. (1988) 'Managing the 'Practical Curriculum: headteacher responses in Tanzania and Britain', in DAVIES, L. and ORAM, R. *op.cit.*, pp. 203–210.

SCHILLING, C. (1988) 'The Dialectics of educational control: the MSC, schools and industry', Paper presented at the *International Sociology of Education Conference*, Westhill, Birmingham, January 1988.

SCRIBBENS, K. and DAVIES, P. (1988) 'Organizing for Marketing', *Management in Education*, 2, 1, pp. 41–45.

SEAGER, J. and OLSON, A. (1986) *Women in the World: An International Atlas*, London, Pan Books.

SHA (1986) *Equal Opportunities — Policy into Practice*, London, Secondary Heads Association.

SHARP, R. and GREEN, A. (1975) *Educational and Social Control*, London, Routledge and Kegan Paul.

SIKES, P., MEASOR, L. and WOODS, P. (1985) *Teacher Careers: Crises and Continuities*, Lewes, Falmer Press.

SILVER, P. (1985) 'Sex Equity in Educational Employment' in HUSEN, T. and POSTLETHWAITE, N. (Eds.) *International Encyclopedia of Education* Vol 8, Oxford, Pergamon, pp. 4550–4555.

SIMKINS, T. (1986) 'Patronage, Markets and Collegiality: Reflections on the Allocation of Finance in Secondary Schools', *Educational Management and Administration*, 14, 1, pp. 17–30.

SIMKINS, T. (1987) 'Finance and the Head', *Management in Education*, 1, 3, pp. 15–17.

SINCLAIR, M. and LILLIS, K. (1980) *School and Community in the Third World*, London, Croom Helm.

SINGH, R. (1988) *Asian and White Perceptions of the Teaching Profession*, Survey reported in *Times Educational Supplement* 2.9.88, 'Teaching Fails to lure Asians'.

SINGHAL, S. (1984) 'The Development of Educated Women in India: reflections of a social psychologist', *Comparative Education*, 20, 3, pp. 355–370.

SIWITIBAU, S., LECHTE, R. AGAR, J., SIMMONS, D. and SOFIELD, C. (1985) 'Women in Development Planning: Fiji', in HEYZER, N. (Ed.) *Missing Women: Development Planning in Asia and the Pacific*, Kuala Lumpur, Asian and Pacific Development Centre.

SMITH, H. (1988) 'National Strikes bring Troubled Year to a close', *Times Educational Supplement*, 23.12.88.

SMYTH, W. (1985) 'An Educative and Empowering Notion of Leadership', *Educational Management and Administration*, 13, pp. 179–186.

SOMERS HEIDHUES, M. (1986) 'Chinese Education in Malaysia and Indonesia', in ROTHERMUND, D. and SIMON, J. (Eds.) *op.cit.*, pp. 48–65.

STEBBINS, R. (1980) 'The Role of Humour in Teaching: Strategy and Self-expression', in WOODS, P. (Ed.) *Teacher Strategies*, London, Croom Helm, pp. 84–97.

STEWART, J. (1976) 'From Luxury to Necessity', *Municipal Journal*, 20.2.76.

STRATHCLYDE DEPARTMENT OF EDUCATION (1988) *Sex Equality in the Education Service*, Strathclyde Regional Council.

STROMQUIST, N. (1986) 'Decentralizing Educational Decision-making in Peru: Intentions and Realities', *International Journal of Educational Development*, 6, 1, pp. 47–60.

SWARTLAND, J. and TAYLOR, D. (1988) 'Community Financing of Schools in Botswana', in BRAY, M. with LILLIS, K. *op.cit.*, pp. 139–154.

TIPTON, B. (1985) 'Educational Organizations as Workplaces', *British Journal of Sociology of Education*, 6, 1, pp. 35–52.

TOMLINSON, S. and COULSON, P. (1988) *Education for a Multi-ethnic Society*, Lancaster, Lancaster University Department of Educational Research.

TOOGOOD, P. (1989) 'Learning to Own Knowledge: Minischools as Democratic Practice', in HARBER, L. and MEIGHAN, R. *op.cit.*, pp. 98–121.

TROYNA, B. (1987) 'Beyond Multiculturalism: towards the enactment of an anti-racist education in policy, provision and pedagogy', *Oxford Review of Education*, 13, 3, pp. 307–320.

TROYNA, B. and BALL, W. (1985) *Views from the Chalk Face: School responses to an LEA's Policy on Multicultural Education* Policy paper 1, Warwick, Centre for Research in Ethnic Relations.

TROYNA, B. and WILLIAMS, J. (1986) *Racism, Education and the State*, London, Croom Helm.

UNICEF (1987) *Unicef and Women: The Long Voyage*, Unicef History Series, Monograph VII.

UNGER, J. (1984) 'Severing the Links between Education and careers: the Sobering Experience of China's Urban Schools', in OXENHAM, J. *op.cit.*, pp. 176–191.

VAN RENSBURG, P. (1978) *The Serowe Brigades: Alternative Education in Botswana*, The Hague, Bernard van Leer Foundation.

VULLIAMY, G. (1987a) 'Assessment and the 'Vocational School Fallacy' in Papua New Guinea', *International Journal of Educational Development*, 7, 1, pp. 49–58.

VULLIAMY, G. (1987b) 'School Effectiveness Research in Papua New Guinea', *Comparative Education*, 23, 2, pp. 209–223.

WALKLING, P. and BRANNIGAN, C. (1986) 'Anti-sexist/Anti-racist education: A possible dilemma', *Journal of Moral Education*, 15, 1, pp. 16–24.

WANASINGHE, J. (1982) 'A critical examination of the failure of the junior secondary school curriculum and prevocational studies in Sri Lanka', *International Journal of Educational Development*, 2, pp. 61–71.

WATKINS, P. (1983) 'Scientific Management and critical theory in educational administration', in BATES, R. *op.cit.*, pp. 119–135.

WATSON, K. (1985) 'Educational Policy and Provision for a multicultural society', in WATSON, K. (Ed.) *Key Issues in Education*, London, Croom Helm.

WATSON, J. (1988) 'Forty Years of Education and Development: from Optimism to Uncertainty', in DAVIES, L. and ORAM, R. *op.cit.*, pp. 137–174.

WATTS, J. (1989) 'Up To A Point', in HARBER, C. and MEIGHAN, R. *op.cit.*, pp. 17–27.

WEBB, R. and ASHTON, P. (1987) 'Teacher Motivation and the conditions of teaching', in WALKER, S. and BARTON, L. (Eds.) *Changing Policies, Changing Teachers*, Milton Keynes, Open University Press, pp. 22–40.

WEICK, K. (1976) 'Educational Oganizations as loosely-coupled systems', *Administrative Science Quarterly*, 21, pp. 1–19.

WEIS, L. (1983) 'Inequality in Ghanaian Secondary Schools: Educational expansion, recruitment and internal stratification', *International Review of Education*, Vol 29, pp. 21–36.

WILCE, H. (1988) 'Unnatural Justice', *Times Educational Supplement*, 4.11.88.

WILLIAMS, J., DAVIES, L. and COCKING, J. (1989) *Words or Deeds? Equal Opportunities Policies in Higher Education*, London, Commission for Racial Equality.

WILLIS, P. (1977) *Learning to Labour: How Working Class Kids Get Working Class Jobs*, London, Saxon House.

WILLMS, D. and CUTTANCE, P. (1985) 'School Effects in Scottish Secondary Schools', *British Journal of Sociology of Education*, 6, 3, pp. 289–387.

WOMEN'S NATIONAL COMMISSION (1983) *Report on Secondary Education*, London, Cabinet Office.

WOODS, P. (1977) 'Teaching for Survival', in WOODS, P. and HAMMERSLEY, M. (Eds.) *School Experience*, London, Croom Helm, pp. 271–293.

WOODS, P. (1981) 'Strategies, commitment and identity: making and breaking the teacher role', in BARTON, L. and WALKER, S. (Eds.) *Schools, Teachers and Teaching*, Lewes, Falmer Press, pp. 283–302.

WOODS, P. (1984) 'The Meaning of Staffroom Humour', in HARGREAVES, A. and WOODS, P. (Eds.) *Classrooms and Staffrooms*, Milton Keynes, Open University Press, pp. 190–202.

WRIGHT, C. (1985) 'Learning environment or battleground', *Multicultural teaching*, 4, 1, pp. 11–16.

YOUNG, M. (1972) 'An Approach to the Study of Curricula as Socially Organized Knowledge', in YOUNG, M. (Ed.) *Knowledge and Control*, London, Collier-Macmillan, pp. 19–46.

YU, V. and ATKINSON, P. (1988) 'An investigation of the language difficulties experienced by Hong Kong secondary school students in English-medium schools. 1. The Problem', *Journal of Multilingual and Multicultural Development*, 9, 3, pp. 267–284.

ZIJP, W. (1983) 'This is my hand and this is my head', in VAN DEN BOR, W. (Ed.) *The Art of Beginning: First Experiences and Problems of Western Expatriates in Developing Countries*, Wageningen: Centre for Agricultural Publishing and Documentation, pp. 85–99.

ZAMBIA MINISTRY OF EDUCATION (1986) Personal Correspondence, Deputy Permanent Secretary, Ministry of General Education and Culture.

ZIMBABWE GOVERNMENT (1984) *Annual Report of the Secretary of Education*, Harare, Government Printer.

Index